Organizations and Archetypes

Organizations and Archetypes

Monika Kostera

Professor Ordinaria, Faculty of Management, University of Warsaw, Poland and Professor, School of Business and Economics, Linnaeus University, Sweden

Edward Elgar

Cheltenham, UK • Northampton, MA, USA

First published in Polish as *Organizacje i archetypy*, Warsaw: Wolters Kluwer Polska
© Monika Kostera 2010
Translated by Adam Zdrowski and Monika Kostera

Translation to English financed by the Scientific Publishers of the Faculty of Management at the University of Warsaw.

Published by
Edward Elgar Publishing Limited
The Lypiatts
15 Lansdown Road
Cheltenham
Glos GL50 2JA
UK

Edward Elgar Publishing, Inc.
William Pratt House
9 Dewey Court
Northampton
Massachusetts 01060
USA

A catalogue record for this book
is available from the British Library

Library of Congress Control Number: 2012938067

ISBN 978 0 85793 798 8 (cased)

Typeset by Servis Filmsetting Ltd, Stockport, Cheshire
Printed and bound by MPG Books Group, UK

Contents

Figures and Tables

FIGURES

TABLES

Acknowledgements

I would like to express my thanks to the Scientific Publishers of the Faculty of Management, University of Warsaw, for providing the funding for the translation of this book to the English language. The Dean of the Faculty of Management, University of Warsaw, Professor Ordinarius Alojzy Nowak receives a special thanks for endorsing the project.

I would also like to thank Wolters Kluwer Polska, who are holding the copyright of the original Polish version of the book, for their kind cooperation and making it possible for the publication of the English version to happen. My warmest thanks to the desk editor, Bob Pickens and the copyeditor, Cathrin Vaughan from Edward Elgar who took such good care of the text and its English flow.

Shadows like roots
Connecting people
Never trust someone
Shadowless

(Monika Kostera, 2011, Fast Poetry)

PART I

Culture, organizations, inspiration

1.   A humanistic manifesto for sustainable management

Indeed, we live in interesting times. To me, it does not sound like a curse. Life is like a book one cannot put down; sometimes alarming, sometimes tragic and sometimes funny, fascinating, happy; never boring. So much has happened during my lifetime up until now: the revolution of rock music of the late 1960s and the 1970s, the increasingly more obvious full admission of women into public life, unisex culture, a revolution in the way we dress – the worldwide popularity of the most democratic garment, jeans. In 1989 the Eastern Bloc collapsed, and we all felt that the world now stood open before us; everything seemed to be possible. Europe grew larger and we were now allowed to live, work or study anywhere we wanted, with minimal formalities. Travel became so easy, though maybe not all the way to the Moon, as we kids once believed, watching Neil Armstrong's famous small step for man on the TV. When we grew up, we would spend our holidays there, we were sure. Well, that dream has not come true, but the flight from Warsaw to London, that used to be so expensive one could only afford it on special occasions, is now cheaper than the train ticket on the same route. And, what is perhaps even more amazing, one can cover all that distance by train, including under the English Channel.

But the dream of computers for everyday use certainly came true. From the stuff of science fiction and, in real life, extremely expensive machines, available only to rich institutions, they have become popular consumer goods, eventually even among those who are not particularly affluent. When I was a child, I did not know mobile phones existed. Much later, I learned about the products of Soviet and American super-technology, used only by the absolute elite. Today, everyone owns a cellular phone, even the unemployed and the poor. I'm not sure whether mobile phones make me happy or not. But the fact is, one cannot avoid them. Last year I saw a homeless beggar in Lisbon sending SMSs on her phone. People carry them everywhere, even little children take them to the kindergarten tucked in their backpacks along with their teddy bears. Like it or not, we are made to eavesdrop on private or even intimate phone conversations on the tram. Phones interrupt parties and dinners, and sometimes I wish they were still expensive toys for presidents and special forces. But then,

3

there is also technology one loves, such as the tape recorder. As a teen-ager, I regarded this piece of technology as something precious and only just available, in its cheap Polish version. Then everyone suddenly owned Western tape recorders of various shapes and formats. And since then they have been gradually put out of use, first by CD players with or without a slot for tape, and more recently by digital MP3 players that do not need tapes or CDs. Their memories also grew increasingly capacious. Today my miniature microSD memory stick can accommodate 160 of my 1993 computers, and I do not know how many music CDs.

Another invention I appreciate, and even cannot do without, is the Internet – what would I not have given for having access to something like it when I was a lonely immigrant teenager in the grey, windy Malmö of the late 1970s. This incredible communication network connects an increasing number of people in an increasing number of countries and we can send each other letters without paying for stamps or, indeed, waiting in queues in the post office. It is so easy now to publish, read and find information. Even being an introvert and phonophobe I can contact people and institutions and deal with many formalities online, by writing instead of using the phone. In my school years, if one wanted to quickly find a piece of information, one had to use an encyclopaedia. This often meant visiting a library. It was great fun but it took a lot of time. And instead of looking up what I intended to in the first place, I often ended up spending long hours reading something else altogether. Today, it suffices to type the word in an Internet browser and, there you go, Wikipedia or even *Encyclopaedia Britannica* visits me at home, while I am sitting in my swivelling IKEA chair. To look at books, touch them, let myself be surprised by them, I still visit the library. It is now a special treat, an experience. The Internet has become the mundane reality instead. The spread of WiFi (wireless Internet) enables the constant use of the net. We have got used to it as something obvious and ordinary. Only our bodies protest now and then. We can access the Internet anywhere and the technology works in all weathers, but our spines, shoulders and wrists protest and demand to be used in a more traditional way.

And yet, not everything is so good with our changing world; it also has a gigantic shadow side. What we once took for granted, such as lasting relationships, fresh mountain lakes, cheap running water, have ceased to be givens. The natural environment is increasingly polluted and damaged; the solutions to problems such as famine, poverty and inequality, which we once thought were close at hand, are nowhere in sight. Every day some of the diversity of the Earth's fauna and flora diminishes; and culture ebbs as well, as old languages, dialects and stories are forgotten, and neigh-bourhood cafes are closed down, giving way to increasing uniformity and standardization. There is so much to choose from, that choice is becoming obligatory; there is no choice to refrain from choosing. Choice is indeed the proof of social competence, and the abundance of things – disposable, precarious, fleeting – ceases to make us happy and often becomes a mere irritant. In Zygmunt Bauman's (2000) words, consumption nowadays is a 'lonely activity' (p. 165), consisting of a constant floating or drifting from one unsatisfying product to another. When I was a teenager, receiving a new pair of jeans from my Dad was something that made me ecstatically happy, and both the jeans and the happiness lasted for years. Nowadays things do not do much for many of us in the West. They bore us rapidly, and wear out perhaps even faster.

Some of the key sociological problems of the contemporary West have been addressed by thinkers such as Zygmunt Bauman, Richard Sennett and George Ritzer. I have selected their work to present these problems because it is particularly pertinent with regard to the topic I intend to deal with in this book: organizations from the human point of view. So this is the story of what we have forsaken in the quest for progress of the last century, and of the sad human consequences of that neglect.

First, the rejection of stability. Zygmunt Bauman (2000) describes our times as highly uncertain, deregulated, individualized and privatized, where nothing is supposed to last and where change occurs incessantly in an ever accelerating tempo. In Bauman's terms our times can be portrayed as liquid, that is, ever flexible and free from restraining stable structures. The simultaneous fragmentation renders sense-making a precarious and perhaps futile effort for many, giving the illusion of freedom, yet delivering further injustice and suffering instead (Bauman, 1998). The authentic increasing global freedom of capital is not accompanied by a similar increase in the freedom of human movement. Parts of the production process that demand labour are subcontracted to poorer regions of the world, failing to distribute wealth but enhancing the disproportions. Poverty has become exported and also privatized. No one wants to take responsibility for the underprivileged; indeed, they are becoming ever more marginalized. Alienation has become the core of contemporary life (Bauman, 2000). Cooperation and solidarity are diminishing; indeed, they are redundant in the liquid society (ibid.), and, at the same time, bonds between individuals become as liquid as any other relationships, making responsibility, commitment and intimacy unlikely (Bauman, 2003). Strong bonds would hinder the individual from being permanently on the move, and in a society where impermanence is the core and transience the imperative (Bauman, 2000), this would be harmful to the individual's social success and career, or perhaps even their ability to find useful employment at all. The sense of impermanence and superficiality which permeates everything in contemporary society is leading to suffering and feelings of insecurity, as well as destroying any meaningful social bonds. This has become a serious problem, which needs to be addressed practically (Bauman, 2000).

Second, we have got rid of the past. In Richard Sennett's (1998) view, this results in a loss of balance, characteristic in particular of the modern organization. Flexibility has become something of a managerial dogma. However, this fashionable word is used in a different way from its original meaning, which implied a temporary change of shape and then return to the original form. Currently change is ever present, but no return to anything original is even considered. Core identities, shapes and structures are thrown, together with stability, into the wastebasket of what is unprofitable and thus plainly wrong. Without history and identity, organizations become domains of an eternal, changing present. As an effect, all sense of responsibility vanishes: the new organizational leaders lose nothing of their predecessors' power but get rid of the responsibility, dispersing it to the 'team' and the market. The real authority is said to be some impersonal externalized force, such as the market or demands of the environment. Organizations have not become structureless, but their structures are less transparent and dimmer. It is difficult to fight the system, as the system is amorphous, shapeless and abstract, and is reminiscent more of a delusion of the mind than of a concrete reality. Such organizations have a demoralizing effect on their managers and employees. People are no longer attached to their employees; indeed, such attachment is nowadays a sign of failure. They have no lasting responsibilities towards them, and the best solution to any disappointment or complaint is to change one's job. Indeed, managers themselves also have no sense of lasting obligation toward the company they manage, or any enduring responsibility (Sennett, 2006). People cooperate by acting superficially rather than by working on the establishment of difficult, profound bonds (Sennett, 1998). Nowadays an ironic approach to everything is valued the most in organizations. Such an approach is costly in moral terms, as it leads to social disintegration. It promotes disengagement from social and problems and the problems of others, and a fixation on one's own well-being – understood in the short term basically as a kind of detachment. The contemporary organization may be extremely profit-oriented but in fact it produces costly pollution, not just in chemical and biological terms but also, very much so, in social and moral terms. Rich Sennett (ibid.) hopes that this trend will not last forever, that it will meet resistance sooner or later. In fact, he is quite positive that such resistance will take place.

Third, our times have forsaken irrationality. George Ritzer (1996) famously painted a portrait of the emergence of a fully rationalized society, a process he labels 'McDonaldization'. It encompasses the prioritization of four key elements: efficiency, quantification, predictability and control, followed by fake fraternization. The end goal of this process is to turn all of society's activities and forms into a fully rational system, modelled on the famous fast food chain. All temporal and spatial aspects of social processes, as well as people themselves, are increasingly managed. Management colonizes every aspect of human life and invades ever new territories with imperatives of efficiency. The sense of making everything efficient is indisputable, it is a dogma. Quantification is another indisputable ideal, which every activity and organization should strive to achieve. Regardless of whether it is useful or not, if it indeed makes sense or not, all aspects of human activity are subject to measurement and counting. Predictability means discipline and order and the striving towards the perfect standardization. How an organization's activities should be carried out is not decided by its individual attributes or indeed its identity and place within the broader context, but by impersonal standards, best practices and routines. Finally, control means that all human elements should, if possible, be replaced by technology, and that control itself is built into technology, as in Henry Ford's famous conveyor belt. Managers try to reduce the tremendous alienation that these organizing principles create, through what Ritzer labels fake fraternization, a play-acting aimed at making the coldness of such an organization at least palatable and not so obviously something to object to.

All these trends apply to modern work organizations, such as factories and service providers, but also to traditional independent professions, as the medical profession or universities. Indeed, Ritzer coined the term 'McUniversity' to describe a machine-like provider of higher education, replacing the traditional all to human university, dependent on personal morality, knowledge and commitment. The McUniversity loses that personal link and the ingredient of professional judgement. Instead, it offers mass education to a depersonalized mass of students and produces quantifiable and predictable research. Knowledge is just another resource for such an organization, subject to efficiency-oriented streamlining and impersonal control. This world, almost perfect in a dystopian way, is not just a problem in itself but also one of the major causes and producers of problems from a social, psychological and, yes, managerial point of view in contemporary times. The McDonaldized organization is like a totalitarian state: smooth and self-referring, but monstrous. Ritzer (1996) encourages his readers to boycott McDonaldized ways of life and to create a non-rationalized niche: an individual response.

At the same time, some of the problems contain powerful possibilities of solutions. Universities that once were sites of social dissent, civil courage and societal conscience have degenerated into pseudo-businesses, of the permanently failing kind. Instead of raising awareness, academics have become seekers of grants from big corporations, which increasingly expect them to subordinate their research projects to their interests. Academics are expected to be almost infinitely flexible, devoid of any sense of the stability and long-term security which are necessary for creative work. Academic freedoms have been more or less completely abolished in Western Europe and the United States and are now undergoing the same process in other parts of the world. Systems of tenure that used to guarantee a security of employment that could result in vocal expression of social criticism are in many parts of the world a thing of the forgotten past. Students, who always used to be the world's most revolutionary potential, are burdened down with learning tasks often beyond their capabilities and which they are told to view as an 'investment'. At the same time, they are increasingly indebted to banks and this weighs too heavily on their minds to allow for any free thinking or protest. From having been the driving force of social change, students have become a bewildered and overwhelmed mass of insecure young people.

Western universities have ceased to be managed collegially, by fellow academics elected for the duration of two terms at a maximum, and have been taken over by managers or manager-like administrators, employed on a contract basis and managing the universities like businesses. And yet it is precisely in this formidable crisis (e.g. Hartley, 1995; Ginsberg, 2011; Ritzer, 1996) that a hope for change is hidden. It has to do with higher education becoming something of a mass phenomenon, no longer directed at the few but concerning millions of people. At the bottom of these processes, asleep but bound to wake up some day, lies the dragon: the democratization and mass emancipation that intellectuals once dreamed about.

Not surprisingly, one of the study programmes that has been gaining most interest (and students) in recent decades is management. When in 1980 I began to study at the University of Lund, management was not a popular field of study. It was considered to be rather narrow and not too interesting and, besides, suitable mostly for kids of rich parents. At that time, there began appearing new interfaculty programmes aimed at a potentially larger group of students and offering a wider range of subjects, including the sociological perspective that I ended up studying, by sheer and utter accident I have to add, as never would I have dreamed of choosing to study anything to do with business if I had a choice. Yet the discipline grew, as did I and others who embraced it. Nowadays[1] there are circa 182 000 people studying 'social sciences, business and law' solely in the United Kingdom (UK), and almost 970 000 in the US (OECD, 2011).

According to the same source, over 86 000 people study business and administration in the UK and over 531 000 in the US (OECD, 2011). In my own country, Poland, the corresponding figure[2] amounted to 450 000 (GUS, 2010). Yes, management and managerial education seem to be making their way into everything in our lives. While I agree that this is a colonization process, it also makes of management something of a potential mass movement.

It is already unabashedly interdisciplinary, influenced by many other academic disciplines, from sociology and cultural anthropology, to biology and mathematics (Hatch et al., 2005). The twentieth century belonged to managers who systematically took control, first of organizations and then of all of organized society (Burnham, [1941] 1960). Yet, having penetrated all milieus, such as public services, health care or the academia, managerial culture itself could not help being influenced by them and has increasingly snowballed into a gigantic hybrid, made up of bits and pieces of almost everything there is under the sun. This cannot have failed to happen, management being studied by all, from managers and their employees, to entrepreneurs, farm owners, to members of the clergy and artists. The number of people involved with managerial tasks, regularly or occasionally, is constantly increasing and can be expressed in the hundreds of millions (Hatch et al., 2005). The managerial culture has thus long stopped being reserved to the elite of mercenaries administrating large corporations on behalf of their owners; instead, it has become a mass culture: popular, eclectic, and created by people from different milieus, representing different views and walks of life. The biggest challenge, as well as potential blessing, that this situation creates is a culture of diversity (Özbilgin and Tatli, 2008). Management has become a kind of common denominator, a return to holistic thinking that we associate with the Renaissance, not with modernity, in the midst of tendencies in academia and professional life which were running in the opposite direction for most of the last century – toward specialization, fragmentation and separation from other disciplines and professions. Management, by taking a revolutionary, democratic, emancipatory and counter-hegemonic turn can, I am sure, become the solution to many of the urgent global problems I have sketched above. To do this, it needs to acquire a critical mass, which I believe can only be found in the humanities.

I will now briefly present five selected areas, not necessarily the most prominent or mainstream, but rather selected by me as illustrative of how this can be done. Inspiration from the humanities is already being used, and the difference it makes is colossal. I intend this book to be an example of such humanistic thinking in the area of management and organization. The five areas below have inspired me, as they did many other authors, to come up with a new way of conceptualizing the whole of our discipline and its main aims and missions in a fluid global world.

First, there is a need to find meaning in organizations, one of the most pervasive phenomena of contemporary society (Perrow, 1991). Organizations have always been multifaceted and complex, and people have been spending an increasing part of their lives dealing with them. According to Karl Weick (1995, 2001) processes of organizing occur through continuous processes of sense-making. Sławomir Magala (2009) argues that sense-making through wise managing is the force that underlies all innovation in organizations, the crucial factor behind the dynamics of changes in contemporary world. People abhor meaninglessness much as nature abhors a vacuum. Without a sense of shared meaning, action, especially undertaken in organized ways, is impossible. According to Linda Smircich and Gareth Morgan (1982), managers need to define symbolic reality for the organization, for example through stories, drama and images. Managing meaning draws upon diversity: the better one can adopt and understand different perspectives, the greater the potential one can put to use. We need to learn how to use the complexity and, with its help, achieve synergetic effects. An open mind befits the contemporary manager. As Smith and Elmes write: '*Things are more integrated, more connected, than they appear*. Our situation . . . is akin to seeing a great tapestry from the back' (Smith and Elmes, 2002, p. 457).

If we can only see individual threads, we cannot comprehend the whole and appreciate the beauty and the harmony; also, we are unable to solve problems which transcend the level of the narrow and fragmented. Organizations as part of human experience make more sense if regarded in their context and wholeness. Being human means not only being greedy, egoistic and aggressive, but also empathic, understanding and compassionate. Today practitioners as well as theoreticians call for open concern with the meaning of organizations in our lives and within the ecosystem of the planet. This is a time which calls for taking a stand against greed, shortsightedness and striving only for what can be measured, with no consideration for the consequences, and for compassionate management. The humanities can teach us where and how to look for these qualities; how those who walked the Earth before us have gone wrong and right in this regard; what they have left for us to learn, left there as a free resource for all to share.

Second, scarce and depleting resources are one of the most vital problems of our times. People, especially those engaged in questions of ecology, are increasingly alarmed about the state of the environment due to overexploitation. This is a real problem that calls for action. People representing business organizations and states are worrying where and how to acquire resources, how to manage them and avoid wastage, and some voices are heard calling for responsibility towards the environment and others. This coincides with an era of unprecedented concentration on one side of business performance only: profit and the dogma of the necessity of ever-increasing rates of growth of what is known as shareholder value. Organizations typically react to these problems not so much by a greener and more ethical approach but rather by downsizing: radical 'cost-cutting', getting rid of everything that does not immediately generate profit, outsourcing corporate functions, limiting the number of employees and letting many contributors work as outside contractors, and so on. Indeed, such single-mindedness has become the norm, the current mainstream in management, due to a separation between management and long-term interests after the fall of the domination of the bureaucratic system (Sennett, 2006). These corporations have grown ferociously fixated upon one dimension of their life only, cutting down not only on functions generating cost but also on those aspects that do not generate income such as ethical values, human happiness, sense of belonging, responsibility, care and inspiration. It also is a strategy that contributes to depletion of resources and degradation of the environment as no concern is shown for anything else than short-term growth and profit.

Yet this is not the only way. Richard Cyert's and James March's (1963) classical idea of organizational slack as a strategy of redundancy intended to adapt creatively to changes in the environment may serve as a guideline and an inspiration for the new holistically sustainable strategies. Now is the time to work against lean and mean organizations, devoid of all human sense, anorectic machines for profit production, and to work for ebullient, baroque organizations which thrive on redundancy, recycling and reusage. The humanities can give us an ethics and aesthetics for this agenda and offer a language to talk about things that cannot sensibly be calculated and maximized or minimized.

Third, there is the big question of our and our organizations' ability to live with change. Change, authentic and profound, and not the superficial and disposable managed solutions, must take into consideration the needs and abilities of people involved in it (King and Nicol, 1999). Change is becoming increasingly problematic and difficult to manage, especially in our times, characterized by chaos, turbulence and unpredictability. Some authors suggest that the kind of change that nowadays is needed in many organizations is not of the superficial, planned kind but rather a profound transformation (Smith and Elmes, 2002). In order to achieve it, one needs to experience the organization as a whole, with its light and dark sides alike. Leadership is, under such circumstances, about taking responsibility for organizational maturation and transmitting the experience of change to others (Hatch et al., 2005). A leader should not force change upon the organization but rather be able to read the signals that tell whether the moment is right for it or not (Durant, 2002). Another important element in the process of such transformative change is play (Sandilands, 2010). Play is spontaneous, cannot be planned, and it sets free powerful creative energies, as well as stimulating human cooperation and sharing. It makes new ideas possible and it gives people a space to test them, try them on and try them out, inspire each other and think in terms of many simultaneous aspects, goals and perspectives. On the other hand, quick fixes and linear turnarounds, based on one or a few factors only, have a tendency to make our collective problems as inhabitants of Planet Earth more, rather than less, profound and urgent. We need to take into consideration aspects that are dark, hidden, shared, non-linear and seemingly irrelevant. Instead of linear planning, we need to develop a sensitivity towards multi-dimensional, creative and profound change. It is time to speak out against manipulated, planned change, driven through forcefully without consideration for the environment; and to speak for transformation, a change that is affirmative of play, the cycles of life, death and rebirth. The humanities can help us to find the way through play, as well as darkness and obscurity, and learn the lessons we so much need to learn for our collective and organizational futures.

Fourth, there is a growing interest in learning. Increasingly, people concerned with organizations and management appreciate learning beyond the superficial accumulation of information and data. Real, lasting learning, as Chris Argyris (1999) has pointed out some time ago, has to be concerned with understanding rather than memorizing, with problematizing rather than receiving models and ideas, with contextualization rather than fragmentation and only definition of separate parts. The learning process takes place in the social space which can be understood through symbols and cultural interpretations of interpersonal interactions (Raz and Faldon, 2005). Knowledge, although it is often treated as such by mainstream management, is not an ordinary resource that can be managed and used (Styhre, 2004). Its usefulness is restricted to certain social and cultural circumstances. Knowledge is always contextualized and does not mean anything in itself. This is particularly true about tacit knowledge (Polanyi, [1958] 1974), that is, knowledge that is not formalized, and is acquired in the course of gaining experience. A rational approach, devoid of intuition, is hardly helpful with concern to such knowledge. Much of the knowledge management area seems to be a new way of further dividing work content from the workers, and as such it serves to subdue the knowledgeable to managerialist systems, Dariusz Jemielniak and Jerzy Kociatkiewicz (2009) warn us. What is needed is an interdisciplinary and holistic approach and that is exactly what the humanities can offer us. It is time to act against a new Taylorism called knowledge management (ibid.), and for the development of wisdom in organizations. The humanities have much to bring in this sphere: a broad, redundant, inspiring education, where history, art, ethics and philosophy play a vital role, and which actually helps students to look for their own answers, use their imagination and sensitivity, which inspires them to reach out of the shells of their egos and of what is known toward new horizons and senses of community.

Fifth, intuition has been something of a taboo in the last century, not least among management professionals and theorists – even though the old masters such as Chester Barnard recognized the importance of intuition for the good manager (Novicevic et al., 2002). Yet if we are to work out solutions to the growing ecological problems, managers need to learn how to think beyond the domain of pure logic and rationality (Reason, 2007). Intuition cannot be learned but it can be reinvited into the managers' way of thinking by the inclusion into their curricula of such themes as aesthetics, systems thinking, sensitivity to others and diversity.

Ecology in the broad sense, such as proposed by Gregory Bateson (1979), is a unity described by patterns of information. These recursive patterns of communication form the foundation for biological and human realms. According to Bateson, ours is a world of flows and relationships that can only be understood in their context. Managerial intuition is necessary in order to grasp these contextualized perspectives and to follow relationships and flows in organizations. Such a view stands in sharp contrast to the now prevailing fixation on the short term, often by forcing or manipulating people to work and preventing them from acting in ways they feel naturally inclined to. This fixation is devastating for the ecosystem, seen both as natural and human resources. Furthermore, it is good to follow natural rhythms, as they often lead towards maturity and genuine growth. Dealing with time is about not only the ability to judge rationally, but also the ability to receive impressions and read synchronicity. Synchronicity is a Jungian notion referring to a meaningful but acausal relation between external and internal events (Jung, 1993). Synchronicity is located in time, but it can be neither planned nor measured. Encountering it through rational planning is not very likely, but it is possible to learn it through the study of aesthetics. Sensitivity towards synchronicity can balance the managerial skill, by taking into account both the effects of rational reflection and intuition.

Such a holistic approach is beneficial not only to people who want to lead organizations but also to the employees, consumers and other stakeholders. It enables communication and action, interwoven naturally within the broader context: right things, right people, coming together in right time, which is, in fact, the very point of organizing (Czarniawska, 2000). The humanistic tradition of social sciences can help us see the human being and organization in a fuller context, as processes of mutual becoming (Letiche, 2000). In teaching management we need both intellect and intuition to deal with the problems of our times, some of which I have listed earlier. Pure logic will only tell us that a solution is impossible, and it is not good enough to leave it at that. We need the humanities in our curricula, to redirect our attention away from an artificial rationalization and streamlining of processes and toward the putting things into their context once again. We need to take a stand against just-in-time management, and for synchronicity in management. The humanities can offer a way of discerning signals that show that the time is right for certain actions and ideas, when such signs cannot reasonably be forecasted by means of statistics and mathematics.

To fulfil these ends we need to take inspiration from the humanities. They are capable of leading us towards the holistically sustainable management that is so desperately needed in our times. This kind of management incorporates a broad ecological awareness that Gregory Bateson (1972, 1979) called the ecology of mind: according to him, ecosystems consist of both natural and human spheres and it is only by understanding the complete informational patterns and thus grasping the ecosystemic unity that we can avoid eco-crisis. Holistically sustainable management is about Batesonian ecological awareness, and it incorporates what is often regarded as dichotomies: the human and the natural, the spiritual and the material. Instead of forcing human activity and talent into predetermined forms – an activity seen as 'management' by the mainstream theories and practices of the previous century – holistically sustainable management uses natural flows of the inexhaustible human activity and imagination. It is not the same as leaving people and organizations to their own devices. Laissez-faire all too often results in chaos and further impoverishment of the poor. What instead is needed is a conscious, thought-through and carefully balanced approach to management that is based on following natural needs and activities and drawing energy from renewable sources, in terms of fuels and energy as well as labour and creativity.

If the times of the nation state have passed (Bauman, 2011), then perhaps it is the time to occupy the space it has freed while shrinking and organize globally for much-needed global solutions. Not states and not businesses but perhaps global non-governmental organizations (NGOs) will be able to serve as the much-needed counterweight to totalitarian corporationism that is now threatening us. They can act to stop the abuses of power by corporate businesses, tackle real social problems and take over health care and universities. Also all kinds of non-corporate economic organizations are needed as fund generators, employers and producers of real value (as opposed to value generated by the banks and other financial giants of today). This is not such an impossibility as it was only 100 years ago: thanks to the Internet we now have a democratic and free communication and knowledge-sharing system, and thanks to the global explosion of management education millions of people in all walks of life now have the competence, the knowledge and the networks needed to manage such organizations worldwide.

But there is one thing that such managers need to gain before they can begin their work. They cannot be short-sighted technocrats – rather, they are to be the new Renaissance people. Many years ago, Abraham Maslow ([1965] 1998) encouraged such an approach to management which he expressed in his idea of the eupsychic manager, and today his thought returns as a very relevant idea and starting point for the development of compassionate, sensitive, long-term-oriented approaches (Payne, 2000). This is a time for holistically sustainable management. Such management needs humanists, and humanists need such management.

2. Culture and organizational stories

2.1 ORGANIZATIONS IN THE CONTEMPORARY WORLD

Charles Perrow (1991) described the contemporary times as a world of organizations. Organizations have existed since time immemorial; they came into being the moment people started cooperating in an ordered way to reach goals unavailable to a single person. What makes our time different, however, is that organizations have become omnipresent. An organization, public or private healthcare, usually welcomes us when we are born; we are raised, taught and employed by organizations; they provide us with entertainment and enable us to do things together. Even those who 'are against organizations organize themselves to protest against them' (Czarniawska-Joerges, 1994, p. 16). People may not spend their whole lives in organizations, but their entire lives are totally organized and there is no way to avoid it (Burrell, 1988). Definitely, organizations are an important part of life for contemporary people, to which they devote much time, attention and energy. No wonder that it is within organizations that people place and find their hopes, efforts, dreams and aspirations. This book is dedicated to meaning in contemporary organizations, workplaces: how people look for it, create it and talk about it. But first, I will briefly explain what organizations are, as seen by organization theory.

Organizations, like many social phenomena, can be regarded in two different ways: as structures or as processes (see e.g. Hatch, 1997; Czarniawska, 2009). Both approaches are equally valuable, and equally true. Organizations are indeed complex phenomena that cannot be directly experienced or described (see Morgan, [1986] 2006). One cannot touch, measure or weigh them; neither can one easily separate them from their environment in order to define them, or even list some of the main laws that govern them. In their everyday lives, people cope with organizations intuitively, but those who deal with them best are those who can think about them and interact with them in many different manners, sometimes in manners different from the traditional and most popular ones, paradoxical and contradictory (Morgan, 1993). Knowledge can help to develop imagination. This is the aim of this book – it proposes a language and symbols that may be of use in developing organizational imagination.

If seen as static 'things', sets of structures and elements, organizations can for example be considered as systems,[3] that is, as complex wholes in which parts are linked to each other by intensive and complicated connections. An organization understood in this way is an open system and it works within its environment which provides it with resources, and in return expects products or other effects of its functioning which it regards as beneficial or desirable. The organization has boundaries that make it possible to differentiate it from the environment. It consists of subsystems, usually including the so-called managerial subsystem, responsible for controlling the entirety. Organizations change as a result of their interactions with the environment, which 'selects' the organizations that are better adjusted to its demands and expectations and eliminates those that are worse adjusted. There are populations of organizations that fulfil the needs of the environment in a given time and place. The aim of organization studies is to come up with general theories that could be true of the population: theories that describe the organizations' states and features, such as their structures. These problems can be investigated through quantitative studies, that is, studies that deal with examining a sample, chosen in a well-specified way, and drawing general conclusions.

Such a notion of the organization is found in numerous mainstream theories and applications but is not being adopted in the present book. Instead, this book is based on a perspective that views the organization as a process. One of the most famous models for such a type of organization is the one proposed by Karl Weick ([1969] 1979). According to Weick, organizations are organized – that is, meaningful – sequences of actions, the results of which are cycles joined in loops that are repeated in a similar shape. Processes give the impression of being stable, and even look as if they were things because they are incessantly repeated in much the same fashion. Only after some time has passed may the observer realize that they are processes leading somewhere, that a change is constantly taking place, albeit slowly. There are exceptions in the shape of an abrupt, top-down restructuring, transformation or breakthrough, when the change can be seen right away and directly.

Weick distinguishes three stages that make up the cycles of organizing processes. The first is enactment, consisting in choosing a fragment of the environment and relating to it through a series of actions. Here, the social actors outline what they mean by 'environment' – what is 'outside'. They also define what is important for them in the environment, and then they establish connections with those chosen fragments of reality. The second stage is selection, encompassing actions with the cognitive schemes available to people in the organization. Parts of the meanings are selected and joined into a meaningful whole. The third state is retention, consisting in recording the results of the actions, of retaining them in cognitive schemes. In this way, an organization remembers what happens inside it and, most importantly, which actions are successful. The process of retention can have a more or less formal character. Karl Weick (2001) points out that these processes are held together by sense-making. It consists of looking back, in order to find criteria that can be applied to the present. Symbolic processes limit the scope for interpretation and enable the participants to envisage the organization and its context. There are a multitude of subprocesses, or stable groups of activities, that are internally similar to one another, which together form the larger organizational dynamics. For instance, Mary Jo Hatch (1997) distinguishes technological processes, processes connected with the social structure, those linked to the physical structures, and cultural processes. They all overlap and interact with one another, often producing synergies that in themselves make important organizational processes.

Organizations are often, though not always, managed. Managing is about specifically coordinated organized action, taking care of reaching a goal, and striving for the organization as a whole to survive. The condition for the rise of management is the perception of uncertainty. When uncertainty has been identified in the environment and social actors within the organization want it to survive, they may bring into being a subsystem responsible for the achievement of this aim. This is the managerial subsystem, which endeavours to protect the organization from influences of uncertainty. The most sophisticated form of such activity is strategy. It consists in the concentration of resources and the energy of the participants on the direction chosen by the management; in other words, they concentrate on reaching a superior goal (Obłój, 2001). According to Krzysztof Obłój, strategy is always connected with making choices: the company decides to take certain actions in order to maximize its chances of winning, resigning at the same time from other paths of development, paying for the lost possibilities. The building of a good strategy should be based on an accurate and intelligent analysis of the environment, which makes possible the reduction of uncertainty.[4] A strategy is a specific, formalized, conscious case of top-down managing of the organization's goals. Organizations realize numerous other goals that have to do with their subprocesses. For example, in sphere of social structure, they may introduce order, and in the sphere of culture they may satisfy social needs. The last category of goals is what this book is mainly about.

2.2 CULTURE AND ORGANIZATIONS

Culture in organizations has been a subject of study at least since Elton Mayo became interested in the dynamics of cooperation between people in a Western Electric factory in Cicero, IL called the Hawthorne Works (see e.g. Wright, 1994). A real explosion in the studies of culture in organization theory came much later, in the 1980s (Alvesson and Berg, 1988). Numerous books on the subject were being published, and there appeared professional scientific journals[5] as well as special issues of existing journals[6] devoted to the problem; conferences promoting a cultural approach were being organized.[7] The growth of interest in the subject in the academic world was accompanied by a wider interest manifest in practice. Corporations started perceiving culture as a resource and they were forming new departments and creating cultural programmes[8] (Alvesson and Berg, 1988). Consulting did not stay behind, and even tried to be the leader of the new trend. The 'new wave in management' was accompanied by an explosion of popular consulting publications and implementation offers that were to bring an attractive 'recipe for success' and, thanks to culture, reach for resources that had not been used earlier in the Western model of management (Koźmiński, 1986). Possibly, we owe the hype over culture to these popular publications that proved immensely successful in the book market worldwide and convinced a lot of people who had not previously recognized the importance of organizational culture in management.

However, these publications shaped the public imagination in ways not always in agreement with what researchers were learning and describing, and often, quite contrary to the research, promised people impossible, even absurd things. For example, popular publications often expressed the conviction that culture is a resource like any other and that it can be managed, while researchers were revealing that attempts at a more rigorous culture control proved ineffective or even dangerous (for an overview, see e.g. Alvesson and Berg, 1988; Hatch, 1997). One definite advantage of the hype was, however, many milieus taking an interest in culture; and some interesting discussions emerging on the utility of culture and its role in management. Numerous ideas were presented and quite often implemented, which were often incongruent or mutually exclusive. Even researchers disagreed among themselves; there seemed to be quite a few different views on what culture was and what its role in management could be.

One of the most widely quoted publications that is an attempt at systematization of the academic publications on organizational culture is the article by Linda Smircich (1983). She distinguishes three main definitions of culture: culture understood as an independent variable, as a dependent variable or as a root metaphor. In the first approach, viewing culture as an independent variable, culture is characterized as a dimension of the organization's surroundings. The aim of research is to work out the best management style: a style best suited to the surroundings, or working out a cultural competence. Culture here is a frame of reference explaining the differences in management styles in different countries, or drawing the boundaries for managerial actions and providing inspiration for these actions. Understanding culture as a dependent variable is based on the assumption that culture is one of the organization's subsystems that can be managed in order to improve efficiency or that through culture can be a kind of communication channel for the whole system if change is needed to be introduced. The notion of culture as a root metaphor is the most interesting one from the point of view adopted in this book. It consists of adopting a wide perspective where the understanding of culture has been borrowed from cultural anthropology. This approach makes it possible to concentrate on the human side of an organization and to regard the actions of the organization's participants from the perspective of sense-making (Weick, 1995, 2001). Researchers who adopt this perspective often use the definition of culture proposed by the anthropologist Clifford Geertz: 'Believing, with Max Weber, that man is an animal suspended in webs of significance he himself has spun, I take culture to be those webs, and the analysis of it to be therefore not an experimental science in search of law but an interpretive one in search of meaning' (Geertz, 1973, p. 5).

Defined in this way culture is, then, a symbolic system that makes communication and sense-making possible. This approach does not assume a full unanimity among people who belong to the same culture; on the contrary, from this perspective such uniformity seems unnatural or unreachable. Even in total organizations seeds of resistance and disagreement can be found (see Goffman, [1961] 1991; Kostera, 1997). Culture does not have to unite everyone, and it certainly does not have to connect people in an identical fashion. There are subcultures linked with different functions and structural layers and there is also a general, usually rather loose, organizational system that makes it possible to reach an agreement despite differences. All such manifestations of culture are important from the point of view of this approach, but they are not seen as static 'systems of norms and values'. This is a way of looking at culture focused on processes and as such it conforms with the processual perspective in organization theory. The researcher is interested in processes taking place in time, such as rituals, ceremonies, ways of lending meaning, sense-making, and so on. The most popular approach to research in organizational culture from this point of view is ethnography, which is briefly characterized in the last chapter.

Symbols are expressions of culture that can be directly experienced by people. They enable us to decipher the meaning of what goes on in the social world. Humans can do this with the help of webs of meanings existing within cultures. Symbols are neither stable nor unambiguous in the long term, but in a given time and place they carry particular meanings and that makes it possible to understand the symbols for people socialized within a cultural system. People from other cultures, however, tend to have minor or major difficulties in understanding foreign symbols. An example of a symbolic system is, above all, language; other examples are gestures, behaviour or recognizable images and signs, such as organizational logos. Elements essential to culture, such as rituals and ceremonies, contain numerous symbols. Among the symbolically loaded cultural phenomena there are myths and archetypes, to which this book is devoted. They constitute the foundations of culture, its deepest layer that joins a culture's participants throughout time and space. They are a fundamentally important part of culture.[9] They are expressed and communicated in the same fashion as other, more superficial, layers of culture, such as in particular narratives. Stories that refer to the sphere of the sacred are called myths. Other narratives containing archetypes I call archetypical tales. Before I proceed to discuss the two forms of expression, I will briefly explain how narratives are understood in social studies and what role they play in organizations.

2.3 STORIES OF ORGANIZATIONS AND IN ORGANIZATIONS

Once again stories are becoming the centre of attention of social sciences after they had been declared not scientific enough and of slight interest in the last century. They are, and always were, abundant in social reality and they play an important role in the shaping of culture. Also they appear at all levels in organizations, constituting a part of everyday life, a tool of management, as well as an instrument of resistance. During the last few decades, we have witnessed a renaissance of stories and storytelling in social sciences, a vital narrative turn, bringing people's attention to and expressing itself in terms of stories and narratives of various kinds (Czarniawska, 2004).

Stories are 'narratives with simple but resonant plots and characters, involving narrative skills, entailing risk, and aiming to entertain, persuade and win over [the listeners]' (Gabriel, 2000, p. 22). Traditional stories have a plot, that is, they represent the transition from one state of equilibrium to another (Czarniawska, 2004). There are also protonarratives, devoid of structure and plot, fragmentary and created ad hoc; such stories, very common in living organizational contexts, are called antenarratives (Boje, 2001). They leave space for improvization and adjustment to context. They are an ideal method of sense-making in contemporary organizations, where both the pace of action and the complexity of structure make it essential for people to deal quickly with uncertainty and the enormous number of pieces of information flowing in ceaselessly from all directions. David Boje and Rita Durant (2006) have observed that all live narratives play several fundamental roles in social contexts. First of all, they make possible the expression of the speaker's identity, anchoring it in relation to the listener, that is, to the social environment. They enable people to share emotions, creating borders around them so that they become possible to express. The ability and skill in handling narratives and listening to them help create ethical attitudes, thanks to the fact that the narratives give rise to sympathy and teach empathy – the listener can learn to understand others, without engaging in their negative emotions. Moreover, they support collective learning as they are a natural way to share experience and are easily remembered. They are perfect ways of expanding imagination; they support innovation and inventiveness. Apart from creating human bonds and a feeling of belonging, they let people experience their uniqueness. Narratives support cooperation and enhance relation-building much better than formalized reports and documents mainly because they do not exclude the context, are easy to remember, engage the listener and make them a virtual participant in the events, teaching how to be open for other people and their different points of view. Stories strengthen the sense of agency as they give meaning to events in people's lives. Therefore in all types of organizations narratives, being live media of communication at all levels, are irreplaceable.

Organizations are made up of multiple narratives, happening ceaselessly and simultaneously. David Boje (1995) presents, in the example of the Walt Disney company, a narrating organization where narratives play a vital role: from the official image-shaping to the ways in which the employees cope with a strong normative pressure and the management's invasion into their moral and emotional spheres. 'Stories discipline by defining characters, sequencing plots, and scripting actions' (ibid., p. 1000), but they also facilitate communication and leave people freedom for interpretation, and thus, probably completely unintended by management, have an emancipating potential. Narratives in organizations structure the actions of people in organizations, giving them also the freedom needed for reinvention and liberation, even in totalizing organizations (Kostera,

1997). People in organizations do not tell stories just for the sake of telling: they also do it to play their social roles and represent the social context in which they are placed. Listening to different voices and gathering different narratives enables a deep and multilayered insight into the functioning of the organization as well as an understanding of the processes taking part behind the façade of a stable image.

Yiannis Gabriel (2000) distinguishes four basic types of narratives in organizations: the comic, the tragic, the epic and the romantic. In the comic story the protagonist goes through disagreeable vicissitudes and adventures which are unpleasant, but which they rightly deserve. The protagonist, then, is a victim, but the listener does not sympathize with them, but laughs at them; often, the laughter contains aggression. The listener feels superior to the protagonist and this feeling may be tinged with contempt. The tragic story also describes unhappy vicissitudes of the main protagonist, but these are undeserved and unfortunate twists of fate and the results of other people's actions. The listener is sympathetic; the story invokes sorrow, perhaps also anxiety and indignation at the unjust fate. The tragedy ends, just like comedy, with the protagonist's failure, but while the ending of the comic story can be viewed as happy because it teaches a lesson and restores equilibrium, the ending of the tragic story brings fear and sorrow. The epic is different in that it presents a protagonist who achieves victory and gains glory. The listener feels admiration, respect, an uplifting joy, but the plot may also invoke envy. The epic story closes with the protagonist's success and victory, which is interpreted as a happy and just ending. Finally, the last type of narrative, the romantic story, shows the triumph of feelings; it presents a protagonist who deserves love and who, despite adversities, manages to unite with their beloved, friend or child. If not, they gain happiness connected with yet another, emotionally important, reason: a successful life project, the creation of a company they have dreamed about, a new ingenious product, and so on. The story awakens empathy and love in the audience, as well as feelings of friendship or gratefulness. The listener expects a happy ending, overcoming all the adversities and the triumph of love and involvement, and feels happy when they can witness such an ending.

In living organizations, all of these narratives are common along with hybrids, that is, combinations of two or more story types. For instance, our analysis (Hatch et al., 2005) of the narratives of the managers interviewed by *Harvard Business Review* identified mainly epic stories of heroes and their exploits, typical success stories. The second most popular narratives were hybrids, combining the epic with, usually, one other story type. There was a manager, who we thought was a very talented storyteller, who successfully combined three types of narratives in a single story. The remaining narratives, less than 10 per cent of all the stories, belonged to categories other than the epic; usually, they were tragedies and comedies, and only in two cases were they genuinely romantic stories. Perhaps managers do not know how to talk about feelings, or perhaps the convention of the magazine interview made them focus on actions and events. We were all amazed, and also quite surprised, by an unquestionable narrative talent displayed by nearly all the managers in the sample we examined. The managers used the narratives with great agility and tact; they skilfully employed metaphors and other stylistic devices, built tension, and created convincing characters. It was all the more notable as in the last century from which our data came, narrative skills were not taught at managerial courses or during managerial studies; moreover, back then, experts on the subject tried to lessen the importance of storytelling by claiming that rationality and calculations were 'the truly managerial skills'. It turns out, then, that even under the most unbecoming of conditions, the art of storytelling is still going strong. This should not be a surprise, given all the diverse and important roles narrations play in many spheres of life, including the world of organizations. I will be mainly interested in a certain type of stories, ones that transmit very deep content, feelings and states of mind. Stories that move the deepest recesses of the human psyche have been with us since time immemorial; in anthropology, stories that belong to the sphere of the sacred are called myths.

2.4 MYTHS AND ORGANIZATIONS

Ernst Cassirer (1946) understood myths as a kind of language used to describe spiritual reality or the religious experiences that cannot be expressed in ordinary words. The language of myths abounds in symbols and metaphors. According to Martin Bowles (1993), myth is a powerful story reaching to the deepest recesses of the human soul, touching 'in ways that we are not able to articulate, our feelings, thoughts, consciousness, or sense of our own behaviour' (idem., p. 414). A myth is, then, a sacred story, and a way for culture to reach our spiritual sphere. In colloquial speech, however, myth still stands for something that is not true: an illusion, an overt lie, an erroneous conviction or, at best, the religious beliefs of other, usually distant peoples. The disciplines that deal with beliefs, religious studies and cultural anthropology[10] understand myth in a completely different way. Myth is a type of narrative where the notion of truth is treated differently than in a realistic narrative. Whether something really happened or not is inconsequential in a myth (Campbell, [1972] 1988; Armstrong, [2005] 2006). Myths do not refer to events, but they use stories, real and fictitious, to express the truth hidden in the spiritual sphere, telling us about:

> matters fundamental to ourselves, enduring essential principles about which it would be good for us to know; about which, in fact, it will be necessary for us to know if our conscious minds are to be kept in touch with our own most secret, motivating depths. In short, these holy tales and their images are messages to the conscious mind from quarters of the spirit unknown to normal daylight consciousness, and if read as referring to events in the field of space and time – whether of the future, present, or past – they will have been misread and their force deflected, some secondary thing outside then taking to itself the reference of the symbol, some sanctified stick, stone, or animal, person, event, city, or social group. (Campbell, [1972] 1988, p. 24)

According to Joseph Campbell (1988), myths connect two realities: the internal and external. The external reality provides images and symbols; it gives us the language and cultural system that enable us to communicate with others. The internal reality provides understanding and conscious-ness. Myths are based on metaphors; they *are* metaphors – they point to something beyond their immediate content. Myths are true as long as that to which they point is deeply meaningful to human beings; they are true as long as they inspire us to a genuine spiritual quest. They refer to what we perceive as essential, though impossible to be meaningfully uttered in any literal and direct way. Karen Armstrong ([2005] 2006) finds a similar-ity between myth and art: both spheres can transform the human psyche; not through persuasion and discursive methods but through immediate experience.

No wonder that myths have been with us since time immemorial and they are still alive, despite the hopes of the Enlightenment that in the future science would explain everything and mythologies would become obsolete. But the role of myth has never been limited to the attempts at explaining the mechanism of the material world. Myths concerned merely with the material world are untrue in the sense we have in mind here, that is, they do not refer to anything deep and vital in the other, non-material sphere. Myths in the proper sense narrate experiences in the spiritual reality; they let the listeners participate in this reality, if they are ready to accept them. According to Joseph Campbell (2004), myths play four main roles. First, they establish a link between current and primordial con-sciousness. Also, they may constitute the only universally available con-nection between the non-material reality and embodiment. Second, they inspire respect, reverence, deference for the cosmos and creation, letting people experience something larger than themselves and their world. Moreover, they help to maintain a certain sociological system, with its order, norms and values; thus, they are the guardians of the social order.[11]

Finally, their role is to guide the human being through life, through its different stages. Myths accompany human beings in their life's journey. It should not be surprising, then, that despite the disregard for mythology so common in our time, myth has not lost its attraction. Karen Armstrong ([2005] 2006) claims that myth has never died – it continues to live in the human psyche.

Myths are needed in various contexts, sometimes unexpected ones for those who divide the world in two disparate domains: the sacred and the profane: 'Contemporary business organizations are usually considered to be models of laicism. It may seem, then, that they do not have much to do with the domain of the sacred from which myths originate' (Kostera and Śliwa, 2010, p. 195). However, whole organizations are sometimes mythologized and granted an extraordinary, nearly sacred status. It also happens that they are attributed supernatural qualities. For instance, an organization can become 'a symbol of a country, as in the case of IKEA and Sweden; an embodiment of a virtue: solidity and integrity in the case of Mercedes; a carrier of supernatural abilities: this is the popular image of the CIA, Mossad or MI5' (ibid., p. 195). Even more often, people mythologize particular organizational skills, abilities or attributes, like power, grandeur, leadership or pioneering (Kostera, 2008a).

Also, organizational heroes become objects of mythologization. The protagonists of myths often represent powers that are important for people engaging in different actions and at various stages of their lives (Campbell, 2004). The hero sacrifices his or her sense of security – everyday life, possessions and status – to embark on a long and difficult journey. On the way, the hero meets various characters, quite often endowed with supernatural powers, characters who either help the protagonist attain his or her goal or try to make it difficult (Campbell, [1949] 1993). Figures that are mythologized most often are leaders who fit this script best. Real-life leaders may enter mythological paths, try on their roles and, more or less consciously, compare themselves to heroes and deities from traditional mythologies (Hatch et al., 2005). But other organizational actors are mythologized as well: entrepreneurs (perhaps as often as managers), clients, independent professionals or professionals (Kostera, 2008b). Nonetheless, cases of genuine mythologizing are rare. I agree with Yiannis Gabriel (2004), who warns that even though myth is important and valid in contemporary organizations, the category should not be blurred too much and applied to all kinds of narratives. It should be kept in mind that myths refer to the sphere of the sacred. They may inspire organizational narratives closer to the sphere of the profane, supplying characters, motifs, threads or central metaphors. Such stories may be essential but not necessarily linked with the experience of the sacred. This broader category of narratives, appealing to the deepest recesses of the mind and helping to cope with fundamental existential questions, albeit not directly located within the sacred sphere, I call archetypical narratives. In this book I deal predominantly with such stories. The next chapter explains what archetypes are and in what the power of archetypical narratives consists.

3.   Archetypes in organizations

3.1   ORGANIZATIONAL ARCHETYPES

Stories that touch us in an exceptional way, that resonate in the most profound layers of the human soul, have such a strong influence because they use archetypes. Carl Gustav Jung ([1959] 1990) believed in the existence of a collective unconscious, a spiritual domain connecting all humanity. It is this space that contains archetypes, or empty slots, ready to accommodate images, characters or plots important to culture and individual development. They are universal in time and space and do not become obsolete with passage of time – on the contrary, they remain vividly alive, and their role is to inspire new ideas and interpretations. Jungian archetypes are very general; they neither specify nor evaluate their content. They activate the imagination to engage in continuous crossing of the boundaries of what is known and familiar. Archetypes as such are neither good nor bad; they all have their bright and dark sides. They are universally shared ways of understanding the world but on a very profound level, without giving it any concrete shape or ascribing values and norms to it. They actualize themselves only when they are filled with the content of conscious sensations and experiences. They exist simultaneously in two spaces: the intersubjective, common to all people; and the individual, internal spiritual space. They can be perceived as pathways connecting us to something larger than ourselves, as well as windows overlooking meanings.

It always seems to us as if meaning – compared with life – were the younger event, because we assume, with some justification, that we assign it of ourselves; and because we believe, equally rightly no doubt, that the great world can get along without being interpreted. But how do we assign meaning? From what source, in the last analysis, do we derive meaning? The forms we use for assigning meaning are historical categories that reach back into the mists of time; a fact we do not take sufficiently into account. Interpretations make use of certain linguistic matrices that are themselves derived from primordial images. From whatever side we approach this question, everywhere we find ourselves confronted with the history of language (Jung, [1959] 1990, pp. 32–3).

According to Jung, all the most important ideas, in both science and religion, originate in archetypes. People acquire archetypical images and notions and consciously convert them to ideas, art, technology, and other products of culture and civilization. Archetypes also play a crucial role in the development of the individual. They realize themselves in the individuation process, that is, in the process of becoming a distinct individual, of actualizing what one indeed is (Jung, [1921] 1971). Archetypes are the opposite of stereotypes, because while the latter close down areas of interpretation, the former inspire original understandings, they stimulate to look for what is individual and unique. Typical archetypes connected with individuation are the archetypes of transformation, like birth, death and rebirth. Closely connected to the archetypes of transformation are the personality archetypes, that is, mainly the Shadow, the Anima and the Animus, and the Self. There are also personified archetypes, referring to characters that can overlap and refer to the same person. These are typical family archetypes such as Mother or Father; the archetypes connected with stories, such as Adventurer, Virgin or Sage; or animal archetypes such as Lion, Dog or Wolf (Jung, [1960] 1981, [1964] 1968).

Archetypes as such are not made up of any content but one can say that they 'attract' certain contents. Therefore, some motifs tend to be repeated in myths, legends and traditional stories as well as in private fantasies and dreams (Campbell, [1972] 1988; Jung, [1959] 1990). These motifs fascinate people, they capture their attention, and provoke discussion and ponderings. Also in this respect they are the opposite of stereotyping: the latter, despite the fact that it is also shared by the majority of people participating in culture, lulls the attention and disactivates conscience, because it allows people to communicate without an active use of judgement and consciousness, as if automatically. In contrast, archetypes wake consciousness and engage deep feelings in the process of experiencing. These feelings are often powerful, ambivalent and complex, connected with the necessity of making difficult decisions. They may invoke profound sadness or ecstatic joy so different from the soothing, thoughtless feeling of satisfaction. Archetypes contain great power; they are an inexhaustible source of action and deep motivations.

Jung has not presented a uniform theory of archetypes; his views constantly evolved. As I am not interested in final definitions and orthodox statements, I do not consider it a problem; it makes it possible to be inspired by Jung's ideas and yet formulate one's own interpretations and form one's own views on the functioning of archetypes in culture. I agree with Jung that archetypes originate in the sphere of the collective unconscious and I am convinced of the existence of such a sphere that is closer to spirituality than culture. However, it is not even necessary to assume the existence of a collective unconscious to be able to make use of archetypes. They work just as well if understood as 'strong plots' (Czarniawska and Rhodes, 2006), or ideas from popular culture which, through its popularity and persuasive power, is able to influence social practice, including organizational practices. They may also be seen as cultural themes equipped with extraordinary narrative and symbolic potential. Their capability to inspire continuously novel ways of interpreting the images that are ascribed to them makes it possible to interpret them as an open work, a work whose 'poetics . . . tends to encourage "acts of conscious freedom" on the part of the performer and place him at the focal point of a network of limitless interrelations, among which he chooses to set up his own form without being influenced by an external *necessity* which definitively prescribes the organization of the work in hand' (Eco, [1973] 1989, p. 4).

In texts on management and organizations the notion of archetype is found to be understood in two ways: archetypes can either be read in the Jungian sense, that is, as described above, or as structural patterns. In the latter sense, they are a 'set of structures and systems that reflect and are underpinned by a single interpretive scheme or a "set of values and ideas as to what ought to be" (Greenwood and Hinings, 1988, p. 298)' (Pinnington and Morris, 2003, p. 86). The term 'archetype' can also be used in a similar, albeit more general way, as a taxonomical ideal type (e.g. Rutenberg, 1970; Lemon and Sahota, 2004). This structural understanding of archetype is different from the one used in the present study and will not be referred to further in this book.[12]

The uses of archetypes understood in the first sense, that is, in the Jungian way in organization theory, are depicted in Table 3.1. The table orders them according to how myths and symbols, through motivation and sense-making, contribute to culture creation. The aim of research is an in-depth and/or holistic understanding of organization in a broad cultural context. The first use refers to the depiction of gaps and problems or to the dark side of the organization. For example, contemporary corporations, and particularly big corporations, are artificially devoid of the feminine side; they look in vain for the missing part of their culture, the collective Anima, by using various half-measures and substitutes like quality management (Höpfl, 2002). A classic text on organizational archetypes is Martin Bowles's article (1991) on organizational shadow – the dark side of the organization that develops in hiding and sometimes explodes with great, destructive strength, astonishing and terrifying both outside observers and the members of the organization. During organizational change, organizations try to control people's behaviour in a certain manner. The stricter the control, the more favourable the opportunities for the development of the shadow that starts influencing the process of change and the very culture of the organization as such (Carr, 2002). Another use of archetypes is communication between individuals in the narrative process. For instance, ancient gods and goddesses embody the values and virtues that are important for an organization but are impossible to be unambiguously codified. They are embodied, in diverse ways, by the organization's participants (Bowles, 1993).

Louhi, a goddess from *The Kalevala*, is characterized as a very ambiguous, but powerful, role model for organizational loners, people who prefer working alone and are therefore rarely represented in today's management literature dominated by 'team spirit' (Aaltio, 2008). Professionals are depicted as witches – independent characters, with a strong autonomy ethos, who will not easily let themselves be organized; in fact, they will lose their magical powers if they are subjected to excessive control (Jonnergård, 2008). Finally, relating the attributes of mythological gods and goddesses – like mortality and immortality – to the features of organizations and its members makes possible a discussion of these features which would otherwise be difficult to conduct in rationalistic terms (Sievers, 1994). Another use of archetypes in the literature is to shed light on the issue of mythologizing organizations through the stories of organizational virtues and vices, exceptional abilities, attributes and skills. Organizational authority is shown as mythological organizational ability which presents it in a new, interesting light, going beyond rational discourse. Often authority realizes itself morally as sin, a dark and destructive power leading people astray (Lee, 2008). Computerized organizations are described as a cosmogonic struggle between protagonists endowed with supernatural powers, thanks to which the cooperation between people and machines is depicted in a new way, which in turn lets us look with more optimism at the possibilities of transforming technicalized organizations into environments more friendly to people (Kociatkiewicz, 2008). Redistribution is depicted as a natural feature of organization, sometimes rather beneficial, as the examples of Captain Jack Sparrow and Robin Hood clearly show (Parker, 2008). Finally, the last use of archetypes in organization studies is inspiring, motivating and enlivening the imagination. Managers dealing with strategic management can resort to archetypes, for example the archetype of competition, to enhance motivation, to stimulate themselves and their subordinates to a stronger involvement in the processes of change (Matthews, 2002). The archetypes of ancient Greek gods can help managers develop their leadership potential: referring to these archetypes, managers can become more effective and more sensitive (Hatch et al., 2005). The archetype of the Aegis, a powerful shield of magical qualities, can help us understand the way in which professionals go about autonomously creating their social roles, but it can also help

Table 3.1   Uses of archetypes in organization studies

	Uses	Example
Archetypes	Depiction of gaps and problems or to the dark side of the organization	The loss of the feminine side in contemporary organizations (Höpfl, 2002); the dark side of organization (Bowles, 1991)
	Communication between individuals in the narrative process	Mythical figures reflecting organizational values and virtues (Bowles, 1993; Sievers, 1994)
	Understanding mythologization of organizations	Stories of organizational virtues and vices, exceptional abilities, attributes and skills (Lee, 2008; Kociatkiewicz, 2008)
	Inspiring, motivating and enlivening the imagination	Tools for managers to become more effective and sensitive leaders (Hatch et al., 2005); tools for enhancing the autonomy in creating professional roles (Kostera and Postuła, 2011)

Source: Kostera and Postuła (2011).

them develop the practical skill of enhancing their autonomy (Kostera and Postuła, 2011).

3.2   ARCHETYPICAL TALES

The way I use archetypes is not connected to psychology but focused on organizations from a narrative point of view. What interests me is, then, not an analysis of the unconscious fundamental motivations of human beings, or even Jungian psychology as such. Instead, I am looking for organizational narratives and their powerful symbols. An archetypical tale is a narrative that is based on archetypes used as a recurrent motif; the archetype can appear in the form of a plot, a character, a setting or the time of the action. For example, stories of magical protagonists or artefacts often belong to the category of archetypical tales. Myths[13] are a special and recognizable kind of archetypical tales. Other popular types of such narratives are fairy tales, fables, legends, folk tales, traditional ballads and epics, as well as stories in or of organizations, gathered during field studies, that rely on archetypes in key moments with the intention of emphasizing or elucidating another side of a problem or explaining important aspects and motifs. In this book archetypes both determine the text's organization and constitute the main subject of the book. Their interrelations, their internal logic and dynamics are the basis for the structuring of the presented material. The archetypical tale is a special mode of narrative – it has its own, often hidden, dynamic, that leads the teller through plots typical for a given archetype, it 'feeds' the right elements, and sometimes it controls the narration. The archetypical tale tends to be dramatic, because its aim is not to present facts in the right order but to move and inspire the reader or listener.

The elements of narration of this book can be described with help of Kenneth Burke's classical dramatistic pentad, used to analyse theatrical performances, the symbolic content of social situations, as well as to present the dramatic aspects of ethnographic material (Kostera, 2007). The pentad consists of five key terms of drama:

> They are: Act, Scene, Agent, Agency, Purpose. In a rounded statement about motives, you must have some word that names the act (names what took place, in thought or deed), and another that names the scene (the background of the act, the situation in which it occurred); also, you must indicate what person or kind of person (agent) performed the act, what means or instruments he used (agency), and the purpose. Men may violently disagree about the purposes behind a given act, or about the character of the person who did it, or how he did it, or in what kind of situation he acted; or they may even insist upon totally different words to name the act itself. But be that as it may, any complete statement about motives will offer some kind of answers to these five questions: what was done (act), when or where it was done (scene), who did it (agent), how he did it (agency), and why (purpose). (Burke, 1945, p. xv)

The pentad is a kind of metalinguistic approach to narration where attention is being paid to the symbolic content. Since the archetypical tale is loaded with symbols, it is perfectly suited to be depicted in this way. I will now present the main elements of this book with the use of the pentad.

Act refers to everything that is the synthetic theme of all the stories that make up this book, its central idea, what the action is that underlies the whole. Scene is the place and time of the action where the story is set. What is the setting of the story and what are the consequences of this fact? Actor is the protagonist: in this case, it is a collection of protagonists presented in subsequent chapters, including the narrator. Agency is connected with a person or a group responsible for acting and it answers the question: how? In an answer to this question, I will explain the typical outline of the particular stories, explain the division of the text into sections and subthemes and clarify the typical narrative structure. Finally, the aim is connected with meaning, it answers the question: why? and shows how the actor looks for meaning in what happens in the story. It will be, then, a story about what, according to the author, is the meaning of this book. Not only are the readers entitled to adopt their own interpretations and ideas, but it is what I hope for in my heart of hearts. Starting a conversation is my ultimate dream as a writer.

Act, or the answer to the question: what? refers to archetypes, understood as root metaphor. Archetypes manifest themselves first and foremost via metaphors. Metaphor is a stylistic device, where one phenomenon or subject is referred to by another one; it is an attempt to understand one fragment of reality through another. Metaphor is a classical rhetorical figure based on a new use of words, whereby the words used gain new meanings (Burke, 1945). Metaphors are used by poets and writers but also by scientists and researchers, including organization theorists (Morgan, [1986] 2006). Finally, it is used by every one of us in everyday speech which is permeated with metaphors governing our thoughts and feelings (Lakoff and Johnson, [1980] 1983). Ernst Cassirer (1946) talks about myth as a form of metaphorical thinking where metaphor is a tool enabling us 'to find, on the one hand, the unity of the verbal and the mythical worlds and, on the other, their difference' (p. 84). This is, more or less, the role of metaphor in an archetypical tale. However, the mythical world is much more consistent than archetypical tales. In the latter, metaphor can refer to different frames of references; it can be fragmentary and episodic. Both archetypical tales and myths should not be read literally. Through metaphors the stories reach different levels of our consciousness, they make a way into the sphere of the collective unconscious or, to put it differently, to the cultural foundations. It is precisely in this manner, by motivating us and stimulating reflection, that the archetypical tale speaks directly to our lives.

The archetypical tales presented in this book share one central metaphor that constitutes their basic content: management understood as inspiration. Until recently, talk about inspiration in management was considered not entirely legitimate. Popular management books often quote the American saying that genius is '1 percent inspiration, 99 percent perspiration', and with that the topic is exhausted. Texts on inspiration in management began to appear recently and are still very rare. For instance, Sanjoy Mukherjee (2007) appreciates the role of inspiration in entrepreneurship, Christine Galea (2006) presents an interview with a high-level manager who claims that employees do not need to be motivated but inspired, and Graham Cooke (2005) believes that leaders can inspire and involve people: both their actions and their thinking. In my opinion, inspiration in management is quite central. The kind of management I believe is important for a sustainable organizational future can be very well seen as inspiration. The almost total fixation upon financial aspects that has dominated mainstream management practice up till now is, I believe, not only becoming obsolete, with its rapid loss of social legitimacy and cultural power, but also dangerous and harmful by its narrow-mindedness and disregard for the needs of humans and the planet. A new, humanistic management is required and it should draw ideas and power from a much broader cultural frame of reference, beginning at least in antiquity, developing through the Middle Ages and Enlightenment, up till the current era. Consideration of that legacy brings a necessary modesty to management, scarcely an invention of modern times, but at the same time it is a treasure trove for the development of new ideas, and the reinterpretation and creative recycling of old ones. In that broad frame of reference, management is about techniques and skills, not a purely economic function, but a kind of uniting service to the managed organization, which I conceive of in this book as similar to that of poets and artists to their communities of thought. But managers, unlike poets and artists, do not have their own Muse. Therefore they have to learn from these traditionally creative groups or, through archetypes, look for a Muse of their own. This book may be, if the reader wishes it so, a first tiny step on their path to finding such a Muse.

Scene is the answer to the question: where is the action set? Subsequent chapters in this book discuss various ideas and theories; their action is set in various real organizations but a common domain where all the stories are set is the space of the imagination. Carl Gustav Jung famously held that archetypes are categories of imagination ([1935] 1969). Imagination plays a key role in the life and mental development of human beings. Currently imagination is not as strongly appreciated as it once used to be, but that is something that should change, if we as humanity are to face the challenges that currently stand ahead of us. Also in this case we can make use of the inheritance of ideas offered by the humanities, as many great thinkers of the past devoted their attention to the question of imagination. Immanuel Kant ([1781] 2008) wrote that imagination is 'a blind but indispensable function of the soul, without which we should have no cognition whatever, but of the working of which we are seldom even conscious' (p. 211).

For Kant, imagination is a cognitive faculty which enables creating a synthesis by reproduction of experience, as well as linking ways of understanding and perception into schemes, and based on that, drawing conclusions and making generalizations. Being an inherent element of the process of perception, imagination makes images conscious. According to Adam Smith (1799)[14] the philosopher is a person of noble imagination, capable to see connections between things that had seemed ordinary and mundane; thanks to this ability, the philosopher is able to repel mental laziness. C. Wright Mills ([1959] 2007) defines sociological imagination as the ability to combine the experiences of an individual with their place in society and history. People tend to see only a fragmentary picture of their lives, limited to their everyday world that consists of their family, job and the place where they live. Imagination lets them overcome the limitation that makes them slaves of destiny. Imagination enables them to see the relation between the particular and the social, it builds a bridge between the dimension of everyday life and the dimension of national and world history. This connection makes it possible to gain the distance that lets a person overstep the limitations of his or her everyday life and gives space for experimenting with new forms of activity in the social sphere. Imagination is more than just reaching for information: it is a state of mind, a mental perspicacity, a feeling of meaningfulness. The development of imagination can be stimulated by three types of questions: about the social structure, about the place of a particular society in history and about which individuals dominate in this society at a given time. Imagination is the ability to struggle with these questions by turning attention from the sphere of politics to that of psychology, and vice versa.

According to Karl Weick (2001), in everyday sense-making within organizations imagination plays an important role. It is all the more significant, as processes of organizing actively rely on sense-making – organizations happen thanks to people constantly making sense of their actions. Gareth Morgan (1993) believes that practical and theoretical imagination helps people to deal better with managing and participating in the rapidly changing contemporary organizations. The author believes that it is possible to learn how to think creatively, for example with the help of mind games, by testing unusual ideas in one's mind, using metaphors and artistic visualizations. The training of imagination is as important as practising managerial techniques and it helps in innovative management, of a kind that goes beyond the stereotypical and the banal. Gibson Burrell (1997) argued that unimaginative thinking is still prevalent in the field of management theory, and warned that 'linearity kills'. Thinking that is based on purely reductionist frameworks can and does bring about harmful consequences. Karl Weick (2005) claims that a failure of imagination in organizations is a problem and can be dangerous, quoting the examples of the failures of imagination uncovered by the 9/11 Commission and by the Columbia Accident Investigation Board (CAIB) that studied the Columbia Space Shuttle disaster. Imagination is lacking in part because organizations give preference to a related ability, fancy, which is about the reshuffling of remembered experience. Imagination is, instead, the ability to create something completely new based on associations beyond linear sequencing:

[P]rimary imagination is about the formation of meaningful images that are associable, then secondary imagination is about an associating principle that reorders, fuses, and moves these associables around, which enables them 'to form around and encrust any new object or experience with which they have an affinity . . . From an internal fund, ideas and feelings rush to surround any object that presents itself to the mind' [(Engell, 1981, p. 201)]. 'Surround' is a key word in this description because it signifies that the associating principles involve more than simply assembling discrete episodes, steps, and objects. Secondary imagination gathers experiences and images into 'more comprehensive schemata' (ibid., p. 14). The products of secondary imagination are like original paintings whose images have no visible joints or seams and no suggestion that they were assembled from multiple constituent parts. Such seams, however, are visible in the products of fancy. (Weick, 2005, p. 428)

People engage in fancy, work in a linear and sequential way and produce associations of adjacency. Imagination is based on concurrence and ideas grow exponentially, producing associations of simultaneity.

Agreeing with James Hollis (2000), I believe that without the archetypical imagination we would have neither our culture nor our spirituality, and humanity would not be able to leave the confines of biological existence where the only thing that counts is physical survival. We need imagination to rise from the dust thanks to good poetry, philosophy, art or, as I argue in this book, good management.

The place of the actor in this book is occupied by organizations as well as the managers who control them, entrepreneurs, employees and stakeholders. Organizations are understood as processes[15] that consist in assembling 'ongoing interdependent actions into sensible sequences that generate sensible outcomes' (Weick, [1969] 1979, p. 3). What results from organizing are interconnected cycles in the shape of sequential loops that do not constitute cause-and-effect chains. Organizations always have many aspects, for example they are companies functioning in the market, micro-political systems, and places where people become friends and compete with one another. It is impossible to separate only one of these aspects without disturbing the meaning of the whole because all the aspects are the facets of one totality. Apart from formal aims, organizations accomplish many other goals: for instance, they satisfy social needs connected with the fulfilment of the participants' dreams and aspirations, they realize ecological aims, and so on.

As both managers and entrepreneurs are central actors in this book, I need to say a few words about who they are and the differences and similarities between them. Thus, a manager is a person responsible for joining individuals and resources in a coordinated way, in order to attain a goal or a set of goals (Sjöstrand, 1998). The manager tries to limit uncertainty; their main concern is to protect the company from the

dangers that result from its actions. The manager works with the creation of structures corresponding to the division of work and the strategy, and their decisions are based on systems that enable them to gain
a proper orientation in the functioning of the company. Basically, the
manager's aim is to ensure the safety of the organization; and, at the end
of the day, to ensure the organization's survival in conditions of uncertainty. The entrepreneur's role is in many respects the opposite of this.
The entrepreneur thrives on uncertainty; they use it as a resource that
enables the company to gain other resources (Hjorth, 2003). They are
most effective working outside structures; they limit the scope of control
and often fiercely try to avoid it as a person. An entrepreneur works best
beyond the reach of rules, and enjoys shattering existing structures in
order to construct new ones in their place. The entrepreneur's job is constantly to gain new territories for the organization through innovation in
production, appealing to new clients and markets, as well as introducing
new production methods.

The participants of organizations are people adopting a variety of different roles, from subordinate to mediatory, to professional and expert.
In the contemporary world, often called the 'world of organizations'
(Perrow, 1991), organizations are the most popular ways of structuring
time and human activity. For the participants, organizations are ways to
do things that are unattainable for a single person; vehicles for transmitting knowledge; bridges linking people to previous generations through
structures and knowledge. At the same time the participants fulfil their
social needs of belonging and friendship by taking part in the functioning
of organizations.

Finally, the stakeholders are a wide group of actors including managers,
employees and other important characters acting outside the organization or on its margins, or participating in the organization not through
personal involvement but via other relationships, such as by custom or
cooperation. Among them some are more and some are less influential or
engaged: owners, shareholders, trade unions, journalists, central and local
authorities, and so on. The decision about who the organization considers
to be its stakeholders is connected with what the organization considers to
be an important value (Gabriel et al., [1992] 2000).

The actors that appear in the following chapters of this book have
not been invented by the author. Partly, they originate in literature: they
appear as individual or group characters in the work of authors writing
on management. And partly, they come from my own field studies, but
because they are to be the protagonists of parables and not fragments of
empirical material to be used in theory construction, I have turned them
into fictional characters, sometimes made up of several real people that I

have encountered in the field. Other characters are people known from the media – the press or television – and appear under their real names.

Agency specifies how the act was carried out. The way this occurs in myths has been the subject of Joseph Campbell's famous book, *The Hero with a Thousand Faces* (Campbell, [1949] 1993). They are often tales of the road: the protagonist leaves home, encounters various adventures and finally learns an important lesson, often together with acquiring a powerful artefact, and then goes back home to share his or her prize with the others. In a secular simple archetypical tale, such as those presented in this book, the plot does not have to be either elaborate or consistent. Each of the following chapters adopts a structure similar to the mythical quest narrative but they do not stick to the unity of the character and they are not always based on the same model. The subsequent archetypes are the central theme, they 'lead' the narration, the aim of which is the telling of an archetypical tale, and not fully elaborating the subject or making a complete literature review. This book is neither a handbook nor an overview of literature on the subject. It does not aim to present the whole or a significant part of scientific literature on each of the presented subjects. Neither is it a reflection of the mainstream research in management. I do not give an in-depth analysis or synthesis of current or classical theories. My narrative aims at something else: I want to present ideas that correspond with the discussed archetypes and that can invite the reader to follow certain paths. I will say more about those paths when characterizing the purpose of the tale.

Each following chapter starts with a presentation of the discussed archetype as it manifests itself in everyday culture and in organization theory. Then, I discuss those directions in scientific and practical research inspired by the archetype, or conforming to it symbolically, that I deem the most interesting. Just like Campbell's mythical hero, the protagonists of my stories leave the domain of familiar thoughts and ideas, and experience intellectual and organizational adventures, some of them dangerous and dark, and others more cheerful. But these adventures are not in themselves the purpose of their quest. The aim is defined by the narrative leaning of particular archetypes: towards a closure consisting in synthesis. The last fragment of each story presents such a synthesis; one could say, using a metaphor taken from Campbell's structure of a typical myth, that the protagonists come back home equipped with new experiences and valuable artifacts gained during their voyages. The last fragment shows the directions in which a full and enlightened use of the archetype's potential can develop. Some of the presented archetypes, like the Self, are personality archetypes, others, like the King, are the archetypes of narrative protagonists. The chapters devoted to them close with a demonstration of how the archetypes' potential can be realized. Other archetypes, like death, are transformation archetypes and the chapters devoted to them close with the description of the transformation undergone, its ultimate border. Each chapter starts with a presentation of the context in which the given archetype functions. There follows a discussion of different aspects of its manifestation in management. Each chapter ends with a story, taken from experience, that shows an example of how the archetype works in organizational practice.

Purpose answers the question: why? In this book the ultimate purpose of the presented archetypical tales is change: presenting the meaning of a new mode of understanding (theory) and of an organizational change (practice) and, finally, the synthesis of these two spheres in the shape of a new form of organization coupled with new ideas for controlling them. Genuine change is not a trivial thing, nor a fix than can easily be applied, even though the amount of mainstream management literature proclaiming subsequent 'ultimate recipes' for change may have led many into a belief that managers and organizations change daily and effortlessly, in the same way as human beings breathe. However, when it comes to adopting revolutionary ideas, genuinely new ways of doing things or simply innovating, practice tells us quite a different story from the popular books, which are often full of wishful thinking or normative postulates. Real change requires something difficult, close to impossible – it may occur 'when a person or a group acts in such a way as if future rules were already in effect or as if the change had already taken place' (Czarniawska-Joerges, 1993, p. 118). It needs a person inspiring the change, somebody who sets an example, a practical visionary. We talk about visionariness when somebody's actions are based on rationality, not of today but of tomorrow. In other words, a visionary acts irrationally from the perspective of current frames of reference, convinced that what they do is rational thanks to a future context, the creation of which they contribute to. In practice, a change is most probable when the managers realize their symbolic role in the organization and are willing to use it to introduce a gradual change, through systematic learning.

There is also the possibility of a more radical change, consisting in reaching a different stage through intensive learning. Such a change can occur when assumptions are symbolically undermined by symbols. Mary Jo Hatch (1993) proposes a dynamic understanding of change, based on natural mechanisms present in culture. Managers may use the mechanisms of gradual natural organizational changes when they want to introduce a radical change. The processes of change are continuous and they take place in four stages. The first stage is the manifestation of cultural assumptions consisting in the fact that norms and values are created on the basis of deeply rooted cultural assumptions, often unconscious ones. The second stage is the realization of the norms and values in the form of objects: artefacts. The third phase is symbolization during which some of the artefacts gain cultural importance: they become symbols. The last stage is interpretation: symbols are explained inside the cultural system. This does not always happen in a conscious manner. Culture 'explains itself' with the help of existing assumptions. Symbols can support or subvert deep cultural assumptions. Symbols that do not comply with assumptions may be explained in an old manner or banned from the system – unless they are supported, made visible and celebrated by authorities in a special way. In that case there is a chance that they will be incorporated into the processes of cultural reconstruction and a radical change will occur, triggered by a permanent subversion of old assumptions with the use of new symbols. This latter process is accompanied by a gradual creation of new assumptions (fitted to new symbols) that will replace the old ones. In other words, managing change should take place at the stage of symbolization.[16] Managers themselves are symbols of organizations and they have great symbolic power in culture. A manager should have a vision of change and they should put it into practice in a way that is visible to the whole organization, enabling identification and following of the example. To do this, the manager needs practical vision; that is, apart from a creative disposition, the courage to think and to act. All three traits are popular and very human. To awaken them, we need inspiration.

And now to Part II of the book, which presents 12 key organizational archetypes.

PART II

Organizational archetypes

4.   In search of the organization's Self

4.1   THE ARCHETYPE OF THE SELF

The Self is one of the main Jungian archetypes (Jung, [1921] 1971, [1959] 1990), and the development of the Self, the realization of individuality and unity in the process of individuation, is the purpose of human efforts and actions throughout the whole of one's life. The process may be sometimes associated with self-actualization (Maslow, [1962] 1968), the reaching of the fullness of one's being. The Self coordinates energy and combines the energy coming from the conscious spheres with the energy of the unconscious. According to Carl Gustav Jung ([1921] 1971), the Self is a whole uniting consciousness with the unconscious, whereas the Ego is the centre for the content residing in consciousness. The Ego is, for an unintegrated personality, the centre of free will and decision-making. For a full personality the broad Self might become such a centre instead. Both the consciousness and the energies coming from the unconscious (such as those known as intuition) may become an expanded field of free will and conscience. The Ego is a smaller entity, comprised in the bigger circle of the Self:

> As an empirical concept, the self designates the whole range of psychic phenomena in [humans]. It expresses the unity of the personality as a whole . . . it is a *transcendental* concept, for it presupposes the existence of unconscious factors on empirical grounds and thus characterizes an entity that can be described only in part but, for the other part, remains at present unknowable and illimitable. (Jung, [1921] 1971, p. 789)

The Self can be known only partly, but it is fully experienced, though not necessarily 'here and now'; it also contains past and future experiences. Its dark part is the Shadow that will be discussed in the next chapter.

The protagonist of William Shakespeare's *Hamlet* ([1600–1602] 2007) can serve as an illustration for the archetype of the Self. Prince Hamlet is the son of a murdered Danish king. In the castle of Elsinore, a ghost appears and reveals to Hamlet that the king was killed by his brother, the prince's uncle. The uncle, having married his brother's widow, became the new King of Denmark as a result of the murder. The young prince decides to avenge his father, as custom demands. He is, however, torn by

45

Figure 4.1   The Self
(photo: Jerzy Kociatkiewicz)

contradictory feelings and stimuli coming both from conscious philosophical reflection and from premonitions and the unconscious sphere of intuition. Under the pressure of overlapping and rivalling impulses he loses his mind – or maybe decides to become mad, or just feigns madness. The playwright depicts the plot in an ingeniously ambiguous way, giving generations of actors and directors the possibility for interpretation and reinterpretation, and showing a lively and credible story about what happens to the self of a person torn by contradictory energies coming from consciousness and the unconscious. Hamlet's indecision, his wavering and quandaries that make him the victim of other people's assaults, are the reason why for centuries readers and theatrical audiences have identified themselves with the story. The protagonist faces diverse disasters that seem to be mystically linked with his state of mind. Finally, Hamlet has to confront his fate. It takes place in dramatic circumstances when, duelling with Laertes, the brother of Hamlet's recently deceased fiancée, Ophelia, Hamlet witnesses the moment when his uncle's treachery and murder come to light. The uncle had replaced Laertes' sword with another, one that had a poisoned blade, and had poured poison into Hamlet's wine glass. As a result of the conspiracy and confusion, all die: Laertes, Hamlet's mother Queen Gertrude, and Hamlet himself, having avenged his father. Do we have a choice? Is human life fully determined and our quandaries cannot change anything? Or maybe it is the other way around – the more we are conscious, the more control we have over our destiny?

Similar questions began to be asked by researchers of organizations, especially at the end of the last century when the science was dominated by the concept of population ecology, which concentrated on describing patterns of successes and failures and the conditions for survival in the face of competitors' actions (Hannan and Freeman, 1977). In their widely quoted article Lawrence Hrebiniak and William Joyce (1985) discuss the problem of the efficiency of explaining reality in two main concepts: those of strategic choice and adaptation. It was commonly believed that the two concepts are mutually exclusive, that they are two alternative and incongruent ways of explaining reality. The supporters of each of the concepts were convinced that they held a monopoly over the truth and they tried to find shortcomings in their opponents' views. However, both these perspectives can be treated as concurrent variables that, only when taken together, describe the spectrum of the organization's behaviour, including the four most characteristic points: full natural selection; a differentiation consisting of a large-scale determinism and a major influence of strategic choice; purely strategic choice; and an undifferentiated choice based on incremental adjustment decisions and an adaptation through chance. The authors show how all of the known organizations' behaviours are located between the four basic moments. They are linked to a broader pattern of the organization's functioning, characterized by the following phenomena: conflict, decision-making style, interactions between the organization and the environment, managerial activity, and many others. In other words, the fate of the organization is influenced both by the environment and by the organization itself. Adaptation is 'a dynamic process that is both organizationally and environmentally inspired' (Hrebiniak and Joyce, 1985, p. 347). Simplified dichotomies cannot account for the diversity of concurrent types of organizations and their behaviours. Raymond Zammuto (1988) comes to similar conclusions. On the one hand, the author presents empirical evidence to support the thesis about concurrency of determinism and organizational choice, and on the other, he shows how the awareness of external conditions broadens the range of organizational choices. It is important to realize the limits in a given period and the changes in the scope of these limits. Thanks to this knowledge the decision-maker can not only help the organization survive but also effectively expand the scope of conscious choice.

I agree with those researchers who think that an organization's fate depends on both conscious choice, usually made on behalf of the organization by the management subsystem, and the forces active in the environment which the organization cannot influence but which it may try to accommodate. I also believe that the awareness of these conditions broadens the field of conscious choice. The archetype of the Self, referring to an individual, can with advantage be used as a metaphor for the organizational culture, and thanks to this the area of conscious choice can be made larger.

Below, I present several conceptions which benefit from using of the archetype of the Self in envisaging the organization, in that it brings the possibility of enhancing the organizational consciousness. The main idea that is useful in this context is the notion of organizational identity, directly linked to the archetype. Then I briefly discuss the problem of extending the limits of consciousness through learning. The chapter concludes according to the archetypical tale, that is, with looking for an ending and a completion that would fit the archetype. In the case of the Self it is individuation, realizing the potential and the individuality of the subject. Can organizations become such completions and provide this to the participants? The last section tackles the question of self-actualization of the organization and in the organization.

4.2   ORGANIZATIONS AS SUPERPERSONS

Alasdair MacIntyre (1981) claims that human life can be consistent only in the form of a story: an individual's identity seems consistent only when it is narrated in a consistent way. Identity is, then, the ability to narrate oneself, to give an account of who one is. Narrating the identity is necessary to make sense of and to express the human life and its protagonist. Stories have the same structure as human life. Telling one's story, the person introduces unique elements but also draws upon known stories; one both emulates and creates. Because stories are so strongly connected with identity, culture and the feeling of common identity, they provide an important material for the development of consciousness and the deepening of one's understanding of oneself. MacIntyre believes that in the course of narration we create and develop our identity, assuming at the same time that there exist real or implied listeners or readers of these stories. Each identity, then, is inevitably immersed in current and past contexts. It should also have narrative coherence: to talk about a moral we need a coherent story in which events are intertwined in a meaningful way.

Recently, a great deal has been said and written about organizational identity. This is facilitated by the narrative approach which puts more emphasis on the effects of the story effect rather than inquiring after the storyteller's subjectivity. In that sense, an organization's identity is defined by its continuity in space and time, the consistency of its roles and the sense of agency (Alvesson, 1994). As an effect, a popular metaphor has emerged according to which the organization in culture is imagined to be a superperson equipped with its own motivations, attitudes and features (Czarniawska, 1997). The primary reason for the rise of the metaphor in reference to organizations was legal: the aim was to make organizations accountable for their actions (the category of legal entity) (Czarniawska-Joerges, 1994). It is often assumed that an organization's identity is comprised of three kinds of factors: central, endurable and distinctive (Albert and Whetten, 1985). Identity, then, is the core of the organization, something that makes the participants and the outside observers recognize it and, yes, identify it.

Organizational identity can also be understood as the organization's idea for survival in the environment as well as its working principle available to all the participants, that is, its adaptive strategy (Dutton and Dukerich, 1991). The external image and, connected to it, the internal identity, together constitute a tool for measuring the environment's reactions to the organization's activities. The environment expresses its approval or disapproval which is quickly reflected by the image which, in its turn, is visible in the identity impressions. If there is a discrepancy between the image and the identity, forces inside the organization are activated to change either the image or the identity, in this way deciding the organization's strategic orientation. Simultaneously, identity and image stimulate and direct the participants to actions through interpretations of problems and phenomena. After some time these interpretations become patterns. The patterns give the participants the feeling of cultural stability. According to Karl Weick (1995) the organization's identity is a vital element of sense-making processes. A sense of identity together with received images of the organization lie at the core of sense-making processes, and all attempts at interpretation and pursuits of meaning have their beginning in the identity.

Just as with individual identity, the organizational identity can also be seen as a kind of narrative (Czarniawska, 1997). Contemporary organizations tend to talk about themselves in terms of continuity and cohesion, directing the story inward, to the employees, and outward, to the stakeholders. According to Barbara Czarniawska (1997) this is a kind of organizational autobiography, an apologetic narration that is supposed to explain the protagonist's actions and present it in a good light. Modern organizations, apart from presenting themselves as coherent actors – or, to be more precise, social super-actors – want to be perceived as rational, full of good intentions, and effective. More and more often there appear questions of ecology and approaches promoting sustainable growth.[17] An organizational autobiography is a story that is continuous, yet unfinished – as long as the organization is in existence, it is retold and often reinterpreted. If the organization collapses there is usually no need to tell the story to the end.

A dynamic model very well suited for depicting narrative aspects of identity has been proposed by Mary Jo Hatch and Majken Schultz (2002). Identity is a process, a result of other continuous processes of interaction between internal culture and the external image. It takes place in four main stages: mirroring, reflection, expression and impression. In the stage of mirroring the images coming from different stakeholders influence the creation of organizational identity. For example,[18] management, after familiarizing itself with the results of market research, comes to the conclusion that clients are attached to the company's traditional products and are not interested in any new goods. On this basis, the managers decide to concentrate on promoting traditional associations with the brand. Reflection consists in grounding the identity in cultural meanings by consolidating the values issuing from the received identity in the cultural assumptions. For example, the employees accept the outcome and stress the meaning of the company's long tradition in everyday conversations. Expression consists in communicating cultural values through the expression of 'who we are'. These are, then, utterances directed inwards; the culture describes itself through definitions. In everyday conversations the employees refer to traditions, tell new employees 'how it feels to work here' and that the company has devoted fans. Finally, impression consists in exerting influence on what others think about the organization through identity declarations. For instance, the chief executive officer (CEO) gives an interview on public television where he assures the viewers that the company represents everything that loyal clients see in it, and that their expectations towards the company will be fulfilled, with even greater care and attention to quality.

This short example comes from the research presented by the authors in their book *Taking Brand Initiative* (Hatch and Schultz, 2008) and refers to the famous Danish company LEGO which, as a result of reflection over its identity, decided to return to the roots of the brand, toy building blocks. In the course of the brand's reorientation that took place some time ago, management reacted to the employees' demand for the managers to specify what they should actually make of the brand. The managers came to the right conclusion that the complaints did not result from the fact that employees could not connect facts and needed to be guided by simple directives, but that they resulted from people's lack of a meaningful bond with the 'reoriented' brand. In consequence, it was decided that the ongoing staff training programme should be changed to include the expression of the participants' feelings through the construction of building blocks. The employees used the occasion to show their attitude towards the product, an attitude which proved to be very warm but decidedly traditional. New products, the recently launched educational toys, were perceived as unsuccessful. The new CEO immediately made use of these opinions to reassess the assumed strategy. In this period, the company's competitive and financial situation was neither favourable nor promising. New products did not sell well and competitors from the electronic sector as well as cheap products from poorer and developing countries forced LEGO building blocks out of their traditional markets.

Simultaneously, the managers realized that the brand still had a large number of fans among adults who used to play with them as children and for whom LEGO building blocks had great emotional value. These stakeholders were willing to devote their private time to save the brand. The CEO decided to use actively the offers of these important groups: the employees and loyal former clients. Thanks to these actions it turned out that the brand has a rich life outside management and the market. Grown-ups used LEGO building blocks and their symbolic meaning for different purposes: for playing, for relaxing (they built skyscrapers and fantastic constructions using diverse, incongruent building block sets which their children had got bored with), for expressing their opinions and formulating messages (short films and cartoons on the Internet), and so on. The CEO decided to open the brand to precisely these fans and to refer to the company's traditions, directing the products not only to the (children's) toy market but also to the market of puzzles and adult games. The company used many of its fans' ideas and the brand's supporters were encouraged to send their proposals. In cooperation with the research and development (R&D) section the fans proposed, among other things, the creation of the LEGO Mindstorms NXT, which became one of the most popular lines in the sets that serve to build robots and electronic models (programming and the construction of advanced electronics). The line is still immensely popular and inspires the creation of other successful lines of products. The company's board is deeply convinced of the rightness of this strategy towards the brand – a strategy that has been redefined nostalgically as the market of design and construction games. It plans to take similar innovative actions in the future.

Looking at this example from the perspective of the categories adopted in this chapter it can be said that the behaviour of LEGO is based on the use of all the stages of the company's identity construction process, using valuable elements coming both from outside the organization and from within, and a conscious shaping of an identity conforming to the dynamics of these processes. Instead of fighting against existing energies, it is possible to utilize them to reach goals that are constructive to the organization. A dynamically understood identity has a wider scope than the managers' conceptual sphere: it includes the whole of the organization as well as, sometimes, parts of the environment. Not taking the environment into consideration causes, after some time, serious problems.

Mary Jo Hatch and Majken Schultz (2002) distinguish two characteristic identity dysfunctions: narcissism and hyperadaptation. Narcissism consists in an excessive concentration on internal subprocesses, reflection and expression. The organization grows excessively convinced about its uniqueness and perfection, it concentrates on itself and on expressing the same content repeatedly. Such attitude perseveres regardless of what happens in the environment or even in an increasing isolation from the environment. Like a pathologically narcissistic human being, the organization quickly loses the sense of reality. For example,[19] in a certain European radio station the feeling of excessive self-admiration became increasingly manifest. Both the board and the employees concentrated on endless discussions about the quality and the message of the shows, completely forgetting about the listeners' reactions. The problems were aggravated by political conflicts that consumed a lot of energy, at the same time as strengthening in the people involved the feeling that the organization was unique and the game was worth the candle.

Hyperadaptation is an opposite identity pathology. It results from the domination of external processes, mirroring and impression. It leads to the erasure of culture, a complete blending with the environment and the loss of identity. In the above example the new CEO of the radio station resolved to put a stop to the self-admiration and decided, with the consent and active help of the new board, to change the organization's functioning radically. All decisions regarding the programme and the line-up were to be based on opinion polls and market research. Eventually, the station's offer became similar to the offer of competing private stations but its quality was worse due to smaller financial resources of the station. The CEO, quite predictably, decided to look for a solution in another opinion poll which, however, suggested liquidation or commercialization of the public broadcasting station. Both strategies would lead to the station's definitive end; surely neither surprising nor sad, since in the polls the viewers said that they did not know what distinguished the station from others.

4.3   ORGANIZATION AS PSYCHIC PRISON

In his famous work *Discipline and Punish* Michel Foucault ([1975] 1991) argues that contemporary societies have abandoned direct invigilation and corporal punishment. Instead, observing and controlling through normalization have become increasingly common. According to the philosopher, the discipline system, based on Panopticon, spreads onto all spheres of life, such as the educational system and the army. Panopticon was an architectural form designed in the middle of the seventeenth century by Jeremy Bentham to be used in prisons. The innovation consisted of the fact that the prisoners were to be under constant scrutiny, as the architecture made it possible to observe all of the prisoners' activities, while the guards remained unseen. Constant observation was quickly internalized by the prisoners and formed into a sort of internal Panopticon, a normalizing voice of social control regulating the life of contemporary people. The tool of control is knowledge:

> We should admit rather that power produces knowledge (and not simply by encouraging it because it serves power by applying it because it is useful); that power and knowledge directly imply one another; that there is no power relation without the correlative constitution of a field of knowledge, nor any knowledge that does not presuppose and constitute at the same time power relations. (Foucault, [1975] 1991, p. 27)

Foucault remarks that other people's definitions of ourselves can create a wall around us, depriving us of our freedom and the awareness of an exit as if the wall was built of bricks and mortar. Many researchers of organizations (see e.g. McKinlay and Starkey, 1988) believe that such a model has been universally adopted in contemporary management. Gareth Morgan ([1986] 2006) presented, among other metaphors for organizations, a metaphor based on Panopticon – of the organization as psychic prison. People and organizations have much more freedom than they realize. Sometimes they are limited by their own constructs, such as management systems. They seem to them an external barrier that they have no influence on. In fact, however, the systems are based on modes of thinking, on the type of knowledge adopted as binding and on behaviour conventions. Some of these barriers are unconscious or subconscious – they result from psychological processes that have consolidated among the participants in the socialization process and which they have never questioned nor even realized. Other barriers are strategies of control of the employees introduced intentionally by the superiors, aiming to broaden their influence. In such cases management, by manipulating and acting in a calculating way, uses the employees' good faith to achieve their own goals. In addition, sometimes the managers and the employees rely on conventions because it provides them with a feeling of security and enables them to find shelter in the common identity; they act like a child who puts its trust in its teddy bear:

> This is the fundamental psychodynamic of totalitarianism. It alienates people from themselves and gives them over to others. Whatever victories may ensue must be pyrrhic. Whatever happiness is to be attained here is not the happiness of the individual. Indeed, it is to happiness at all. It is the drama of happiness attaching to a role that the person performs in a play in a play that is written and directed by others. (Schwartz, 1990, p. 16)

Michael Pratt (2000) describes an organization which builds its culture by modelling it on an ideological fortress that is to be a safe and impenetrable protection against any attacks from the outside. The beliefs that this direct marketing organization adopts in its everyday functioning are the bricks and mortar used in the construction of the fortress. Management claims to give over control to a higher force but it is only a way to preserve control over the employees and not a reliance on spiritual flow, typical for mystical organizations such as contemplative orders. Rather, it is a strategy of avoiding uncertainty and at the same time answering all the important questions with the help of formulae enabling more control. This international direct marketing company bases its activities on the involvement of the participants. Products are sold individually, by 'distributors' who are not officially employed by the company but work as 'independent entrepreneurs' connected to the company by an agreement which also includes a list of a seller's ethical principles. The organization is a network which adopts a rule of internal hierarchy of the sellers, and a mechanism of sponsoring new sellers by more experienced ones. There are strong bonds between the co-workers, both economical and social. The company does not have any separate function responsible for the sales and marketing, nor a set of rules or procedures regulating this aspect of the company's functioning. The function of sales is the domain of individual collaborators who are obliged to self-control on the basis of the common ideology they have accepted. It is this 'voluntary' ideology that constitutes the metaphorical bricks and mortar, culturally constructed in the company. First of all, it transmits to everybody a complete, ready-made worldview. The participants do not need external opinions to cope with the majority of problems, whether connected with their work or not. The company's ideology answers the questions regarding finance: how to earn money? Career: how to be successful? And existential issues: why do we need to make an effort? What is the meaning of life? The company aims to recruit all the people close to its participants: their friends and family. In this way the company becomes a totalizing presence and, similarly to greedy institutions (Coser, 1974), it defines all the participants' social reality, simplifying their lives and depriving them of role conflicts as well as lending their lives an unusual coherence and limiting the diversity of viewpoints natural for the majority of people who have contact with different milieus.

> Organized groups are always faced with the problem of how best to harness human energies to their purposes ... Such competition for loyalty and commitment is a perennial problem because these are scarce resources. Not only do human beings possess only finite libidinal energies for cathecting social objects, but their resources of time are similarly limited. As a consequence, various groups having a claim on individuals' energies and time compete with one

another in the effort to draw as much as they can, within normative limits, from the available pool of resources. The struggle over their allocation is as much a root fact of social life as is the competition among users of scarce resources in economic affairs. (Coser, 1974, p. 1)

The company described by Michael Pratt (2000) harnesses the energy of people's private lives to realize the goals connected with management and the pursuit of economic goals, so that the employees' private lives no longer compete with the company's goals. Moreover, the company dictates moral rules to the participants, ordering and stabilizing their lives. For example, they claim to preserve the 'traditional' family values in accordance with the types of Protestantism popular in the so-called Bible belt in the United States of America. Simultaneously, to these quasi-religious values are added other economic values and rules such as the belief that gaining a lot of money in the company is one of the criteria for being a good friend, spouse and parent. Financial success is equated with spiritual success; it is a sign of a higher force's approval of a person. The company seeks to define all the employees' social roles through the perspective of its own roles and tasks, connected with work done for the company. In contrast to ordinary conflicting and rival value systems that people encounter in their everyday lives, the value system offered to the company's cooperators is surprisingly coherent. 'Business', 'religion', 'family' and 'friendship' intersect and support one another in the activities undertaken for the company's sake. It results in life being more predict-able, but also much more limited, than an ordinary human life outside the company. All incoherencies are explained by references to 'spirituality': for instance, when a co-participant works hard but is not successful, it is explained as the result of 'God's will' and the person is advised patience and the resignation to God's design that must certainly carry some useful content even if it consists of painful experiences. This is how the organiza-tion fully encompasses a person, controlling him or her as well as entrap-ping them within the borders of its complete and coherent ideology. By such an approach the organization may offer the employees a sense of meaning, but it happens at the price of cutting them off from a whole spectrum of impressions and experiences that await people outside of the fortress the company symbolically becomes for its participants.

Przemysław Piątkowski (2007) tells the story of an organization that also limits the lives of its participants but does so as if from 'the oppo-site side' – it is a religious organization that gets involved in the private, professional and financial spheres of life of its participants. The dualistic character of organizational culture is present in all spheres of the social life of the organization's participants. It neatly divides reality into two spheres: us and them. The central motif is the battle between the forces of good ('us') and evil ('them'). Following Pratt, Piątkowski also adopts the fortress metaphor in reference to the organization. It expresses the same facets of the organization and, in addition, it shows how the organization is a realm of constant battle. The members fight battles on the organization's walls, and these battles touch upon the professional and economic spheres as well as the strictly religious because, just like Pratt's company, Piątkowski's religious organization has totalizing ambitions. The members are expected to limit most their lives to working inside the organization, which will offer them in exchange a complete set of norms, values and beliefs for every occasion, eliminating the necessity of making decisions and, in a way, letting the organization act as their conscience.

4.4   LEARNING AS ORGANIZATIONAL LIBERATION

In the 1940s Gregory Bateson (1972) introduced the idea of deutero-learning, a higher level of learning that refers to the organization of the learning process, that is, learning how to learn. This level of learning consists in its contextualization through generalization (taking place at the first level). The learner puts together the rules that enable him or her to learn as effectively as possible. It is possible to proceed from the level of ordinary learning to the second level through reflection, problem-oriented learning and the development of intelligence. In taking the thinking to a higher, more complex level the problems are given a frame of reference and situations are more easily understood. There is also a third, highest, level of learning (trito-learning), beyond knowledge and understanding, a spiritual and existential level. On this level the learner asks about the sense of his or her experience, and tries to understand it in a context as well as comprehend his or her role in the reality he or she studies. There is also a possibility of a change of identity, a redefinition of personality. On the first level one gains skills; on the second, knowledge; and on the third, wisdom.[20]

Chris Argyris and Donald Schön (1978) applied Bateson's ideas to the organizational context. They distinguish two levels of learning: of a single and a double loop, corresponding roughly to Bateson's first and second levels of learning. Learning of the first loop consists in adjusting the means to desired aims. It works like a thermostat: when the temperature of the surroundings changes, the system adjusts itself, producing the required amount of heat. The double loop of learning introduces a new quality: asking about the purpose, questioning it and, possibly, changing the purpose. In organizations it can mean a strategic change, a shift in thinking about organizational aims. According to the authors this is the basis for the development of learning processes within an organization. For example,[21] the detection of a recurring fault in services, such as failure to meet deadlines, results in a re-evaluation of rules and management systems in the company, a decentralization and an increase in the responsibility of workers who are in direct contact with the clients. The company abandons cost-cutting and invests in improving quality. Simplifying the way of decision-making can hasten the services and help in meeting the deadlines. The double loop means questioning the organization's strategies and aims and comprises 'those sorts of organizational inquiry which resolve incompatible organizational norms by setting new priorities and weightings of norms, or by restructuring the norms themselves together with associated strategies and assumptions' (Argyris and Schön, 1978, p. 18).

Argyris and Schön (1978) consider the question of how an organization can increase its abilities to develop learning of the double loop. An organization can be perceived as an expression of the shared knowledge of how the whole of the system functions in its environment. The knowledge is expressed in a dynamic way in the processes of thinking and problem-solving. Therefore, learning organizations should also have a dynamic character; static procedures and objectives are not enough, even if they are formulated in a most rational fashion. The participants should be encouraged to get to know, and even question, the organization. For the learning process to take place the 'learning agents' discoveries, inventions and evaluations must be embedded in organizational memory' (ibid., p. 19), that is, in the common action maps, constructed in cooperation with other participants. If the process does not take place, only individuals learn, not the organization.

Peter Senge ([1990] 2006) is, likewise, interested in organizational learning, but he stresses other aspects than Argyris and Schön. He focuses on systems and structures rather than interactions and cooperation in groups. People are naturally disposed to learn, whereas organizations have to be taught how to. In order for the organization to be made to learn, two conditions must be fulfilled: the first is the ability to design the organization in such a way that it could realize the assumed purposes in the best manner possible; and the second is the ability to see where the organization's functioning diverges from the desired objectives, and to take the necessary steps to correct the discrepancy. A skill that supports organizational learning is system thinking, which means that individuals are always seen as parts of a broader context of the system, and organizations as parts of an environment. At the core of system thinking are the reactions and relationships between parts of the system and between diverse systems. Problems are always considered in such a broad, dynamic perspective and never in isolation, without reference to the whole system. There is a classical maxim, dating from Aristotle (1998): 'The whole is more than the sum of its parts'. This saying has been taken as an axiom by system theorists, who stress that the solving of problems on the level of parts is a misunderstanding since an element of the system taken in isolation is something completely different than it is within its broader context. This idea also lies at the basis of Peter Senge's ([1990] 2006) concept of the learning organization: learning should be built into a broader context of the system. The learning organization gains the ability for autonomous self-creation in time: it can 'create the results [it] truly desire[s], where new and expansive patterns of thinking are nurtured, where collective aspiration is set free, and where people are continually learning how to learn together' (ibid., p. 8).

Such an organization is said to be more flexible and its participants have more freedom than in other organizations. It is connected with a change in thinking, with the passage from the level of individual ideas, things and people to a systemic level, as well as a change of perspective where people are no longer perceived as elements but as active co-creators of the system. Moreover, the learning organization should take care of two essential aspects necessary for the continuity of learning: it should provide helpful leadership and sensible cooperation. Cooperation does not exclude conflicts. On the contrary, a learning organization should be open to conflicts, because they are the sign of a diversity of ideas, attitudes and methods of achieving goals. People should be free to act and make mistakes. Defensiveness is one of the most serious barriers in learning. The system should also give managers the right and the freedom to be ignorant. Managers' defensiveness is a colossal barrier in learning. People who are managers often assume that their role encompasses a kind of infallibility: that they should know everything about anything that is connected with his or her organizational unit. As a result they often create an appearance of an organizational omniscience that is connected with an inflexibility in behaviour issuing from the belief that a manager should not be influenced by anything. Behind the façade of self-assurance lurk defensiveness and uncertainty. Abolishing defensiveness can often unblock the ability to learn. It is not enough to attempt learning at the individual level: organizations need a systematic building in of diversity in the hierarchy and the inclusion of the employees in the empowerment on a larger scale than at the moment.

Karl Weick (2001) stresses the importance of continuity and identity for learning processes. He warns that a compromising of the sense of identity and memory of the past in the name of economy (for example, cost saving) can have seriously deleterious effects on an organization's ability to learn at all. It also potentially blocks an organization's adapta-

tion capacity. An organization with a good learning potential is, therefore, one where there is a strong enough and shared sense of stability and
connection.

Aleksander Chrostowski (2006) portrays a learning organization. The
managers of a Polish company in the restaurant business asked academic
consultants for help in introducing radical changes. First of all, it was
decided that the employees should participate in management processes
much more actively than had been the case before. A strategic session was
organized with the participation of the representatives of all the groups of
employees from all the hierarchical levels. The participants together considered the current and the possible future objectives of the company and
presented a general outline of the new strategy. The emphasis was put on
teamwork and a decision was made to transmit a part of the rights and
responsibilities to the lower levels of the hierarchy. It was agreed that in
the future all important decisions will be made with the participation of
a wide representation of the staff. The knowledge and experience of the
most important people in the organization were to be used as effectively
as possible in the management process. The management agreed that a
real chance of creating and introducing a good strategy may appear only
when it is worked out by the people working for the company. A wide
range of privileges for teams have been formally written into the new
structure. Changes have been made in the assessment and remuneration
systems. Managers have been obliged to consult the employees' teams.
System thinking was also introduced, thanks to which, in the words of
one of the managers, people now '[c]ould define their place, the scope of
their competences, their responsibility – they could see and feel it' (ibid.,
p. 147).

The feeling of a shared responsibility combined with the lack of anxiety
concerning the possibility of making a mistake made the organization
much more open and enjoyable to work for. The new strategy together
with the new rules for collaborative work made learning one of the basic
rules of interaction with the environment. According to one of the board
members the changes activated a huge potential in people:

> The change in the company's mindset proved a great thing. The change in the
> rules of cooperation, a wonderful school of communication, a wonderful way
> of introducing a new philosophy in which the company is treated as a coherent
> organism, where everyone, regardless of his or her position, has a common aim.
> Thinking from the perspective of the product that will ultimately be judged by
> the client shows the real purpose of the company's multiple functions and posts.
> We succeeded in making people see their place in the organization, understand
> their problems and shortcomings and cooperate – I believe it is a great success.
> (ibid., p. 149)[22]

4.5 THE WAY TO ORGANIZATIONAL SELF-ACTUALIZATION

The story of the Self has its own archetypical narrative gravity, like a river that flows to the sea. In this story the gravity is the fulfilment to the point of transcendence, what Jung (1921/1977) calls individuation. This is also what the psychologist Abraham Maslow (1962/1968) had in mind when he spoke of self-actualization. He was interested in healthy, happy people and the basis of their happiness. He considered the steps that need to be taken in order to make it possible for each human being to experience genuine satisfaction, and came up with the famous concept of the hierarchy of needs. According to this theory people move upwards in the hierarchy of their needs as the more basic needs are fulfilled to a satisfying degree. The last degree is the need for self-actualization, the counterpart of individuation. It is a full actualization of one's potential and one's individuality. It is manifested in the ability to experience and express reality from the unique perspective of the subject. A self-actualizing person takes nothing for granted; they can live in the present without forgetting about the past or losing touch with the flow of time. According to Maslow, a healthy personality is characterized by unity, coherence and integrity, the awareness of the existence of different aspects of reality together with the capability to integrate them. People who actualize themselves are realists: they are open to reality and they do not use defence mechanisms and beliefs to guard themselves from experiencing it. They can accept themselves and others just as they are. They are spontaneous, they do not live in a programmed way and they will not let themselves be limited by imagined necessities. They concentrate on the problems they encounter and not on themselves; therefore it is easier for them to solve the problems – they do not view them as personal misfortunes that they have to cope with or overcome. Self-actualizing people have a strong need for privacy, for personal space, but at the same time they feel a deep need to share their thoughts and feelings with other people – they are very empathic. They make autonomous decisions and judgements and are not easily influenced. Since they are resistant to outside influences, including acculturation, they tend to be perceived as nonconformists or eccentrics, which they do not mind. Self-actualization is characterized by occasional peak experiences, moments of unity with the world and life accompanied by a feeling of liberation and happiness as well as an inner serenity. According to Abraham Maslow, all healthy people have the potential and inner motivation for self-actualization, for using the natural, spontaneous energy that:

> consists of free, uninhibited uncontrolled, trusting, unpremeditated expression of the self, that is, of the psychic forces, with minimal interference by

consciousness. Control, will, caution, self-criticism, measure, deliberateness are the brakes upon this expression made intrinsically necessary by the laws of the social and natural world, and secondarily, made necessary by the fear of the psyche itself. (ibid., p. 197)

Maslow's model is the basis for the recent field of transpersonal business studies (Boucouvalas, 1999) that deals with the questions of self-actualization in business. Apart from Maslow's writings, the theory draws on flow theory in business. Mihály Csíkszentmihályi (1990) describes a state called 'flow' resembling the peak experience of a self-actualizing person. The state is favourable to creation but also to everyday work, if it is done particularly well. A person in this state is fully concentrated on his or her work, on the present moment, and feels happy. The person loses the sense of time and place and experiences an intense awareness of the work being done. A person in this state immediately spots the mistakes made and corrects them. To reach the flow state concentration is needed, as are the skills needed to perform the work, and also talent. The environment should be appropriately adjusted and it should not disturb the person at work. Flow can also become a collective experience, if a group of people creating or working collectively has appropriate conditions (Csíkszentmihályi, 2003).

'Good business' cannot be reduced to the urge to maximize profit. One of its essential goals should also be the contribution to human happiness. A good company gives people a true satisfaction with their work, contributing simultaneously to social prosperity, both material and non-material. The manager of such a company should create attractive work conditions and make sure that the work makes sense. Another strategy for the development of appropriate work conditions is encouraging and rewarding those people who are naturally prone to feel the flow and can derive joy from their work and share it with others. They set a good example for other employees. Other factors that can help managers in creating a good company are: cultivating a good sense of humour and a humorous detachment from one's ego; showing respect to people, regardless of their position in hierarchy; and providing good workers with the freedom of action and movement. A good company should communicate its objectives clearly and its management should create an atmosphere of trust. Everyone should know the objective connected with their specific job and position. This facilitates the functioning of the monitoring system that shows what the current standards are and whether the work of each employee is in accordance with the standards. It is also important to select the right employees for particular jobs so that everyone can realize their skills and predispositions. It is important to keep in mind that people follow the example of the managers: empathic, visionary leaders draw people to themselves and make others develop similar qualities. Hypocrisy and cynicism are deadly for the morale of the environment. Respect, in contrast, can work miracles in creating a culture open to flow: the culture of good business is the best stimulus for the creation of collective flow (Csíkszentmihályi, 2003).

Drawing on the theories of Maslow and Jung, Richard Schott (1992) presents the model of the eupsychic manager,[23] that is, a self-actualizing manager who, at the same time, takes care about the self-actualization of the organization as a whole. The author observes that many self-actualizing persons tend to shy away from managerial positions. The question why this is the case remains open to researchers and authors. Indeed, more managers of this kind are badly needed in the morally and aesthetically desolate business world of our times. In *The Quest for the Self-Actualizing Organization* (Kostera, 2005) I describe the self-actualizing organization as the modern organizational utopia which many people, both practitioners and theoreticians, long for but which remains a dream, an ideal unreachable in practice for the people I interviewed. My interlocutors created short fictional stories regarding various aspects of the self-actualizing organization. Put together, the stories formed a narrative collage[24] that presented the image of an organization open to flow, interested in the unique potential of its collaborators, unbound by its hierarchical structure, heading for holistic development and supporting personal development of its participants.

Such an organization seemed to me most similar to an entrepreneurial organization,[25] although there I have also spotted some important differences mainly regarding the use of uncertainty. In the entrepreneurial organization uncertainty is treated as a resource to be used in the company's development, understood as gaining a better position in the market and increasing income (profit). In a self-actualizing organization uncertainty can be accepted as long as it is in agreement with the flow. This means that such an organization's development can be, but does not have to be, regarded in categories of profit and market position. Another difference refers to the role of the individual: in an entrepreneurial organization the individual counts as much as they contribute to the company's development. In other words, only those employees who are completely involved in fulfilling the company's aims can actualize themselves there. In a self-actualizing organization everyone can find their place and be appreciated. Of all existing types of organizations, a self-actualizing organization is best suited to a certain type of entrepreneurship – social entrepreneurship (e.g. Milczarczyk, 2008). Social entrepreneurship consists in combining social work and mission with gaining profit (Bornstein,

1998). A social entrepreneur is: 'a pathbreaker with a powerful new idea, who combines visionary and real-world problem-solving creativity, who has a strong ethical fiber, and who is "totally possessed" by his or her vision for change' (ibid., p. 36). To make it happen, the social entrepreneur organizes and supports the work and the personal development of others. All employees in such a company have to be really personally engaged in the company's objectives. The social aims come first, and the individuals later. If someone is not convinced by the cause, they will be left out; it is not, then, a true self-actualizing company.

A good example of an organization which engages in social entrepreneurship is provided by David Bornstein (2007). He presents a Hungarian organization working for the disabled, Összefogás Ipari Szövetkezet, established by Erzsébet Szekeres, the mother of a disabled child, the now grown-up Tibor. Erzsébet could not count on her family's help in the upbringing of her son. After several years of lone struggle with adversities she decided to set up an organization that would help parents in a similar situation and their disabled children. Together with other people who shared her experiences and vision, Erzsébet started looking for funds and eventually succeeded. The money was spent on employing disabled people, constructing apartments for them, setting up a shop, buying production technology, and so on.

The first serious contract for Összefogás Ipari Szövetkezet was a commission to install aerials for the army. After that the organization started to get further contracts and to grow. During the times of transformation the organization did just as well as under the previous system, and still does now. It combines passion and social mission with economic momentum. So far, the company has managed to create 21 centres throughout Hungary that provide training, work and accommodation for more than 600 disabled people. Összefogás Ipari Szövetkezet has also gained wide recognition – the Hungarian President has honoured it for the work towards improving the conditions of life of the people with disabilities, and Erzsébet Szekeres advises the government about legislative solutions. The organization gives the disabled, as well as volunteers and employees supporting the disabled, a sense of development and actualization. Bornstein's impression of the organization's participants was that they live full lives, fulfil their dreams and constantly develop. The organization's founder is a source of inexhaustible energy; she keeps adjusting the company's actions to the clients' needs; she fights for the rights of the disabled in society. Within the organization, she tries to create conditions for them to pursue their interests and better integrate with the society. The organization creates new worlds, both spiritually and materially.

5.   The organizational Shadow

5.1   THE ARCHETYPE OF THE SHADOW

The Shadow is one of the main Jungian archetypes ([1959] 1990; [1921] 1977) and it refers to the negative, dark side of the human soul. The archetype contains unwanted, unaccepted traits, inclinations, aspirations and predilections discarded in the process of socialization. Jung believes that the shadow is a universal subsystem of the psyche, and that it accompanies every person. It is contained within the wider circle of the Self mentioned in the previous chapter and constitutes the Self's unconscious elements. This means that it is not always seen by its owner. The majority of people concentrate on their Ego, trying to make it socially accepted and best suited to the environment. The Shadow, however, plays an important role in human life. It can be an unconscious source of nuisances and misunderstandings.

Unfortunately there can be no doubt that man is, on the whole, less good than he imagines himself or wants to be. Everyone carries a shadow, and the less it is embodied in the individual's conscious life, the blacker and denser it is. If an inferiority is conscious, one always has a chance to correct it. Furthermore, it is constantly in contact with other interests, so that it is continually subjected to modifications. But if it is repressed and isolated from consciousness, it never gets corrected (Jung, 1938/1966, p. 93).

In certain pathological cases, the Shadow can cause serious problems. If it develops excessively and remains entirely outside the light of consciousness, it can take control over a person's life and make the individual change suddenly, become 'mad', become someone else, someone dark and incomprehensible, like Doctor Jekyll changing into the terrifying Mr Hyde.

Robert Louis Stevenson's novella ([1886] 2007) tells the story of the London lawyer Gabriel John Utterson who tries to solve the mystery of the death of his friend, Doctor Henry Jekyll. The protagonist learns that the gloomy Mr Hyde is the main heir to Doctor's Jekyll's fortune. Therefore, Hyde becomes his main suspect. But soon Hyde is found dead. Gradually, the protagonist discovers the truth – Jekyll and Hyde are in fact one and the same person. Doctor Jekyll desired to separate good and evil in man and created a potion that changed him into either the good Doctor Jekyll or the bad and depraved Mr Hyde. After some time, however, the stock of the potion ran out and its particular composition, the result of a mistake, could not be replicated. It happened at the moment when Hyde needed the potion to change into doctor Jekyll. Hyde sees only one way out of this deadlock: suicide. The decision is the last flash of self-awareness, the last desperate effort of the mind. Hyde had never been guided by reflection or empathy; he was evil to the bone, wicked, violent and aggressive. He embodied Doctor Jekyll's dark side which the latter had up to then been suppressing. After Jekyll separated the dark side from himself, he could be fully good. However, now and then he could feel that his role as the good doctor was false and that his dark side was becoming more active and genuine. Mr Hyde was increasingly powerful, and he needed the potion to return to his good and bright form. The story can be read as depicting the forming of the Shadow, and shows what happens if the Shadow separates completely from the conscious personality.

Jung ([1938] 1966) believed that all people create a Shadow when they shape their personality, want to perfect it and win social approval. Organizations, too, create shadows. The Shadow is the more intense, the more the management tries to gain absolute control over the organization

Figure 5.1   The Shadow
(photo: Monika Kostera)

(Bowles, 1991), which is neither exceptional nor limited to pathological cases of mismanagement. Just like a person striving for perfection but unable to see his or her limitations, such organizations lose the ability to see their mistakes. Any negative signals they receive are projected onto others: competitors, clients, trade unions, their own employees. People in such an organization frequently feel uneasy, depressed, often terrified or desperate, but they always imagine that the source of these feelings is a force external to the organization; it is never 'us' but always 'them'. An attentive observer of culture will notice that the feelings, as well as their cultural sources, come from inside the organization. It is the organization's cultural system that entangles, lures and oppresses. Just as in the case of a person, the organizational Shadow is a moral problem.

To solve the problem one needs courage and determination to confront one's own demons and accept the fact that they are as much 'ours' as what makes people in organizations proud and that they like to identify with. Only the light of consciousness can defeat the darkness of the Shadow. The way towards the integration of the Shadow is difficult but it is worth the trouble. The Shadow may also contain beneficial elements – the so-called Golden Shadow. Often, some positive traits and talents end up in the Shadow, together with the unwanted traits. This may happen because a person, or an organization, cannot cope with these traits or because they are connected to manifestations of traits that are socially unacceptable. Often, this is the case of people who consider letting loose their creativity and think they may want to self-actualize their unique potential.[26] Creativity requires stepping out of the crowd, becoming an eccentric or a freak in the eyes of the others. Quite often people cannot accept this; they prefer to be 'like everyone else' at the expense of giving up their individuality; they choose mediocrity for fear of social rejection, or losing their friends or a source of income. Organizations behave in a similar way and their behaviour is governed by similar motifs. They also worry about losing the approval of important groups in their environment, like clients, investors, creditors, shareholders and other stakeholders. An organization that does not enjoy a good reputation can easily lose support and be forced out of the race for survival. Numerous organizations give up their dreams of experimenting and creative management, favouring mediocrity and an existence devoid of fantasy, made attractive with the help of labels like benchmarking or the NIH[27] syndrome. Yet without creativity we are not fully human, and our organizations become sterile and destructive. Realizing the existence of the Shadow, and its integration with its light side, can become an important matter for many organizations.

I will now present the organizational Shadow in its three most predominant forms. They refer to its origins: excessive control, negligence and violence. At the same time the three mechanisms are manifestations of the Shadow, the result of its functioning in the organization's culture. One can say that each of these phenomena is a self-propelling vicious circle, a cultural *perpetuum mobile*. Excessive control, the lack of care for people, as well as violence feed and strengthen the Shadow; simultaneously, the existence of the three mechanisms proves that the organization already has a developed Shadow that in turn generates the very mechanisms that cannot be stopped with ordinary measures usually applied in healing an organization, such as courses and training sessions. Even though the mechanisms are discussed separately, it does not mean that they do not occur together in one organization. Unfortunately, one aspect does not protect from others.

5.2 THE SHADOW AS A SIDE EFFECT OF IDENTITY MANAGEMENT

In her famous book *No Logo* (2000) the Canadian journalist and activist Naomi Klein presents two different faces of international organizations. Companies that invest their enormous resources in creating and supporting brands at the same time contradict the rules they propagate. The brand has become much more than a guarantee of quality – it symbolizes values, lifestyles, attitudes. Attracting clients through the promise of the satisfaction of their needs and the fulfilment of their dreams has become a classic function of advertising. Recently, companies have started offering people the symbolic capital of the brand.[28] People tend to trust famous brands, believing that they stand for quality, solidity and civilization. Naomi Klein demonstrates that for many companies brand-building has become much more important than the process of manufacturing the product or providing the service.

While the stakeholders concentrate on brands, the decisions made behind the scenes are unethical, treacherous and highly cynical, far from what we are accustomed to view as civilized. Brand products are manufactured at extremely low costs in developing countries, in settings that do not resemble those that people are used to seeing as good and safe working conditions and often regard as the social achievements of the contemporary world. Often children are employed to work in sweatshops, made to work long hours for starvation-level wages, and have no rights that would protect them. Nobody pays attention to the effects these sweatshops have on the social or natural environment. The units do not belong to the company selling the brand goods, but are contracted as part of the outsourcing plan to minimize costs. Western companies cooperate with local partners to whom they would not wish to be linked officially. Not only do the companies exert no pressure on their subcontractors to improve the work conditions of their employees, but they also purposely and consciously choose those subcontractors that offer the cheapest product, regardless of the means that used to manufacture it. The question of why we, consumers and citizens of what we call the modern and democratic world, accept this state of affairs remains one of the fundamental issues of the contemporary era. Quite often the answer is that people feel power-less with regard to these questions. They feel that corporations rule the world with a power unequalled by any state, organization or, least of all, individual. Companies seem unperturbed. Double standards are blatantly employed by many of them: officially they proclaim that they are symbols of modern and enlightened virtues, while unofficially they are guided by greed, the desire for profit and a contempt for human rights. Vices thrive behind the façade of values that people working for these organizations openly propagate.

However, it does not always have to be so. Hypocrisy is certainly wide-spread, but some reactions to Naomi Klein's *No Logo* show evidence of something else. Many employees of Western corporations did not know or did not want to know about their employees' dealings in the poorer countries. Some of the employees of such companies believed that their companies were progressive, ethical and modern, a reaction I have heard many times from my practitioner students. Even more tellingly, the MBA students of my colleague[29] blamed the poorer countries for the immoral deeds of the companies: the subcontractors, local authorities and even the employees of the sweatshops (the students claimed that if they organized themselves, like the Western employees some time ago, they would gain some rights for themselves). The brand companies were described as victims of the greed and demoralization of their local partners. The example illustrates the omnipresence of Shadow development in brand-creating organizations as well as the social need for brands. Just like in Victorian England, virtue is very much needed in contemporary business. But concentrating just on the light side gives vices excellent conditions under which to grow and flourish, and if they are not discussed in public, an uncontrolled development of the Shadow can be expected, as it thrives in darkness.

The Shadow has also a propensity to prosper as a side effect of identity management. Together with a co-author (Kociatkiewicz and Kostera, 2010), I showed how this can happen based on a model of identity forma-tion by Hatch and Schulz (2002). The Shadow is understood as something more than the pathologies resulting from the imbalance between the image and the identity of the organization. It develops out of the elements that the social actors have discarded parallel to all the conscious stages of identity formation. Some values, feelings and attitudes elude the organization's culture and image or are effaced from it. The process is depicted in Figure 5.2. In the process of reflection some norms and values are not accepted by the culture; instead, they find their place in the Shadow. They become declared norms and values – the managers claim that everyone should follow them, but the participants cannot or will not do so. Kociatkiewicz and Kostera call this process 'imposition'. For instance,[30] an information technology (IT) company that functions in the Polish market expects its employees to meet deadlines and to account for the hours spent working on computer programs. The employees, however, believe that one cannot separate effective work from the hours spent on collecting thoughts and ideas. The time pressure exerted by management does not make work more effective; instead, it is perceived by the employees as entrapment and provokes a feeling of danger. Certain norms and values do not reach the conscious identity through expression but are followed anyway, while remaining undeclared. We call this process 'hypocrisy'. For example,[31] in a certain Polish private higher education institution all teachers know that the only real value is money. Students who pay tend to pass all the exams, even if their knowledge leaves much to be desired. As a result, the predominating picture of a student in the organization is of someone not intelligent but demanding good grades for the money they have paid; thus, the student resembles a child in an amusement park and not an adult person embarking on a sometimes difficult path of acquiring knowledge. This image is never officially verbalized by the dean or the faculty.

The elements of the image that are not reflected in the identity build the Shadow in the process of denial. For instance,[32] a famous Polish company receives signals from the environment, mostly from its clients but also from the supporters of its traditional image, that things are getting worse, the social support is decreasing, and the current actions of the board are perceived as arrogant and directed against the brand they know and like. These voices are immediately hushed up, not only by the management but also by the majority of employees. Culturally, the company is proud to be modernizing and getting rid of old-fashioned content, 'from the bygone era'. This produces dissonances discerned most clearly by the employees who are in direct contact with clients who complain about the deterioration of the services, putting the blame mainly on the employees.

Finally, there are images that the organization sends which are not absorbed by the process of image impression. The images are lost – they are not received by any of the groups of stakeholders. The process is called 'misdirection'. For example,[33] a certain well-known Polish company regularly announces its successes in statements issued by management,

Organizations and archetypes

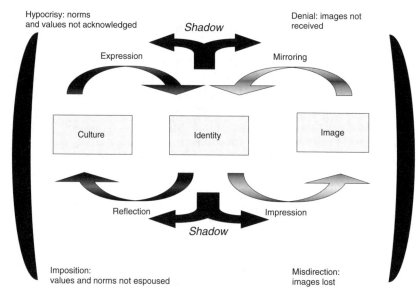

Source: Kociatkiewicz and Kostera (2010), based on identity dynamics model by Hatch and Schultz (1997).

Figure 5.2   The construction of organizational identity and Shadow

and in media interviews. The managers stress the company's outstanding achievements, good press and remarkable results in rankings. The employees, however, whisper to one another that the good press consists mainly of articles sponsored by the company and other public relations (PR) presentations, and the rankings too are more or less directly 'sponsored'. The other readers do not pay attention to the company's bragging.

The process of Shadow development can intensify to such an extent that it ceases to be an accompanying process and begins to suppress the conscious identity processes. It can also destroy the organization through a sudden outburst in the course of one of the subprocesses, or create an atmosphere of blockage that causes a sense of burnout in the participants and sterilizes the organization's culture (Bowles, 1991).

The process of Shadow formation is accompanied by collective negative feelings, the sources of which the participants are usually unable to recognize. These feelings may be very strong and can even trigger an epidemic of depression and phobias among the organization's participants. The existence of norms and values that have not been reflected upon but are instead imposed causes a feeling of oppression, the willingness to protest, or provokes resignation. The feelings can lead to burnout or an outburst of violence. Norms and values that are not accepted but result from hypocrisy cause the feelings of alienation and exclusion, an inner void and indifference; they can also encourage cynicism and aggression directed against one's own organization. Ideas promoted officially, for example, through PR or advertising, but not subjected to impression, not internalized, lead to the sense of frustration and impatience and, in extreme cases, to aggression directed at no specific addressee.

The central motif in all cases of the Shadow's expansion is the intensification of control over the identity-building process (Kociatkiewicz and Kostera, 2010). These processes should, like culture, be co-created by various social actors. As far as questions of their identity are concerned, organizations should be even more open than in the case of the creation of organizational culture, since including important groups from the environment – important stakeholders – is vital for keeping the balance (Hatch and Schultz, 2002). Attempts at delineating too clear-cut boundaries, introducing excessive order and exercising direct control turn against the people who make such attempts. In order for the company's identity not to be stifled by the Shadow the participants and the stakeholders should have the freedom to speak and management should abandon obsessive attempts at eliminating all ugliness, sadness and suffering. Even propaganda functions, like PR or marketing, should allow for a measure of darkness, for instance through the use of irony or sarcasm. Swedish advertisements often contain humour and are sometimes violently funny. I sometimes show ordinary TV adverts from Sweden to my Polish students, and I have heard from them quite a few times that this style of advertising not only draws their attention to the product but also does not produce the feelings of anger and impressions of falsehood that so many other standard ads provoke.

Denying feelings that exist in the organization, especially collective feelings, will not efface them; on the contrary, they will accumulate in the unconscious (Sievers, 1994), expanding the sphere of Shadow. Unwanted common feelings often strengthen the tendency to control. Management wants to protect itself from the effects of such feelings by trying to strengthen its power. Unfortunately, the effects are contrary to expectations, denying the Shadow leads to its expansion. For example,[34] the school mentioned above provoked the development of a relatively wide sphere of the Shadow in the shape of aversion and negative feelings, a growing aggression and the lack of initiative and action among both students and faculty. The management reacted by introducing new rules and norms to regulate people's behaviour and prevent demoralization. The new rules, however, provoke reluctance or aggression in the participants. Some accept them passively, devoting all their time to administrative work and neglecting other tasks. Others engage in passive resistance and sabotaging the new rules, for example by interpreting them erroneously. A student representative called his experiences in the school 'a run through the offices': taking care of all the formalities was so time-consuming that he had neither the time nor the energy to study.

5.3   MIASMA, CORRUPTION, RESIGNATION

The Shadow is often developed due to an excessive urge to control the organization; however, a reverse tendency, management's lack of care for the organization's culture, can also generate the Shadow. It is a common contemporary practice in an era which Zygmunt Bauman (2000) calls liquid modernity. In the previous era social institutions were solid and gave people the opportunity to plan their lives and relate their actions to a stable collective framework. Our contemporary reality will not allow for building anything the construction of which takes much time. People cannot organize their lives in a longer perspective; they are doomed to choose temporary, episodic solutions. Human life becomes a collection of short-term projects, often not connected with one another in a meaningful way. The notion of 'career' in this reality becomes meaningless. Uncertainty stops being an organizational abnormality, becoming instead everyday reality. Loyalty becomes a luxury or an illusion, and a deep involvement is replaced with calculation that becomes the main motivation of people's actions. People have to be flexible and their lives undergo fragmentation in all spheres, from marriage and love to work. While many of my Polish students still dream of long-term employment, the Western students I teach express disinterest and even contempt for people staying long with one employer, calling them 'dead wood' and 'old guard'.

Similar observations on the situation of the contemporary employee can be found in the work of Richard Sennett (1998) who presents the phenomenon of the fragmentation of human life and the separation of the contemporary employee from work, calling it the 'corrosion of character'. Regardless of their position in the hierarchy and their social class, contemporary employees do not relate to their workplace or career in a meaningful way. People drift through their professional lives as if unmoved by their own feelings. The experience has been separated from the person who experiences it. The author believes that this results from the shape of today's business, which is increasingly hyperflexible – it resembles a tent that one can put up and fold down quickly rather than the solid stone building to which one could compare business in the past. People do not get a chance to grow accustomed to their workplace, colleagues, subordinates and superiors or, indeed, to develop links and relationships. Growing roots is out of the question, one only copes on a day-to-day basis. Accordingly, one can observe the tendency for privatization of problems and solutions that Bauman (2000) writes about: everyone is expected to cope with their life on their own. Sennett (1998) observes that any difficulty connected with the understanding of a situation or of people becomes obsolete and is even considered embarrassing. Only appearances matter, as well as immediate effect and quick success. Learning ceases to be meaningful, as does gathering experience; growing old becomes just a nuisance, and is no longer associated with gaining wisdom and mastery. Instead of knowledge and understanding, our times expect superficial skills; one can hear voices saying that such skills should be taught not only in vocational schools but also in secondary schools and even at universities. In the workplace everything is based on superficial impressions and temporary effects. One cannot count on anybody or anything except for oneself; the stress put on 'teamwork' is only another illusion of cooperation: actually, the only aim here is a superficial and temporary adjustment of perfectly egoistic individuals.

Building an identity in such conditions becomes highly problematic (Bauman, 2004). Social institutions no longer constitute a stable frame of reference necessary for the building of an individual's identity. Under such circumstances the project of building an organization's identity is difficult to put into practice as well. When the once-stable points of reference become fluid, the process of collective identity-building becomes more or less random and capricious. Quite often, nobody in an organization pays attention to matters important to people, such as greeting new participants and saying goodbye to departing veterans.

The conditions described above may give rise to the development of the variety of Shadow that Yiannis Gabriel (2008) calls 'organizational miasma'. The author refers to the myth of Oedipus who unwittingly brought the plague upon his city. Miasma means pollution, not so much physical, but spiritual and moral. Miasma is contagious, it permeates the whole of a given milieu. The people who brought the pollution to a place, whether they did it consciously or not, are charged with responsibility. Miasma engulfs everyone to the same extent, regardless of the individual person's guilt or intentions. To get rid of miasma, a ritual moral purification is necessary, as it will not go away of its own accord, and neither can people get rid of it by living hygienically. In Sophocles' play Oedipus tries to discover why the city of Thebes was plagued. He gradually discovers the terrifying truth – that he himself is to blame as, unaware of what he was doing, he killed his father Laius, the former King of Thebes, and married the widow and his mother, Jocasta. Jocasta commits suicide and Oedipus, having blinded himself, sentences himself to exile. Still, the miasma remains.

The breaking of taboos, especially those connected with not honouring the dead, brings moral pollution to a society. The cultural taboo linked with paying appropriate respects to the departed was extremely strong in antiquity and was connected with the ceremonies of death, burial and mourning. In smaller, contemporary cultures, such as organizations, the taboo refers not only to death,[35] but also to any kind of departure. After a participant has left, the empty place the person had left must be honoured in some way – after all, organizations are not just systems of transmission gears and cogs, but places where real people work and live. Traditionally, the retirement of an employee who had worked many years for the company used to be celebrated, often by the whole staff. The person was given a diploma and a souvenir, for instance a gold watch. The CEO shook hands with the veteran and uttered a few ceremonial words. Even the group lay-offs caused by crises in the solid modernity era were culturally celebrated: first, through the ritual of negotiations between the trade unions and the board; and then, through expressions of collective sadness and regret, remembering people's merits in official speeches by both the trade union representatives and the managers and by just plain respect for the feelings of those who were leaving. In today's liquid world, flexible corporations dismiss people every day. Quite often, nobody pays any attention to the people leaving; even massive waves of dismissals are treated as something ordinary, demanding no special measures. All this provokes the development of a particular type of Shadow: paralysing, depriving people of the energy to protest; making the employees feel tainted, worthless and dehumanized. This is the type of Shadow that Yiannis Gabriel (2008) calls organizational miasma. Such miasma brings corruption, destroys relations, and kills love, empathy and trust. People start looking for a scapegoat, a person or a group to put the blame on. The process is accompanied by a deepening dejection, collective depression and resignation. According to Gabriel, organizational miasma is characterized by the following three traits: the weakening of the will to offer resistance, a high level of self-criticism and the searching for someone to blame. In a culture plunged in miasma, deep social bonds dissolve, communication fails, and the organization is submerged in an endemic depression. Traditional solutions, such as training, courses or negotiations, fail. There is no easy solution to the problem, and a purification, just as in the case of other types of Shadow, must start with the realization of the problem.

For example,[36] an organization that forms a part of a larger corporation employing well-educated professionals entered a phase of violent changes after the new manager decided to subject the organization to another radical change endeavour. It meant, de facto, a breaking with most of the company's traditions. The past was referred to officially only in extremely negative terms. The former manager was made to take early retirement and many long-serving employees were given an ultimatum: retirement or dismissal. Others were encouraged to accept 'generous offers of leave-taking' and they were made to understand that if they did not accept the offer, their life in the company would become hard. Numerous employees, both those who were encouraged to leave and others, decided to quit working for the organization. The majority of the remaining people felt uncertain; they either considered leaving or were felt threatened by dismissal. For a long period of time 'alive' and 'dead' employees coexisted in the company – some of them were employed, others were dismissed or wanted to leave themselves. The employees in various phases of quitting never discussed the past and they finally stopped noticing one another, except in situations when they had to cooperate to accomplish a particular task. In the course of two years two-thirds of the company's employees left. After some time, a new category of employees appeared – neither employed, nor dismissed, they were former employees who were given temporary jobs or stayed as 'freelance consultants', people doing exactly the same job as before but on the basis of a contract. The new order also meant a new vocabulary, new values and a new identity. During meetings only the new forms of communication were used; the achievements and successes of the company were stressed but only the new ones, none of the pre-change accomplishments of the organization or names of the people who contributed to them were mentioned. People felt lost in the new company and deprived of any driving force. The depression, resignation and the lack of faith in their abilities were deepening. People experiencing these feelings confided in the researchers; at the same time, each person was certain that only they felt this way, that it was a personal feeling, a private complex. People did not share their feelings with other employees. They started looking for a scapegoat – usually particular individuals, regardless of their real involvement in given events. Empathy vanished. Each employee became enclosed in a world of their own, concentrated on their own suffering and plans. The employees who were not willing to give up their empathy had already left, when the changes began.

5.4 VIOLENCE AS THE DARK SIDE OF THE ORGANIZATION

The physicist Robert W. Fuller observed the phenomenon of rankism, the violence encoded in hierarchical organizations in a covert manner, eluding the rational projection of structures. In his famous study *Somebodies and Nobodies* Fuller (2003) presented this type of injustice that typically manifests itself in aggressive behaviour towards people who occupy lower positions in the hierarchy. Rankism consists in using the power ascribed to one's post for other goals than fulfilling one's duties in the organization. As a result of rankism, people are humiliated, offended and intimidated. It is an assault on their dignity, which is particularly serious, as dignity belongs to the basic rights of every person. The organizations that succumb to the pathology of rankism make people become either 'somebody' or 'nobody'. However, this is a transitory state, depending on the position in the hierarchy and not resulting from somebody's traits or aspirations. Every 'somebody' is sometimes a 'nobody' and vice versa, remaining a human being all the time. Rankism emerges from hierarchy, from the hierarchy's potential of power. The violence towards people in the lower levels of the hierarchy stimulates the development of rankism in other places in the organization: people follow the example from above. When the boss treats their subordinates badly, the tendency appears for them in turn to treat their subordinates badly. Rankism in organizations manifests itself in different types of discrimination and aggressive behaviour, such as sexism, racism, homophobia and, mainly, bullying known also as mobbing. Posts become tools enabling the humiliation of others. It is rare for organizations to be openly structured around the idea of combining hierarchy with violence (as in the case of criminal or pathological organizations). Usually, the phenomenon is not supported officially but it develops in hiding, outside the main organizational discourses.

Hierarchies as such are not tools of oppression and they may be very useful, which is stressed by Robert Fuller (2001) in his article for the magazine *Leader to Leader*. It is not necessary to level them completely or opt for strictly non-hierarchical forms of structuring. The problem lies not in the structure itself but in the improper use of the structure. The people whose personal dignity is constantly abused are prone to many psychological problems and the whole organization, after reaching the threshold of its cultural tissue's endurance, begins to fall into decline. Rankism undermines creativity, lowers efficiency, and has a negative influence on the quality of the services and the involvement of employees. The effects were confirmed by the studies carried out in organizations suffering from negative behaviour (Pearson et al., 2000). Fuller also stresses the fact that rankism creates a significant loss of energy in the system. It affects the company's ability to read and interpret signals coming both from the inside and from the environment. Organizations overrun with rankism lose contact with reality and their self-assessment becomes increasingly idiosyncratic. This chapter will deal with rankism understood as the cultural Shadow of an organization, manifesting itself in sudden acts of aggression between people. The question of despotism will be discussed in the chapter devoted to toxic leadership.[37]

The following two examples from my field studies show typical manifestations[38] of rankism in the everyday life of an organization. The first example refers to an organization based on knowledge, employing highly qualified specialists, mainly middle-aged men or men of pre-retirement age. During a meeting one of the few women employed in the company (who had rarely spoken before) presented a critical view that her department had on the reorganization carried out in the company. She spoke calmly, to the point, but with much resolution. Suddenly she felt that something was 'very wrong' and involuntarily leaned sideways. A mug flying in her direction failed to hit her by several inches and broke against the wall. The woman looked in the direction from which the mug had been thrown – one of her older colleagues, still red in the face, was sitting and shaking his head as if something had got into his ear. The other incident took place in an IT company. A young man, who was promoted by the new project manager, participated in a meeting where he presented his project to his colleagues. His presentation did not include any particularly controversial points. It was very professional and interesting; probably, it also lasted longer than a typical presentation by a young employee. Nobody, however, seemed bored or impatient and the speaker was sure that everyone was listening to him with attention. During the break, everyone went out to the corridor. The young manager standing with his back to the staircase noticed the chief accountant, a middle-aged woman enjoying huge prestige in the organization, walking fast in his direction. Without looking his way the accountant approached him and suddenly pushed him down the stairs. Then she left, still, according to an observer, not looking in the direction of the young manager who fell down the stairs, luckily not hurting himself.

Both incidents seem to be instances of pointless outburst of violence. The protagonists are quite different: a female employee of a higher rank and a younger male employee of middle rank. The scenes become meaningful only when put in context – both companies are managed in an autocratic way, important information is not disclosed to the employees, and the humiliation and offending of employees of a lower rank is very common. Uncommonly clear, unapologetic and matter-of-fact speeches and presentations provoked attacks consisting in sudden outbursts of physical violence. Neither of these two people had been attacked previously and I know nothing of any later assaults aimed at them. These were incidental, non-personal attacks.

Matters are different in the case of bullying, that is, a repeated attacking, harassing or humiliating of the same people, usually connected with power inequalities. Bullying may be linked with rankism and in such cases it becomes a phenomenon permeating the whole organization. Bullying is relatively common; it may affect a significant amount of employees in Western countries (Monks et al., 2009). The most popular forms of bullying are insults, verbal violence and aggressive exclusion (Burns and Pope, 2007). Bullying resulting from rankism is not a psychological or purely social problem. The personalities of the parties involved or the characteristics of the group they belong to are of secondary importance or they may only be the spark that triggers violence. The main feature of bullying is the fact that it is deeply rooted in the organization's structure and, as in the case of the incidental outbursts of aggression described above, the cause of such behaviour lies in the organization's Shadow. After a change in the culture consisting in the reduction of the Shadow's domination, violence ceases and the sides engaged in it may stop bearing grudges against each another, as in the example at the end of this chapter. Organizational bullying that is not combated produces strong negative results, not only in the people affected by the violence (Pearson et al., 2000) but also in witnesses, the employees who are neither the victims nor the perpetrators (Lutgen-Sandvik et al., 2007).

Barbara Czarniawska (2008) presents humiliation as a typical side effect of organization. Humiliation refers not only to personal matters but also affects many other spheres of the organization's activities, like budgeting, often considered a 'hard' side of the organization – as opposed to the cultural side, often classified as 'soft', that is, more easily influenced by human actions. The author describes humiliation as the negative result of organizational authority, a phenomenon that is very common but usually not well documented. She cites evidence from her ethnographic research: a situation when a superior reprimanded an older, well-qualified employee in public. He used harsh words, as an adult addressing a stubborn child. The incident, apparently unconnected with the main plots that the research revealed in the field, in fact turned out to be an integral part of the organization's functioning. The situations observed and studied by Czarniawska enabled her to characterize the humiliations as denying employees their basic rights of an organizational citizen. The deprivation of employees of participation rights is a result, on the one hand, of the abuse of power and, on the other, is in itself the source of further power abuse. People who have been humiliated in public are more easily controlled and subjected to negative practices. The spreading of such practices makes it easier for the perpetrators to use them. The observers are accustomed to them and do not protest when they see their colleagues being humiliated. Some take on these practices themselves and use them on those who are weaker than themselves.

5.5 THE INTEGRATION OF THE SHADOW

As Jung observes ([1959] 1990), the Shadow devoid of the light of consciousness spreads and grows increasingly powerful. Fighting the Shadow in order to eliminate it is ineffective; after all, the Shadow constitutes a part of ourselves, our soul, our culture. The only effective method of dealing with the Shadow is its integration. This offers more stability to the person or the organization that opts for such integration. Feelings of one-sidedness and the illusion of the absolute good, the false total correctness, are lost in this process and the person or organization undertaking the quest has to be prepared to give them up. Integration makes an individual or an organization more authentically flexible, not in the way popularized by mainstream management books, but in the traditional sense of the word: able to change and then go back to the original form again. They also become less defensive and rigid in their reactions. Certainly, the Shadow is difficult to accept and its acceptance is not an act but a long-lasting process, demanding significant conscious effort and an openness to people, to their faults and weaknesses, and indeed one's own. The effort is worth making, however, since the Shadow is dangerous precisely because it is unconscious and unaccepted (Jung, [1959] 1990). An important step towards the integration of the Shadow is the realization of its existence, and an acceptance of the Shadow as part of one's self as well as a symbolic integration of the Shadow into one's life. As a result, the Shadow releases frozen life energy that can literally heal the person or the organization, breathe new life into them. A person or an organization balanced in this way will be more open to people and more likely to use their energy to achieve positive objectives.

There are no easy tools that would guarantee success in the integration of the organizational Shadow. Attempts at integration always require a creative approach, courage and effort. Bradley Olson, Debra Nelson and Satyanarayana Parayitam (2006) propose a model of sense-making as a way of dealing with negative behaviour, increasing the chances for coping with such behaviour in a constructive manner. The authors emphasize the fact that the manager should get to know the character of the negative behaviour at the workplace as well as understanding its consequences. First, all the phenomena should be seen in their organizational context and difficult truths need to be accepted, such as the fact that some acts of aggression do not result from particular employees' personalities but are the manifestation of a broad organizational context in which everyone, and especially the management, participate. Then such methods may be used as formal control, informal control or trust in the employee, as well as developing empathy or self-awareness. A continuous reflection on the past and a respect for individual and collective experience are indispensable.

Together with a co-author (in Kociatkiewicz and Kostera, 2010) I point to a different path leading in a similar direction. Like Bradley Olson et al. (2006) we see the necessity of acknowledging the dark sides of culture and submitting them for public discussion. People must start speaking about the aspects of the Shadow that are the most difficult to accept. A perfect way to facilitate such a discussion is to use the principle of carnival. A collective celebration, feasting, allowing for sense of humour, even extreme humour – the more sarcastic, ribald or insane, the darker the Shadow is. Organizational carnival is the best way to meet and acknowledge the Shadow as well as to transform it into a creative potential. It cannot be a one-time event, but must be a recurring motif. Management should encourage the employees to impersonate it, to make jokes and parody their leaders. Finally, the role of a symbolic and public forgiveness granted by the leaders to people who are guilty of the behaviour issuing from the functioning of the Shadow is extremely important. Acts of forgiving can also become a part of the recurring carnival.

Such measures helped to restore a good atmosphere in a certain IT company.[39] The new manager has been an employee of the company for many years. The organization had developed a significant Shadow, especially during the tenure of the former boss who set ambitious aims for himself and the company but neglected communication and good ambience. People were impolite to one another; outbursts of aggression, especially directed at employees of a lower rank, became common; disloyalty, malicious gossip and informing became the new norm. The story of the young man pushed down the stairs comes from this company. The new manager decided not to give up on the realization of many of the goals set by his predecessor but he decided to pursue them in a different way. He simply liked people and knew they could achieve a lot thanks to their own free will – they must want it; success cannot be ensured through re-engineering and 'quality assurance'. Among other ideas he introduced was an annual integration trip, a so-called team-building weekend. In the course of two days the employees tackled obstacles and gained trophies in competitions organized by a team of consultants. In the evenings they dined together. There was a lot of good food, wine, dancing and performances by the employees. There was recitation of ironic poems about the company and its management; the employees set up a cabaret and sang mocking songs. Everything was mocked, but mainly management. The new manager laughed most loudly at the jokes that were on him. He also used the occasion to demonstrate symbolically his forgiveness to those who had played a dirty trick on him or acted in a disloyal and unfriendly manner during the previous era of Shadow domination. Everyone remembered the stories and the new manager did not pretend to have forgotten them either. He referred to them, however, with a humorous distance, and he treated his 'wrongdoers' with humorous sympathy and showed that he did not hold a grudge. In everyday contacts outside of these occasions he was much more distanced but he still showed warmth and a sense of humour. During ordinary company meetings he seemed genuinely happy to see his staff but he was not effusive or excessively direct. The employees were impressed with the way he treated the technical staff: the cleaners, the janitors and the gardener. It was talked about in the corridors, and in interviews people thought his behaviour was really nice. The new manager had also a lot of faults of his own, but who of us is perfect? He did not pretend to be a saint and indeed, was for many reasons not a good candidate for sainthood. However, he had managed to integrate the organizational Shadow. Moreover, the company started gaining new, important clients and its position on the market situation improved again. The manager was glad of the successes and stressed that they should be credited to the employees.

6. Anima and Animus

6.1 THE ARCHETYPES OF THE ANIMA AND THE ANIMUS

According to Carl Gustav Jung ([1934–1954] 1968), the Anima and the Animus are two main personality archetypes. The Anima is the female aspect of the soul, and the Animus, the male. The Anima contains the elements of all the roles women play and the Animus, analogically, carries the potential of all the male roles. Jung claimed that men carry the Anima in their unconscious domain; he claimed that: 'The whole nature of man presupposes woman, both physically and spiritually. His system is tuned into woman from the start, just as it is prepared for a quite definite world where there is water, light, air, salt, carbohydrates etc.' (Jung, [1928] 1972, p. 190).

Similarly, the woman's soul contains in its unconscious domain the archetype of the Animus, an inner warrior who is 'partial to argument, he can best be seen at work in disputes where both parties know they are right' (Jung, [1934–1954] 1968, p. 29). The Animus, however, is a secondary element in relation to the primary Anima, though, similarly to the Anima, it is deeply integrated with the soul and thoroughly rooted in the sphere of the collective unconscious. Jung focused more closely on the description of the Anima as it contains, according to him, a creative potential which can lead a person to true wisdom: this is the image of the Anima as Sophia, the divine wisdom. A similar path and potential also linked with the presence of the Animus. The first step to fulfilling this potential is the realization of the existence of one's own Anima and Animus. Then, one has to let them mature until it is possible to integrate the high level of their development that is characterized by wisdom as well as diversity and dynamism. Immature Anima and Animus may be projected on the environment, on real women and men. The individual who does that attributes the features contained in their inner image to other people. This may manifest itself as admiration, misogyny or the expectation of women that men will make decisions in their stead – but it is always a symptom of the lack of contact with reality. It is a sign of immaturity to respond to the Other, reducing him or her to one's own projections and expectations. David Hart and Neil Brady (2005) believe that in organizations there exist collective images of the Animus and Anima, shared by men and women. The Anima is a stimulus of action, something that encourages effort, an irresistible attraction. In contemporary organizations it tends to manifest itself in its immature form, as a superficial orientation towards career. When mature, it contains a great creative potential. The mature Anima tends to be apparently absent from corporations, it is deeply hidden in the organizational unconscious. The Animus tends to be more distinctive and conscious, but it is rarely integrated and developed. It manifests itself as a more or less graceful spirit of competition or a celebration of success and power. The result of the union of the Animus and the Anima is the Syzygy, an alchemical marriage and unification of the two archetypes (Jung, [1934–1954] 1968). The unification is a source of great power, but also symbolizes communication and the finding of the right complement.

A good example of the two archetypes taken from popular culture is the well-loved Polish novel for children, *Dziewczyna i chłopak, czyli heca na 14 fajerek* by Hanna Ożogowska (1961/2007). The protagonists are siblings: Tosia and Tomek. Born on the same day, they resemble each other physically, but have completely different personalities. Tosia is an embodiment of femininity: gentle, subtle, obedient to her parents and also a little bit frail and rather timid, she is treated at home and at school with kindness and protectiveness. Tosia is a good student, she behaves well at school and is held up as an example for Tomek to follow. Her brother does not like to be nice at all; he is rather naughty and reminds us of the stereotypical boy: belligerent, proud, at times stubborn and disobedient. His father thinks that he needs a heavy hand and the teachers complain that Tomek does not pay attention in the class and that he does not apply himself to study. Therefore, his marks are poor and he has to retake one of his exams.

In the summer, Tosia is going to her Aunt Isia's place in the country and Tomek, as punishment, has to visit his stern uncle living in the forester's lodge. Because of Tomek's sudden and unexpected outing, matters get complicated – the uncle-forester comes to pick up Tomek but he is not there. The desperate Tosia, fearing their father's rage, makes a truly resolute decision – she decides to pass herself off as Tomek and goes with the uncle to his forester's lodge. She leaves a letter to her brother in which she explains what has happened and urges him to be equally courageous and go to the countryside disguised as his sister. Whether he wants it or not, Tomek has to put on Tosia's dress and go to his aunt's house.

This is how an eventful summer begins, full of adventures, surprising in many ways to both siblings. Tomek has to look after little children and realizes how difficult it is to be a girl. At the same time, he shows

Figure 6.1   Anima and Animus
(photo: Monika Kostera)

to his cousins and their friends in the countryside that 'girls can be cool too' – he impresses them with his ideas, his sense of humour and his courage. And Tosia has to pass a real test and show the boys from the forester's lodge that she is a boy and not a sissy; she combats her fears and becomes stronger.[40] Both Tosia and Tomek are successful. They return home knowing how it is to be 'the other gender', they become more loyal to each other, and less one-sided. After the adventure, Tomek becomes more Tosia-like, and Tosia, more of a 'tomboy'.

In organization theory the archetypes of the Animus and the Anima have been referred to by, among others, Janice Thomas and Pamela Buckle-Henning (2007). The authors have carried out their research among successful project managers of both genders, asking how they perceived their work. Then they compared their speakers' opinions with the official publications of the Project Management Institute (PMI). The publications are used in training, standard-setting, the registration and accreditation of university curricula and in the assessment of project managers' work (they specify the 'best practices'). To analyse both the interviews and the rest of the material, the researchers resorted to the Animus and the Anima. The Institute's materials visibly contained the ethos connected to the archetype of the Animus. The management conforming with the recommendations consists in a clear, linear definition of the project and separating it from the context. Some managers preferred exactly such an approach to their work but there were some who defined their attitude in a way characteristic of the Anima, that is, as inextricably interwoven with the context and having less clear boundaries. In practice both the 'male' and 'female' management styles are used; what is particularly interesting is that the 'female' style is willingly used by successful managers of both genders especially when problems and uncertainties appear and when the carrying out of the plan is endangered by unexpected events. Thus, both the logic of the Anima

and that of the Animus are important in the practice of project management. Good managers know how to change their actions from the ethos
of the Anima to that of the Animus and vice versa, depending on what the
situation demands. It is not reflected in any way in the PMI materials that
promote the 'masculine' style to the virtual exclusion of the 'feminine' one.
It means that the managers who prefer the 'feminine' style may be assessed
as less successful than their results show. Most importantly, however, the
PMI materials overlook the important ability to combine styles. If managers learned managing solely on the basis of these documents, they would
not cope with many situations that demand a more 'feminine' approach,
that is, with situations where uncertainty and unexpected events lessen the
effectiveness of the Animus.

6.2 THE ABSENT ANIMA AND WOMEN IN MANAGEMENT

Simone de Beauvoir's classic *The Second Sex* (1949/1997) portrays women
as the gender traditionally having to come second, a deviation from
the norm which is constituted by men. It is culture, from philosophy to
popular culture, that defines them as women. The social and economical
conditions in which they live posit who they are and who they should be,
always in contrast to the masculine role: as 'the second', different, 'that
which men are not'. A man is; a woman becomes, always referring to him.
These mirrored traits are rhetorically justified by biology, which is invoked
as their primary determinant. Woman is denied the freedom of the
transcendental subject which man is. A man is destined to have creative
freedom, whereas a woman is fated for the dependency of maintaining,
supporting. Women are always situated vis-à-vis a potential future that is
both unreachable and necessary, they are unable to reorient themselves in
a different direction or specify their objectives on their own. The woman's
future is defined through her biology, understood rather as a source of
possibility, a condition for creation, than a creative impulse in itself. The
man also has a biological aspect but it does not define the boundaries of
his identity. 'Woman, like man, is her body; but her body is something
other than herself' (ibid., p. 61).

The body delimits for a woman what she is and what she should be.
It is not biology as such but biology in its cultural and socio-political
context that delineates femininity for the woman. Masculinity is depicted
as primary and active, against the background of the secondary and
passive femininity. This is a way of seeing that is strongly informed by
the perspective of culture, and not any objective reality. The history that

defines the woman's role in such a way is written from a male perspective. Therefore femininity, understood as female subjectivity, is absent from the definitions of reality in general and from the definitions of femininity.

Much has been said about the absence of the feminine element in the theory and practice of organization and management. A traditional corporation is an unambiguously 'masculine' workplace, both literally and archetypically. In the 1970s Rosabeth Moss Kanter ([1977] 1993) carried out ethnographic research which showed that in corporate practice women are rarely given the same chances as men. The reasons are twofold. First, the definition of a manager was formulated in traditionally masculine categories. Women were to provide support and backup, both at the workplace and at home. Second, women used to occupy positions that usually did not give them any chance of promotion. In the higher levels of the hierarchy they were represented by a handful of token women who, in order to be promoted, had to adopt many traits traditionally considered masculine. Moss Kanter claims that organizations are to blame for this state of affairs, and not individual people. In order to make the chances of women and men equal it is the structures that should be changed, and people exchanged for others. In the 1993 edition of her book Moss Kanter added a chapter that shows the current situation in the company under examination. The researcher concludes that women's chances considerably improved in the organizational practice, although the chances of the two genders are still unequal. The changes that appeared in the corporate structures influence the careers of the representatives of both genders, bringing a greater uncertainty but also causing women to be less frequently placed in positions that give them no chances of promotion. Thanks to these changes there is more space in the higher levels of the hierarchy for women whose position does not depend on adopting male roles in their professional or private lives. Women, however, have not yet broken through the glass ceiling barring their way to the highest positions in the organizational structure.

Lisa Zanetti (2002) argues that contemporary management is based on the principles associated with the Animus, whereas the Anima is eliminated. For instance, success is measured quantitatively; organizations concentrate on results and on reaching clearly specified goals. Power is perceived as a limited resource and is used for exclusion. One of the main projects of organizational power is maintaining and deepening the division of human life into work and private time. An ideal employee is a person deprived of personal life and especially family, because it is perceived not as a benefit to the organization but as a burden. Very often both the management theory and practice define the employee as a traditional man, although this is not voiced openly. Instead, the employee is described as a successful person, competition-oriented, willing to fight, to sacrifice private time for work, and so on. Certainly, this role can be successfully adopted by both men and women, but it is very tightly linked with the traditional role of the man. Organizations tend to exclude the female element much more forcefully than they exclude women as such. 'Success people' in organizations tend to be the epitomes of the Animus, regardless of their gender: they are assertive, aggressive, often forceful, with sharp views, holding their positions by virtue of their will. To change the situation it is not enough 'to let women in the organization' – instead, organizations should open to diversity, both masculine and feminine. First of all, one should show more openness to the traits associated with the Anima, such as intuition, creativity, cooperativeness, and so on.

The mainstream of organization and management writings is dominated by what can be termed a masculine ethics. This is especially true of rationalistic schools that give 'matter-of-fact' answers regarding the fulfilment of goals (Kanter, [1977] 1993). The Anima, though present, is not represented to a sufficient degree. It influences the development of some of the less dominant fields, such as the psychology of organization (Lyons, 1997). In this context the work of William Foote Whyte and Eric Trist should be mentioned. These authors are men, but what matters here is not their gender but the fact that they draw upon both feminine and masculine archetypes in their research and scientific work. Denise Lyons (1997) believes that the creation of the Tavistock Institute of Human Relations in London proved to be a crucial moment in the process of organization theory's opening to the voice of the Anima. The researchers from the institute looked for an equilibrium between the perspectives of the mind and the heart. Eric Trist (quoted in Lyons, 1997) argued for the importance of the ability to combine one's life with one's work. For him the context was of crucial importance, and perfect management was based on the ability to create good personal relations. William Foote Whyte (quoted in Lyons, 1997) stressed the role of understanding and empathic research, the researcher's deep immersion in the context. His idea of action research and a compassionate, involved approach to management also introduced a breath of fresh air into consulting services. These fields of study are popular today and yield interesting results, although they still function outside the mainstream of research and many management graduates are ignorant of their existence.

In an article entitled 'Reflections of the Other' (Kostera, 2003) I quote instances of the marginalization of women in the discourse of mainstream management as evidenced in the Polish business press of the 1990s. The professional press of the time wrote much less frequently about female managers and entrepreneurs than about male ones. If women were presented at all, they were shown in a different way than men: the emphasis was put on their extra-career roles, they were shown as mothers, grandmothers or wives. They were often asked questions on how they managed to combine their traditional family roles with their work. The articles described the women's appearance and personal likes and interests, which was not common journalistic practice at the time in the case of male managers and entrepreneurs. The men appeared only in their professional roles and their family and emotional life was not discussed. At the end of the 1990s there appeared stories about strong women, the 'iron ladies' of business (ibid., p. 328). Their professional roles were characterized more closely than the profiles of the female managers from the early days of the Polish transformation. However, the practice of describing men as completely concentrated on their professional roles persisted. It is also visible in the pictures, where the men are dressed formally, very rarely smile and assume serious poses. This changed after 2000 when photos of more colourfully dressed, smiling, even laughing men began to appear. Simultaneously, the interviews with managers, both men and women, now concentrated on their professional roles. There appeared a new type of interview and, although still rare, it is interesting from the point of view of the role of the Anima in organization, where managers of both genders are shown both as a private person and a business person. A good example is the article describing a female entrepreneur as 'a girl with a passion' (ibid., p. 329), a person to whom work is a genuine source of joy; an individual who is creative and daring as well as professional and successful. I consider this article a possible herald of a new management discourse, introducing a space for talking about features typical of the Anima.

6.3   THE QUEST FOR THE ETERNAL MOTHER

The archetype of the Mother is presented either as a separate archetype of the family or as a part of the Anima. Here, I will opt for the second interpretation as I am more interested in the archetype's role in work organizations than in the social structure in general, and so a broader approach is more relevant.

Henrietta Moore (1988/1995) describes motherhood and the mother's role in culture from an anthropological position. Apart from the natural processes, like pregnancy and childbirth, motherhood is associated with an exceptionally elaborate symbolism and cultural status. The characteristics of the mother's role differ depending on culture. In some cultures the mother is full of warmth, protective, and takes care of the child all the time; in others she is distant, authoritarian, and looks after the child during a limited amount of time. Everywhere, however, the mother occupies a central, elevated position. In many cultures motherhood is one of the important aspects of femininity in general. In other cultures, it is not an element of femininity, but a separate social role. The biological and cultural roles of the mother may, but do not have to, occur in pairs. 'Mothering' does not always have to be connected with the involvement of the biological mother. Children are often raised in extended families or they are looked after by carers. The carers and the children often develop a close and intense relation. In some tribal societies the whole tribe assumes the role of the mother, that is, the whole society looks after children and shares various aspects of mothering and motherhood. Sometimes this role is also assumed by men, for example in the rituals that consist in observing the food taboo or even in the symbolic participation in the childbirth (*couvades*).

Motherhood being such an important and universal cultural theme, it could seem that it would be beneficial for contemporary organizations to support the archetype of the Mother. They could do so either directly, through supporting motherhood and using the experience of the mothers employed in the organization, or symbolically, through referring to protectiveness and care for young or newly hired employees by experienced employees or the whole collective. The archetype of the Mother is, however, perhaps even more openly ignored in contemporary organizations than the Anima. Heather Höpfl (2002) writes about how organizations suffer a cultural emptiness resulting from the elimination of the Anima, and especially its motherly component, from their structures. Organizations become involved in futile attempts at finding a replacement for the lost motherhood, such as benchmarking or continuous improvement. The aim of the new strategies is a ceaseless betterment and education, but without the maternal element. The mother educates and perfects the child, at the same time rewarding the child for each improvement; she 'saves' the child, finding perfection in the child's every effort at betterment. Patriarchal organizations introduce continuous improvement but without the possibility of finding satisfaction, without the happiness of being appreciated and in this way they perpetuate a permanent inadequacy, a constant frustration as the dominant state of mind in the culture. Perfection seems a sterile vision, more of a threat than hope, rather a measure of one's weakness than a reward. The attempts at finding a substitute for the mother are ineffective as they have been emptied of the rich content: warmth, care and attention. The archetype of the Mother is rejected by contemporary corporations because it does not let itself be managed – it is complementary to patriarchal management models and is not submissive to them. Therefore:

> Organizations, as collectivities, have understood the sense of loss of the femi-
> nine and have tried to construct it in symbolic and in representational terms.
> This is a profound conceit as is evidenced by the contradictions of contem-
> porary organizational life and the pervasive melancholy that arises from the
> knowledge of an ill-defined loss. (Höpfl, 2002, p. 20)

An organization models itself into an abstraction but cannot make its real, living employees abstract. The inability to acknowledge feelings as a rightful part of the process of organizing, and the constant awareness of the loss of femininity, have the effect that the most common feature of corporate culture is a barely conscious melancholy, a state resembling indifference, passivity or laziness, which gives rise to a constant struggle of the organization with its participants' inertia, a ceaseless imperative to 'motivate' them.

Kaaren Hedblom Jacobson (1993) points to a different consequence of the elimination of motherhood from the conscious management processes. The archetype instead takes control over unconscious processes, leading to many characteristic and common pathologies of contemporary corporations, such as an excessive strife for safety, depriving the participants of independence, limiting their autonomy and responsibility; as well as an inability to cope with feelings. Eventually the participants lose the capability of undertaking independent moral actions, as the organizational culture prevents maturation, leaving people at the stage of development characteristics of a young child. The organization becomes for the participants an unconscious substitute for the mother. It is only a substitute construct – it does not give warmth or support, but it seems omnipotent and makes all the important moral decisions for the participants. The existence of collective standards encourages people to give up their own. The temptation to submit to dissolution in the collective identity can be irresistible, especially when the archetype that exerts the influence is unconscious. In this way, one not only loses the chance for individuation but also one risks losing one's 'I' in the collective unconscious, a dark and hostile domain, thus depriving oneself of the ability to find one's way out again. Organizations in turn not only deprive themselves of the chance to draw on the employees' unique potential but they also introduce chaos into the questions of responsibility. A collective responsibility is no responsibility at all, as organizations do not have a conscience. Such a situation invites abuse, dishonesty and in extreme cases violence, even murder. Everyone is only 'doing their job' and nobody feels responsible; usually nobody dares to protest openly when the limits of morality are overstepped. This does not have to result from fear but it can be the effect of the loss of contact with one's conscience that is the only efficient motivation for acting against the collective.

Not only do organizations try to exclude motherhood but also they do not build an environment favourable to mothers (and nurturing fathers). Mats Alvesson and Yvonne Due Billing ([1997] 1999) conclude, presenting abundant evidence, that there is no place in organizations for people who want to have a career and take care of their small children at the same time. Among high-level managers that are also parents, men are much more numerous than women, and these men usually do not take care of their children very intensely. Women occupy managerial positions less often than men, and women who raise children are even less common in such posts. This seems to suggest organizations' reluctance to treat motherhood and nurturing fatherhood as an important experience that can be used for the benefit of their culture. Taking care of small children is perceived as an obstacle, something that distracts from work and, at best, can be tolerated. Care and a managerial position seem to be perceived as a bad combination.

The question of motherhood in and of organizations is not popular in the dominant discourse, nor visible in practice. However, there are exceptions. One of them is the specialist magazine *Working Mother* which presents the profiles of working mothers who are successful in business, and provides a ranking of companies favourable to mothers. The 2009 ranking (Finnigan et al., 2010) rewarded those companies that managed to protect working mothers from the negative consequences of the world crisis. These companies, despite the difficult situation in the market, spend money on healthcare, childcare and other family-aid programmes. They also enable mothers to organize their work in a more flexible manner, they let mothers help one another in their duties connected with work, and often support their employees in difficult situations such as a child's illness. One of these companies, Accenture, has created a separate post to help the employees to combine their private lives with work (Director Work/Life Initiatives). On its website (Accenture, 2010) the company prides itself on having won the prize and publishes the following words: 'The working mothers of Accenture know that they constitute the company's driving force as they set a good example for others showing them how to perform well at the workplace while simultaneously taking care of their family.'

In the passages that follow the care for the working mothers is presented as a part of the company's policy of diversity management and a manifestation of a modern approach to maintaining balance between private life and work. The company's main objective is keeping valuable employees in the company, and supporting them is treated as an investment that will pay for itself in the long run. The dominant approach in the company is rationalistic, more typical of the Animus. One can, however, see some traces of the integration of the Mother archetype in the company's support of the solidarity and cooperation between working mothers and in enabling the employees to have more flexible arrangements.

6.4   ORGANIZATIONS AS MALE BUSINESS

Animus, the archetype of maleness, is by no means a monolith. It can manifest itself in many different ways, inspiring social actors to enact the roles they consider 'male'. The phenomenon has been best described in a new field of sociology called masculinities studies:

> [T]he case we make is for masculinities as plural, changing, and histori-cally informed around dominant discourses or ideologies of masculinism ... [M]asculinities are those behaviours, languages and practices, existing in specific cultural and organizational locations, which are commonly associated with males and thus culturally defined as not feminine. (Whitehead and Barrett, 2001, pp. 15–16)

Maleness is relationally – that is, culturally, and not biologically – linked with authority and power. It is the effect of the identity work, to use the authors' terminology, or in the language of this book, a feature of the archetype of the Animus. Stephen Whitehead and Frank Barrett describe several types of male power, of which the simplest and the most primitive is aggression. Another type of power is the derivative of the close relation between maleness and power positions in society (and this includes busi-ness). Finally, power can constitute a sort of discourse, not in an individual sense, but as a collective source of male identity building. In her exten-sively quoted book on men and masculinity Lynne Segal (1990) writes that the traditional male role common in our culture seems limited by such central characteristics as power and violence, authority and domination. This role has recently been undergoing rapid changes, and the aspects that had been marginalized are now integrated into male identity and so now we can talk about masculinities, not only one masculinity. Modern inter-pretations of masculinity include a wider range of attitudes and behaviour, from a macho type to a father, from a young rebel to a tender and caring romantic, from a hero to a reliable life partner on whom one can always count. All these types constitute various shades of masculinity that had appeared in other cultures, in different time and places. Their coexistence is characteristic of our times.

In management, however, the traditional model of masculinity still dominates. David Collinson and Jeff Hearn (2001) observe that masculin-ity, although central in the context of organizations and management, is often omitted in mainstream discourse and assumed as obvious. Men are the main protagonists of management literature, being at the same time ignored as human beings. This will become less surprising if we see that the main role in management is not played by particular men but by the Animus, not fully conscious and, therefore, more limited than it would be if it was subject to conscious creative interpretations. Also, one does not have to be a man to manage in a 'masculine' fashion. Judy Wajcman (1998) describes how women in high managerial positions adopt male standards and in fact manage 'just like men'. Female managers character-ize their work in terms associated with masculinity and these are similar to the terms used by men. The primary virtues that are valued are firmness, an orientation on tasks, flexibility, a certain 'harshness' and, sometimes, aggression. Managers of both genders are mostly authoritarian and believe human relations are subordinate to the accomplishment of tasks. Such standards are described in literature as 'good management practices'. Wajcman observes that men and women in high managerial positions hardly differ. A book edited by David Collinson and Jeff Hearn (1996) discusses the question of management as a 'male business', showing that in practice the managerial masculinity manifests itself mainly as a 'compul-sive desire to be in control, and thereby, to act instrumentally with respect to everything, including the self' (Kerfoot and Knights, 1996, p. 80). Such an attitude is especially common in strategic management where managers devote a lot of time and energy to setting objectives and proving that these were attained thanks to their efforts. Since masculinity is assumed as self-evident and not subject to any conscious reflection, all departures from the inflexible canon are treated as a sign of weakness.

The canon itself is not totally monolithic as it has a few variants. David Collinson and Jeff Hearn (2001) present five main types of masculinity in management. The first is authoritarianism. It is characterized by the lack of tolerance for disagreement and diversity, the rejection of dialogue and an almost exclusive concentration on task-accomplishment. Aggression is seen as an advantage, and striving to subordinate others is one of the main aims in managing people. Paternalism is a gentler form of mascu-linity in management and consists in playing the role of the father who refers to moral principles and higher purposes, and stresses the impor-tance of cooperation and interrelations within the organizational hierar-chy. The traits that are valued in this variant of masculinity are wisdom, self-discipline and providing care over one's subordinates for their good. Often it is the boss who decides what this 'good' actually is, regardless of the employees' feelings. Paternalism is more common among older men (and women) in high positions. Yet another type of masculinity is entrepreneurialism, or relying on one's ingenuity, coping on one's own in various situations, a penchant for confrontation and a positive approach to conflict. Such a manager most of all values results, accomplishments, profits and other 'hard' results of efforts, usually in comparison with other people's and organizations' accomplishments. There is a certain type of solidarity between otherwise ruthlessly competing individuals and a sort of respect based on the principles of fair play. This type of masculinity is usually preferred by young people. The fourth popular masculinity type is informalism, based on values shared by a group of people. Such a group is characterized by strong internal bonds; it is sharply distinguished from the environment and from other groups. Personal interests, such as golf, cars or angling, also strengthen the bonds inside the group. The members of the group support one another distancing themselves from people from outside the group. The valued traits are loyalty, friendship but also aggression towards outsiders and the ability to resort to degradation rituals. The last of the styles listed by the authors is careerism. It is a rather lonely type of masculinity, meaning that a person competes with others without establishing bonds of solidarity and without respect for competitors. The most important thing is gaining promotions, receiving prizes and an increasing income, which is a continuous confirmation of masculinity through climbing the organizational ladder. This type of masculinity is quite common among people from the middle classes.

Not only management is a purely masculine domain in organizations. Lisa Zanetti (2002) emphasizes the fact that other organizational roles tend to be linked with masculinity: an 'ideal' employee often takes on the characteristics of a hero, is presented as a 'road warrior', a merchant with 'killer instincts' or a salesman 'penetrating markets' (ibid., p. 525). Usually, organizational legends praise the heroes who fight glorious battles in the face of a gigantic crisis, and not the employees who work with care and devotion, preventing crises in the first place. David Collinson and Jeff Hearn (2001) characterize factory organizational cultures as distinctly masculine (this also true of factories that employ only women). New employees are subjected to diverse aggressive, amusing but also offensive rituals that are to check whether the new people are 'all right', whether they would make good members of the collective. Those who skilfully respond to these practices but also know when it is time to show their superiority over others, for example subsequent new employees, become fully recognized colleagues.

David Collinson and Jeff Hearn (2001) observe that organization theory has been quite blind to the questions of masculinity (and femininity). The various management functions are treated as if they were genderless, while at the same time the majority of managers are men. This is true now as much as it was true in the past. As a result, a hidden connection between management and masculinity has been established. The connection was also established in the management writing tradition, as early as in the classical management theories that insisted on the separation of the professional and personal spheres (Roper, 2001). Theorization takes place in the space between the author and the outside world. Organization theory classics, like Taylor, Fayol or Urwick, tried to eliminate all personal and non-linear aspects from their theories and models. The illusion of objectivity was celebrated by younger authors and still pervades mainstream theories. Most importantly, organization theory has been deprived of personal experiences, of both the authors and their objects of study: managers and the other participants of organizations. Also, the writings of the precursors of organization theory, especially Frederick Taylor, were an attempt at raising their status in the eyes of their contemporaries through a display of power, neither physical nor political, but a power in the field of a rational solving of practitioners' problems to show the advantage over the practitioners.

Masculinity may be a driving force of actions and a source of energy for social advancement. Charles Lawrence, a manager in the hi-tech sector, constantly promoted, sets his father as an example to follow and does not want to have anything to do with feminine modes of thinking: 'I can never understand a female, that's for sure, and how they think' (Connell, 1995, p. 168). He was a good student, but not an outstanding one. First of all, he was ambitious and go-getting. He set himself the goal to become a pilot. He managed to enrol in flying lessons but his poor performance prevented him from getting the diploma. Against his family's will he kept pursuing his goal; he worked at fruit picking, collecting money to enrol in flying lessons once again. This time he got a diploma but could not find a job as a pilot. He decided to enlist in the army and develop his skills as a pilot. Without losing heart he completed all the necessary courses but did not become a professional soldier. He began working for civil aviation and was quickly promoted. His family helped him in many key moments in his career, but in Charles's story acting against his family's will, coping on his own and his determination play the most important parts and the rest is either marginalized or shown as something negative. Told this way, his progress becomes a victorious duel of a brave knight with a dangerous dragon.

6.5 VISIONS OF STRUGGLE AND COMPETITION

In his essay on sport as an actualization of masculinity Bruce Kidd (1987) observes that the acceptance of aggression has increased because of the 'civilized' manifestations of aggression and competition, such as in sport. For a long time sport has been considered a masculine domain, a 'manly need', and a typical manifestation of masculinity in action. Even in sport, however, one can see that the boundaries between competition and violence are actually thin and can be easily crossed, that in fact they are two sides of the same coin. The author argues that the main problem is the imperative to win, which indeed is a desire connected with the male cultural role. Aggression can be understood as derivative of a general urge to win at all costs. Aggression in a broader context can also be perceived as a problem of the role as such. In his book on the male cultural role Joseph Pleck (1983) argues that aggression is not determined biologically but is a sort of pathology of the male role, a pathology that is considerably common. Pleck believes that the pathology results from the fact that fulfilling the traditional male role is difficult and sometimes is beyond the reach of men, and the pressure to identify completely and ideally with this role is in some societies very strong. In other words, very often men do not have a choice: their range of inspiration is limited, and to many people the social sanctions against those who do not play their roles in the 'right' way are too difficult to bear. The attitude of social actors to the male role is less personal than it is to the female role. In many societies women have a broader possibility to personalize their roles than men, to interpret it in their own fashion, and their failure to play their role is not as strongly condemned as in the case of men. The male role is strongly normative and simultaneously the many of the norms that describe it are internally contradictory. Moreover, many norms are psychologically dysfunctional, for example the one according to which showing feelings, or even experiencing them, is not masculine. A common reaction to these problems is aggression. Aggression becomes dangerous when it replaces all other feelings or even when it becomes the only culturally allowed feeling. Repressed feelings remain beyond the light of consciousness, where they accumulate and change into violent feats of passion that overcome the person, take control and explode into aggression, which in the case of the male role is often accepted or at least perceived as a 'necessary evil', a sad but unavoidable part of the man's fate.

For a long time competition and competitiveness have been central to organization theory, and they have usually been perceived in a positive light. Robin Matthews (2002) analyses the phenomenon of competitiveness in business and concludes that it is one of the most important archetypes of modern management, applying to whole organizations and their main social actors. The author observes that competition, including rivalry and a sort of chivalrous cooperation, is not only a feature of a free market economy, as it also existed in the socialist system. My research confirms this observation, though competition in the Eastern Bloc applied to different elements of the company's functioning than in the free market system: in the socialist system the political sphere was more important than the economic one (Kostera, 1996). Mathews refers to the notion of archetype because, in his opinion, competition is the principle that organizes the dynamics of the organizations' functioning, and it refers both to actions directed outside and to those influencing the company's internal structure. In the first case one talks of the market's invisible hand, which is an expression from the sphere of economy metaphysics. In the second sense, competition lies at the foundation of organizational actors' actions as they refer in their work to the archetypes of the Hero, the Trickster, the Sage, and so on. One of the rules motivating their actions is the principle of competition, be it fair or ruthless.

Burkard Sievers (2000) discloses the darker side of competition. For him, competition and war are close to each other, not just in a metaphorical sense but, sometimes, literally. The author quotes an example of a German company that, during World War II, treated competition as its contribution to the war efforts of the Third Reich. Apart from manufacturing products that were to contribute to Germany's victory in the war, the company perceived its dominant position on the market as proof of Germany's superiority on all fronts. The company openly promoted Nazi ideology and identified with Nazi symbols, and at some point the swastika was incorporated into the company's logo. After the war this symbolism was abandoned and the new board started using an unambiguous business rhetoric. The company's new successes were still presented as proof of Germany's superiority, only this time it was about technological superiority, gained in the time of peace. The author points to a close symbolic relationship of aggressive and peaceful competition. The situation becomes dangerous when other values become more important than the respect for a human being.

It is quite common in contemporary organizations, not only in time of war, that the spirit of competition is transformed into hostility and aggression. Bardley Olson, Debra Nelson and Satyanarayana Parayitam (2006) believe that every leader, because of the commonness of aggressive behaviour, should know how to manage in the context of violence and brutal conflicts. Managers should aim at toning down the conflicts and preventing aggression through understanding; that is, to use the terminology adopted in this chapter, they should transcend the narrowly understood archetype of the Animus. A manager cannot fight aggression with aggression as it will only aggravate the problem. Impoliteness, an aggressive tone, offensive utterances – these are all types of behaviour that have extremely negative consequences for the people involved, and for the whole organization. Understanding and a firm but polite refusal to tolerate aggression, together with respect for values such as justice, trust and the readiness to offer support, are the manager's proper answer to aggression in organization. Self-awareness and empathy are so important because they make people less prone to act impulsively or aggressively. Often the objects of aggression in organizations are younger people. This is a result of the tradition of the so-called 'pecking order' typical of the traditionally understood masculinity. Joanne Leck and Bella Galperin (2005/2006) demonstrate that aggression towards young employees can have far-reaching negative consequences for the employees and the organization. The authors have noticed that young victims of aggression are less likely to change their jobs than their older colleagues in a similar situation. This may be due to feelings of powerlessness; they are young and thus in a helpless position, for the time being. Behaviour of this kind is well known in the army; for example in the Polish army it is called 'the wave', a pertinent name as it suggests its most depressing feature – it is transmitted to the next generations.

A certain Polish sport organization[41] hired a young person, Kazik, as a coach for children and teenagers. He was experienced, he had worked for several years for a club, had established friendships, and his cooperation with his colleagues was very successful. When he became one of the key figures in the club his relations with people, and especially with the deputy chairman, Jan, suddenly changed. Jan, from having been a kind colleague, changed into a ruthless rival. He started talking about Kazik in a way that was not only negative, but plainly aggressive and derogatory. Kazik had no doubts that he was in the position of Jan's rival: 'His aggression was not hostile, neither did he aim at inflicting pain or hurting me. It was rather an instrumental aggression that was to discourage me from voicing my opinions on the functioning of the club or even discredit me in the eyes of other club members.'

Jan also began making certain gestures. Once, Kazik was asked to leave the tennis court; and each time Jan addressed Kazik, he assumed an aggressive posture and gesticulated energetically. Apart from these incidents and utterances, some organizational measures were taken to discourage Kazik and make his work difficult. Young activists decided that Kazik's presence in the club was a good occasion to present their opinions to a wider public. In a general meeting he was chosen to be a member of the board, which led to an aggravation of the conflict. The deputy chairman managed to convince the older members of the board of his point of view and from then on they all voted against the initiatives of the young people, motioned by Kazik. In the opinion of the young manager, the good of the club was not taken into account – what counted was rivalry and the urge to show the young man 'his place': 'Many times I have been told that Jan talked about me, saying "[Kazik] can be the boss at home, here I am the boss."'

6.6   SYZYGY

Donna Haraway (1985/1991) inspired many readers to think outside of the gender dichotomy with her essay 'A Cyborg Manifesto', where she proposes the cyborg metaphor as an alternative to gender studies based on the strict division into men and women. The cyborg is a hybrid of a human being with technology where the genders combine and change into a being of a different order, a kind of androgyne and hybrid. Androgyny is not only the coexistence of the male and female elements but also the synergetic effect resulting from the combination, a beauty and sexuality multiplied and complemented (Singer, 1976). It should be remembered that originally the Greek deity of love and sensuality, Eros, was an androgyne – one of the four eternal deities[42] that existed in the beginning of time. Haraway believes that due to contemporary technology such an androgynous and hybrid being, known before only from literary fiction, has become common and normal. '[W]e are cyborgs', Donna Haraway claims (ibid., p. 150), in our everyday interactions and social processes that are permeated with technology to an increasing extent. The author argues with the currents of feminism based on a common identity resulting from biological premises and determined by them, and proposes instead a solidarity based on the feeling of cultural affinity. Contradictions and disagreements between people should be reconciled and united and not solved in a linear way through the elimination of elements that do not fit. Technology makes such arrangements possible, it gives us a chance of becoming better persons.[43]

One should examine the cyborg metaphor carefully as it offers solutions transgressing dualism and opens a new perspective for 'transgressed boundaries, potent fusions, and dangerous possibilities which progressive people might explore as one part of needed political work' (ibid., p. 154). It is a unity of a different type, or even a different order, being different from the unity gained by domination or incorporation, typical for colonial discourses. The cyborg as an identity is not totalizing, because instead of pushing into existing frameworks it gives a chance to preserve one's uniqueness and a connection based on the sense of human bond. One of the most interesting voices in the discussion around Donna Haraway's work is that of Katherine Hayles (1999) and touches upon the questions of posthumanism. The author shows how the new communication media let us redefine what a human being is. They make the human being abstract, separating the mind from the body, which seems to be the dominant approach in thinking about the role of technology in the progress of civilization. Information, however, cannot replace the body. But it can be incorporated into the body, changing and broadening the possibilities of everyday actions of human beings in the world. The dualistic division into body and mind is no longer needed in the era of developed technologies as they enable connecting on a different level, which does not have to consist in subordinating the body to the mind. Hayles argues for a restitution of the body's prominent place in the discourse; not as a factor determining identity (e.g. through gender or race), but as a materialization, placing the subject in the context of experience.

Several authors praise organizational androgyny. Alice Sargent (1981) argues that androgyny in management is valuable and desirable. In many spheres of management androgyny, understood as a coexistence of behaviour traditionally considered masculine or feminine, becomes an integrative factor. It enables combining effectiveness with personal development and opens new interesting ways for the maturation of organizations and people. To become more versatile and modern, managers – both men and women – should learn to develop the characteristics which are ascribed to the other gender, but which could have been repressed. For example, men should learn to communicate better with others, to express their feelings and change their attitudes. Women should not abstain from assertive actions, they should solve problems with confidence and not back off when the manager should become visible. The author believes that training for such skills should be included in standard curricula of managerial education, which would add some practical elements to the teaching of management styles, such as the application of models of learning and leadership. This is important, as '[e]ffective use of power in organizations is critical for producing compliance, but effective management also requires alliances' (Sargent, 1981, p. 305).

To attain the two goals one should know how to use one's power in both a 'masculine' and a 'feminine' manner, both through firm leadership and through building the sense of bond and belonging. Androgyny does not only mean an effective use of both types of power but also creates a synergetic effect which reinforces creative potential and opens the way to the development of a whole range of beneficial attitudes and types of organizational behaviour. Moreover, it also effaces the negative consequences of a traditionally male management style's domination, such as lowering the level of aggression. According to Sargent, androgynous management provides a great foundation for creating a management based on competence, promoting the organization's competence thanks to a holistic development of its staff. Also, it lowers the stress level, which is helpful in the learning process.

Jerzy Kociatkiewicz (2004) presents the possibility for a synergetic interaction between computer technology and organizational social actors in terms of an alchemical marriage. The traditional Cartesian division into body and soul (functioning in the physical and virtual spaces) does not adequately mirror the way in which people and computers interact in space. To this traditional division Kociatkiewicz adds three additional types of space: the technical, the domain of the mind; the personal, where experience acts; and the abstract, or the space of logic. The author calls the space where all these spaces overlap, which is a place of special potential for transformation, the alchemical marriage. The contradictory energies meet and have a chance to complement one another dynamically. In other words, it is a space of an interaction of all aspects: body, soul, mind, logic and experience; and their interaction results in the creation of a new quality, rich in new dimensions. Moreover, the space enables a close encounter between people, as shown in an example from the author's research. Andrzej, an information technology (IT) specialist in a software company, intensively used his mind and senses to work on computer programs. Simultaneously, he used an instant messaging (IM) service, Gadu-Gadu, to chat with a person he was in love with. He was simultaneously present in several spaces and in each of them he seemed attentive, concentrated, creative and intensely present. The division of attention into rational and emotional spaces did not diminish his concentration; on the contrary, he seemed the more energized the more he engaged in both: a synergetic effect bringing new potential.

Another example comes from an IT equipment advertisement published in Polish computer magazines. My co-author and I (Kociatkiewicz and Kostera, 2005) distinguished several shades of attraction used in advertising. We described advertisements using the Anima, the Animus, and a combination of the two. The Anima appears in advertisements promoting monitors, Internet services, software and other peripheral devices; it is less common in advertising of computers as such. The Anima appears in different shapes, from a traditional one as in the case of an advertisement of a computer monitor, featuring in the foreground a scantily dressed woman in a pose and with a make-up characteristic of the 1950s; to the less typical, as in the advertisement of a different computer monitor bearing the caption 'depth' and featuring a woman with a mysterious expression, against a dark background. The Animus is used in the advertisements of the same devices as the Anima, with the addition of complete computer systems. Often the advertisement presents an office type of masculinity – a man wearing a suit and a tie looks at a point next to the reader. He is self-confident, matter-of-fact but not involved with any interactions with the person looking at the advertisement. Another type of masculinity can be seen in an advertisement for computer monitors where a tattooed man tattoos another. Both are turned a little sideways to the viewer but seem conscious of their gaze. The advertisements that used androgyny seemed the most convincing. Often, the androgynous element is manifested by images of people shown as ambiguous in their gender identity. A good example of this is a transgender geisha advertising printers. The geisha looks at the viewer in a slightly provocative way, her expression is mysterious, intriguing and eye-catching. Some advertisements present computer equipment in an androgynous and clearly sensual way. For instance, an uninterruptible power supply (UPS) unit is presented against a red background; there is something intriguing and unsettling about it. Its smooth, delicately rounded shape and intensely flickering lights catch the viewer's eye. In our opinion, computer advertising is much more daring and inventive in its use of the images of the Anima, the Animus and the Androgyne than the majority of other advertisements in the Polish media. Possibly, the field of imagination is broadened thanks to IT technologies that inspire and demand thinking outside the box, reaching for associations and the potential that lurks in us, waiting to be awakened, and helping us create new things and reach for the unreachable.

Elsewhere (Kociatkiewicz and Kostera, 2012a) we argue that a syzygic mode of learning, the co-narrative study, is beneficial for management education. It is a way of uniting oppositions without changing them or levelling them out. It enables us to encounter and empathize with the Other, not by means of identification that too readily can degenerate into projection, but by an interest in and celebration of difference and contrast. Co-narrative stories relate different experiences and can be written, told, enacted and interpreted by students. Instead of looking for traditional answers to questions or trying to 'solve' the cases, the students can co-author stories, thus exploring and experiencing situations in different ways without simplifying them. Syzygic teaching can embrace much many senses and modes than traditional teaching, it can pay attention to rhythm, time and feelings. Most importantly, it brings moral issues such as compassion and moral judgement back to centre stage in management education. It enables a dynamic learning process, in accord with cadences of communication and experience.

Fotaki and Harding (2012) argue for an empathetic and conceptual bisexuality in academia, because such a position brings hope of radical change and seriously challenges the old structures through giving voice to the repressed, and undermining apparent stabilities. Scholars would be encouraged to think and speak bisexually, not necessarily engage in cross-dressing or changing gender. The important thing is to be aware of the position of the other and to move between the gendered positions, not letting oneself get caught in either end of the dichotomy, but embracing the whole spectrum. All persons using masculine language should learn feminine language, and vice versa. Then not an exchange but a merger should take place, bringing in new understanding and seriously changing the symbolic order of academia and knowledge.

7.   Persona: the actor and the mask

7.1   THE ARCHETYPE OF THE PERSONA

The word 'persona' comes from the Greek word for an actor's mask in the ancient theatre. There were different masks for actors playing in comedies and for those playing in tragedies. The mask's function was to convey the main characteristics of the role to the spectators, even those who sat far away from the stage. In Carl Gustav Jung's psychology ([1959] 1990) the persona is a mask of character – the role an individual plays in the society: 'One could say, with a little exaggeration, that the persona is that which in reality one is not, but which oneself as well as others think one is' (Jung, [1959] 1990, p. 123).

The Persona is a façade, an image we present to the world and to ourselves. It consists of our attitudes, mannerisms, facial expressions, scripts we follow and co-create as well as appearance, attire and make-up. It is a kind of dress we put on our personality, often devoting considerable effort to it. We derive inspiration from tradition, the lessons we learned at home and at school, social expectations or, more precisely, our perceptions of the latter, and our imagination. Complications appear when the Persona becomes an inflexible armour, preventing the development of a spontaneous personality and making it difficult to experience the world. This happens when defence mechanisms start to dominate or when the perceived external expectations suppress individual expression to such an extent that a person feels alienated from the world and their own image. If this happens, the actor should get rid of the mask and begin looking for their face, try to find something that feels like authenticity and enter the road that leads back to the origins. A full Self uses the Persona in a conscious and creative manner, as a way to help to communicate with the world and to dramatize human expression. It can become a tool for the individual's contacts with the world, making available powerful cultural resources for individual communication such as rituals or symbols. Such a Persona connects instead of dividing; it helps to express a vibrant personality, and it does not limit it. At the same time, it enables a better reading of information that comes from the outside and a greater sensibility for that which the others really want to express. The Persona can help us interact in certain situations, it can tell us what we can and cannot do, such as in the relation between the doctor and the patient or the teacher and the student.

The working of this archetype is described in Oscar Wilde's *The Importance of Being Earnest* ([1895] 2007). The comedy, set in Victorian times, presents two young people, Algernon Moncrieff and his friend, whom Algernon knows under the name of Ernest Worthing. Ernest wishes to marry Algernon's cousin, Gwendolen. The friend refuses to give his assent to the marriage demanding that Ernest should explain the inscription on his cigarette case he had left at his friend's place, which reads 'For Uncle Jack.' Who is the mysterious Uncle Jack and why did he get a cigarette case from a Cecily? Being put under pressure Ernest confesses that he leads a double life. As a protector of Cecily, a girl living in the country, he plays the role of a serious Uncle Jack. But in his spare time he adopts the name of Ernest and becomes a modern Londoner enjoying a rich life, a younger, reckless brother of the severe Jack. Returning his confidence, Algernon tells him about his own similar practices: when he wishes to free himself from everyday commitments, he leaves for the countryside to visit his imaginary invalid friend, Bunbury. Numerous complications and unexpected turns of events involving the two friends follow. Algernon, stealing from his friend the role of Ernest, visits his country estate and falls in love with Cecily. Ernest alias Jack decides to abandon the role of Ernest as it moves him further away from fulfilling his dreams regarding Gwendolen. Therefore, he visits his country estate mourning the death of Ernest, and meets his friend there, impersonated as Ernest. The play concludes with the happy engagement of both couples. But before the happy ending may occur, it turns out that Jack's first name is indeed Ernest, as he is revealed to be Gwendolen's aunt's son, who had been lost as a child. Everyone, and especially Gwendolen, seems very attached to this name and so the final revelation adds both some joy and an ironic turn resulting from the wordplay of 'Ernest' and 'earnest'. The double meaning is a perfect emblem of a consciously used Persona, that is by definition 'just a game', but a game that is in fact earnest, as it enables the expression of the actor's authentic aims and desires. One should add that the other characters, apart from Jack alias Ernest and Algernon, also alias Ernest, are masks played less consciously, less earnestly.

The whole Victorian Age is known for the stress put on the façade. The play's author, Oscar Wilde, famously said: 'give a man a mask and he will show his true face'. His tragic fate can be seen as a consequence of his relationship with the mask he himself wore in order to show the truth about who he was. I have often wondered, like many others, why he did not choose to leave England, as he had the opportunity to do so at least

Figure 7.1   The Persona
(photo: Jerzy Kociatkiewicz)

twice during his ill-fated trials. We will never know, of course, but there might be an explanation in his use of the mask. Perhaps he felt compelled to let the mask lead to a revelation of his truth – and hoped for the best, as in the happy ending of *The Importance of Being Earnest* where eventually all the strong-willed characters accepted each other's metamorphoses brought on by their respective masks. Of course, he must have known that the likelihood of this was minimal and that he was taking a colossal risk, not just for himself but also for those close to him. But a catharsis could bring liberation not only to him as individual but also to a whole culture. Theatre is a sacred cathartic experience not only for the actors on the stage but also for whole audiences – the mask holds a transformative potential, and in the sacred theatre of ritual it makes it possible to communicate with spirits and reveal deeper truths that usually remain hidden. What the Victorians failed to grasp, perhaps we can try to.

Organizations too can put on masks. This can be beneficial but sometimes it can prove destructive for themselves and others. Georg Schreyögg and Heather Höpfl (2004) propose an overview of organization theory writings inspired by the theatrical perspective, where theatre becomes the central metaphor that shows how organizations can play roles and how roles can be played by people in organizations. The authors emphasize the fact that dramatization in organizations is constructive as long there is an openness to all the elements of the performance, as in Kenneth Burke's (1945) classic interpretation: agent (who performs the act), scene (when and where is it done), act (what is done), agency (how it is done) and purpose (why it is done). When management gives permission to talk openly about only one or just a few of these elements, the effect on the culture can be potentially harmful mystification.

In its positive guise, theatricality may be an inspiration for the organization, as it can teach improvisation and thus enable innovative action. It can also help develop a sense of humour, add distance and lightness to human interactions and make communication with the environment more energetic. In its negative aspect, theatricality means faking, falseness, impersonation. The mask helps one to lie more effectively; organizations and their participants abandon themselves to vanity and window dressing. Only the surface counts, the depth is scorned as it requires time and experience and the façade can be easily and effortlessly built. This lets the actors be perfectly flexible: a quick metamorphosis does not cost anything as the end justifies the means. Such an actor is, as Diderot wrote ([1773] 2009), a machine without a soul. Such management becomes a professional lie. In ancient Greek, 'hypokrisis' means acting, feigning.

In this chapter I first present the construction of a façade that, as such, has a positive role in organizations but is often used to limit the expression of the organizational culture: marketing. Then I discuss dress code and show how and why the playing of roles is significant in contemporary organizations. Finally, I let the archetype conclude the story according to its internal dynamics: I present the potential hidden in the persona and propose a project for the dramatization of management.

7.2 MARKETING AS THE CREATION OF THE PERSONA

In his famous book *The McDonaldization of Society*, George Ritzer (1996) observes that in the contemporary world marketing has become exceptionally widespread. Apart from being present in the goods and services market, it has entered spheres of life from which it had been absent, such as politics, and has dominated them instantly. Politicians know that image has an enormous significance and devote to it a lot of their attention, resources and energy. Simultaneously, all spontaneous forms of contact, for example between the candidates in the United States presidential election and journalists, are completely disappearing. Naomi Klein (2000) also argues that the contemporary world has been conquered by marketing. The amount of money spent on marketing actions, and especially on brand promotion, is incomparably more than it has ever been before and it is enormous when compared to the resources spent on production. The tendency has its origin in the 1980s when, as a result of economical stagnation, corporations changed their target clients and aimed their selling strategies at young people. Brand names started appearing in new contexts, not directly connected with retail, as something desirable and attractive. The kind of marketing that consisted in bringing 'associations with a brand' gained popularity in spheres such as culture, sport, even schools and non-governmental organizations. As a result the image, a result of brand marketing, has lost its connection with what is behind it, and gained an independent business and cultural life. The whole world has turned into a marketing opportunity. This did not, however, make the relations between corporations and stakeholders any better; on the contrary, it has made them completely suffused with reckless empty rhetoric and manipulation.

Critical marketing is a relatively new field of study which takes marketing as its main topic of interest. Marketing has grown to a social and economic phenomenon with few parallels, yet it does not enhance social communication, as was one of its founding ideas. Michael Saren (2007) observes that contemporary marketing goes far beyond the activities of the marketing department and is ubiquitous in the cultural sphere. It plays a crucial role in defining and shaping tastes, dreams, aspirations, needs, even morality. It is not an unambiguously negative phenomenon. Clients today do not passively interpret advertisements but reinterpret their content, sometimes creatively, usually from the point of view of their own practical needs and sometimes in order to use it in their everyday communication. Critical marketing investigates the various influences and underscores their diverse aspects, to help increase the awareness of clients, stakeholders and corporations themselves and thus broaden their possibilities for active participation. The difference between critical and traditional marketing also lies in the scope. Critical marketing is not directed exclusively at managers but to a wider audience. Its interest lies in the construction and reconstruction of the bonds between organizations and their stakeholders as well as the role marketing can play in the process. Therefore, critical marketing focuses on the negative effects of marketing actions and often assumes the perspective of the consumer.

The main charge voiced by the champions of critical marketing against traditional marketing is the latter's one-sidedness, its concentration on the needs of business and not on those of the clients or on the social effects of consumption (Tadajewski and Brownlie, 2008). Despite the mainstream definition of marketing which included the identification of needs, informing and communication, the content of the writings published by marketing theoreticians and the objectives aimed for by the practitioners do not have much to do with the declared aims, being instead close to propaganda. Often the aim of marketing is to hide the real face of the organization from the public, especially those aspects that are less attractive or directly repulsive. At its best, marketing is reduced to a set of techniques and tools, which is paradoxical, because its social and cultural roles have gained such overwhelming prominence. Focusing on techniques is also a skilful way to bypass moral problems as techniques are usually considered morally neutral. Techniques are focused on the short term, and evaluated in terms of whether they either work or not. Long-term effects of marketing actions are rarely taken into consideration, and if they are, they are only considered in terms of marketing strategy understood as business actions. Not only the social and cultural consequences are disregarded but also the material side effects, such as the influence of marketing and business as such on the state of natural environment. Such an approach to marketing marginalized many questions that researchers consider crucial today. It is paradoxical, or maybe ironic, that such marketing limits the free market of ideas.

Critical marketing aims to overcome the problems of traditional marketing that have accumulated for dozens of years, and it seeks to return to the constructive aims it was to pursue in the beginning, that is, to communication and information exchange between the organization and its environment. First of all, it deals with reflection, the creating of theory (Burton, 2001). A cooperation that transcends the boundaries of academic disciplines is very helpful. Marketing can benefit from being interdisciplinary in its theories – after all, in its practice it transcended the boundaries of business a long time ago. To understand better its nature and potential, it is a good idea to use diverse attitudes and perspectives. An interesting recent trend to follow is the development of critical management education (CME), especially in Europe. This may help to build a common ground for the practice and theory in management discourse, and to reflect on the role of marketing in society. Critical marketing should question the assumptions on which marketing in contemporary business was built (Böhm and Brei, 2008). It is important to 'see marketing as part of a wider social formation characterized by specific power relations leading to specific development discourses' (ibid., p. 349). Such marketing can contribute to exploring and describing many important tendencies in the organization's environment, such as the development of protest movements, and the disclosure of gaps and inconsistencies in the organization's self-presentation, and thus become a tool of liberation and social change resulting from genuine needs of the organization's environment. Some practices of this kind are already being used: social and green marketing are interesting and promising examples. These are marketing practices which aim at socially desired goals that are not necessarily financially profitable. An example of a practice of this type is the campaign against smoking in public places. Green marketing can be financed with public means or by non-governmental organizations. Often green campaigns are financed by companies that want to show their concern for the natural environment. There are also morally dubious or reprehensible examples of social marketing use, such as the publicly funded xenophobic campaign in one European country.

A good example of a creative use of critical marketing in practice is provided by a Polish lesbian, gay, bisexual and transgender (LGBT) organization[44] using marketing tools to show the population that gay and lesbian people are people just like their hetero neighbours. Big posters showed young and older people, couples holding hands or single people, some fashionably dressed and some quite behind the times, some happy and some serious, some slim and some rotund. They appeared on buses, on billboards, in public buildings, vis-à-vis ordinary ads of clothes and financial services, and it was known as the 'let them see us campaign'. The campaign was warmly received by some, and maligned by others, notably by conservative and religious organizations. The latter claimed that this was an advertisement campaign for homosexuality. My interviewee from the LGBT organization claimed that, if anything, it was an advertising campaign for humanity, based on the assumption that people when faced with another person tend to be more ready to leave aside their prejudices, than if they are constantly reminded of abstract labels. Whether that worked, remains to be seen. However, on the whole, it fulfilled an important aim: it showed that gay and lesbian people are unlike the young, glamorous models usually portrayed in advertisements, but very much like the 'common Kowalski', or the ordinary Pole.

7.3   DO NOT JUDGE BY APPEARANCES: ORGANIZATIONAL DRESS AS FAÇADE

Dress codes, sometimes quite complicated and intricate, can be found in all cultures. They enable us to categorize at sight members of society according to their class, occupation, gender, marital status, sexual orientation, and so on. Many modern societies want to expand the individual's role in the creation of their own image as part of the identity-building process. Our dress communicates our preferences, our belonging to subcultures or minorities, our class aspirations, and many other things. Dress is a powerful symbolic tool, both at the collective level and, to a lesser degree, at the level of an individual. Thorstein Veblen (1899) discusses the question of dress in his famous work on the leisure class. Appropriate dress is one of the most popular ways to demonstrate one's financial position, and it is an example of ostentatious consumption. Dress does not just serve for protection but also, to a much higher degree, for favourable presentation. People will deny themselves much to buy clothes that will make them look good. Moreover, in a cool climate people tend to spend a lot of money to impress others with attire which is inadequate for the weather and does not protect them from the cold. Clothes should be expensive and look this way; a 'cheap' appearance is not desired, in bad taste, and it testifies to the person's moral imperfections. Apart from this, clothes should communicate the social status of the wearer – a high social status is linked with not doing any physical work. Attire that is uncomfortable and restricts movement, impeccably clean but easily soiled, shows that the wearer does not have to do any physical activities. The imperative to follow fashion intensifies ostentatious wastage – clothes are replaced with new ones much faster than they wear out and people get bored with their clothes increasingly fast. The expansion of the leisure class creates the need for a diversification of tastes. The rich class adjusts to these 'sophisticated tastes', following the standards of beauty and elegance as closely as possible. In Veblen's interpretation, then, dress is the most visible declaration of belonging to a privileged social group.

In his famous book *Moral Mazes*, Robert Jackall (1988) stresses a similarly declarative significance of dress in managerial work, far exceeding the protection of the body against natural elements. In the first place, dress is supposed to show that a person identifies with the managerial class, both in the organization and in the society. But there is more to it: 'Proper management of one's external appearances simply signals to one's peers and to one's superiors that one is prepared to undertake other kinds of self-adaptation' (p. 47). In business, dress is also a sign of one's readiness for conformism, one's willingness to adjust oneself to the system of the organization's norms and values, such as the managerial professional culture. Also, people today want to attract the environment's attention. According to Charles Derber ([1979] 2000), who presented his views in his book entitled *The Pursuit of Attention*, the desire to attract attention has today become an obsession. People use different tactics to interest their environment at all costs. One of the most popular ways of doing so is wearing fashionable attire. Such a superficial approach favours privileged classes and social groups, as they, for many reasons, find it easier to create the desired impression with their attire. Contemporary culture promotes actions that promote unbridled egocentrism, but marginalize the significance of empathy, deep understanding and social skills. This observation applies perfectly to contemporary professional life as well. Not only employees try to make a good impression using superficial means, particularly clothes, but also corporations as such use the so-called corporate dress codes to impress employees and stakeholders. This raises many questions on human and workers' rights and the extent to which corporations can interfere with employees' identities. In many work organizations the management's possibilities of exerting influence on the employee's appearance are very wide, often coming close to that of uniformed services, such as police or the army. This, on the one hand, gives organizations significant power over individual persons, and on the other, it promotes the idea that image management is the most important of all, whatever else the official propaganda may say.

The typical dress code for white-collar workers in the private sector in the 1950s included a suit, a tie and a shirt for men, and a skirt with a lady's jacket for women. Today, in many workplaces, the dominant style is the so-called business casual: a tennis shirt and cotton trousers for both men and women. Some employers accept jeans, especially designer jeans, and a jacket, and some companies allow corduroy trousers for both genders. However, there are still many workplaces where a growing tendency towards a formalization of dress and written dress codes can be observed. This also results, in part, from the desire of the candidates and employees to attract attention (Kiddle, 2009).

In her studies carried out through covert participant observation, Barbara Ehrenreich (2005) searched for answers concerning the professional culture of the contemporary American middle class. The author tried to find a job in an organization typical of the middle class. She went through many recruitment procedures, asked the advice of job counsellors, took courses, but still could not find a job. When she was looking for a job, she was often told that an appropriate outfit was of crucial importance. The advisers suggested that employees will get a positive impression if her attire was both formal and complied with the current fashion. Moreover, the attire should be adapted to local preferences: for example, in New York and San Francisco a black and white minimalism is preferred, whereas in Atlanta they like red and gold features. The advisers stressed the fact that one should emphasize those elements of one's appearance that a particular employer may find appealing. The author learned that she should get to know the preferences of the company's culture regarding norms and values, and dress accordingly. She took all the advice into account in her searches. She responded to each offer presenting a curriculum vitae with a description of her qualifications and her rich professional experience. Still, she was not able to find a job.

But, finding a job is just the beginning. Holding it is no small deal, and the 'proper' attire can be an important element in the game. Anat Rafaeli and Michael Pratt (1993) show how crucial 'right dress' is for the management of many corporations. Enforcing a dress code is an indication that the organization desires to control and subordinate the employee. Accepting the employer's demands is a sign of disindividuation. Dress is a tool for reducing diversity – the stronger the control over the dress, the more mechanistic the organization.

Another study by Michael Pratt and Anat Rafaeli (1997) shows yet another aspect of dress code use inside the organization: not by the managers but by the employees themselves. The employees of the rehabilitation unit of a big American hospital used dress as a tool for the negotiation of their identity and the identity of their unit. Some employees emphasized the specificity of the unit where patients stay in order to recover. The wearing of everyday clothes by the staff is a symbol of their patients' return to the world of healthy people. At the same time, this group of employees advocated a stronger role of management and did not object to lowering the position of the nurse, invoking the rules of effective management. The other group believed that the most important thing was the identity of the medical profession and the hospital as a whole, and that the traditional hospital uniform should express this uniform identity. At the same time, this group, the professionals, wanted to preserve their own high position and the relative independence of doctors and nurses from management. Both groups tried to make themselves heard and to get the upper hand in the process of negotiating the official definition of the unit. The example shows how employees try, with the help of dress, not only to express but also to influence the definition of the organization's identity. Two groups of employees had different opinions on fundamental questions: what is the meaning of their work, or what kind of job they are doing, who is their client, what is their role in the organization and what is their place in the hierarchy? Finally, they differed in their expectations as to who was to make the key decisions. Dress was an attempt to control the answers to these questions. One can say that this study shows how the persona can be used by the organization's participants to express the most important elements in their collective identity and to show how they would like to shape this identity.

Finally, the possibility of rejecting corporate dress code and being able to dress in a way preferable to one's own group is sometimes presented by a professional group as an indication of their powerful position. This is the case of the knowledge workers, such as IT specialists, who stress how different they are to employees wearing ties: 'Paradoxically, dressing supposedly carelessly could be viewed here as a sign of power and competence' (Jemielniak, 2007, p. 495). The IT specialists' dress is also a kind of façade and one that shows the world their collective identity. It is an example of a conscious use of the persona that it to testify to the IT specialists' freedom from other people's attempts at defining their identity, especially the attempts of management. Thus, the IT specialists' casual attire is a distinct sign of their independence. It is not surprising, then, that managers often complain about the IT specialists' insubordination and wish they could do without them.

7.4   PRETENDING AND ROLEPLAYING

In *The Presentation of Self in Everyday Life* Erving Goffman (1959) famously holds that '[a]ll the world is not, of course, a stage, but the crucial ways in which it isn't are not easy to specify' (p. 36). People play parts in performances before an audience constituted by others, the society at large, culture, organizations, and so on; that is, they engage in an activity that 'serves to influence in any way any of the other participants' (Goffman, 1959, p. 26). The parts played in this performance are characterized by social roles: 'Defining social role as the enactment of rights and duties attached to a given status, we can say that different parts may be presented by the performer on a series of occasions to the same kinds of audience or to an audience of the same persons' (ibid., p. 27).

Goffman distinguishes the front, which is the stage on which actors play, and the space backstage where they can relax and be more casual. One actor may play many roles on many stages: the role of spouse, manager, amateur basketball player, and so on. A social actor should be convincing in their role, so they should remain consistent. To do this, actors read the signals from the audience and from other actors that tell them what should be the content of the role. Actors want to make a positive impression on others and they try to act in such a way as to be appreciated. If they are appreciated, the audience may want to pretend that they did not see the unsuccessful elements in their acting (for example, a much appreciated waiter who stumbles may be rewarded by the audience with their purposeful inattention: they 'have not seen anything'). In this way the audience supports the actor in their effort at saving face. Sometimes people present a fake façade. They pretend to be someone they are not, using the same means that are used for the everyday enactment of real roles. The audience may reject this play of appearances but it may also let itself be tricked. The social theatre is interactive – actors play for one another and sometimes they test their performance against one another. Sometimes, however, the play of appearances is intended and the audience is supposed to be tricked. One group among them, such as clients, is to be made to believe in an illusion, though other groups, for example, co-workers, know that the reality behind the play is different. There are some relatively stable points, defined by what in a given time determines the roles and the repertoire in the eyes of the society, but even these points are eventually elements of the performance. Actors usually play what to them seems normal and expected, with minor variations. Sometimes, they introduce their own, creative elements. The acting out of social roles is a sort of collective improvisation mixed with negotiations. Barbara Czarniawska-Joerges (1992) points out that social roles are not stable nor preprogrammed, and they are played anew every time that they are being performed. Improvisation is an important part in each performance, which is fundamentally a way of enacting culture and its rules, 'not necessarily in the sense of acceptance, but of recognition' (Czarniawska-Joerges, 1992, p. 126).

Arlie Hochschild (1983) describes professions where acting out emotions is an important element, such as flight attendants, nurses and waiters. Social actors who perform such roles often suppress their real feelings, which in the long run may lead to alienation: people lose touch with their emotions or with their professional role or, often, both. People who do this kind of work adopt typical defence strategies. The first is deep acting, that is, trying to really feel the emotions that are demanded. This protects them from the necessity of lying continuously but may lead to burnout and emotional problems. Another strategy is distancing oneself from one's professional role, a clear differentiation into 'the real I' and 'the professional mask'. This strategy helps prevent burnout but instead it may lead to the feeling that one's life is a constant lie and, in consequence, to the loss of enthusiasm in and pleasure from one's work. Finally, one can distance oneself from one's professional role, but be fully involved in the play, understood as a performance. It is the most sophisticated approach, a conscious acting that protects one from burnout and indifference. The danger in this case is in falling prey to cynicism. Adopting the strategy of conscious acting, many actors eliminate empathy and see themselves as a person essentially different from the audience: the clients, students, patients. The actor may regard him or herself as a more composed person, more balanced than the audience, not gullible enough to believe in the reality of the performance.

Heather Höpfl and Steve Linstead (1993) tell the story of two workplaces of this kind. The first one is an airline demanding from flight attendants a continuous expression of positive emotions towards passengers. Flight attendants often compare their work to acting in a theatre, because of the amount of acting and its importance for both professions. The other company deals with retail and is based on multilevel marketing. Here too the employees must present an enthusiastic and joyful attitude towards clients. The jobs differ from working in a theatre mainly in the necessity of saving the illusion (which is not demanded in the theatre). Even if the employees can admit to other employees that their work is based on playing, they cannot do it in front of their clients. The audience in the theatre knows that they are watching a performance and they consciously participate in the magical illusion of the theatre. Passengers on a flight or the customers of a cosmetics company believe, and even want to believe, that the emotions played by the employees are genuine, that the flight attendants really want to look after them, and the cosmetics salesperson really believes in the miraculous qualities of the merchandise. The organizational performance tries to hide the ambiguities that in theatre often constitute the basis of artistic expression. The aim of organizational performances is unambiguous, and the feelings that do not fit are eliminated. Social actors cannot use all the range of their emotions and experiences to offer a more original interpretation of their roles; some of the feelings are excluded from the start. Employees carry within themselves the contradictions and conflicts of the performance, which may lead to their 'losing themselves' in the enactment of the role or the deepening of their alienation.

Iain Mangham and Michael Overington (1987) present managers as actors, playing on a scene of illusion, where not all the participants realize that it is only a show. Sometimes managers play unconsciously, ambitiously, identifying with their roles. Sometimes they play cynically, ruthlessly trying to produce the desired effect, using all the means available. Sometimes they use their gift for acting and are aware that it brings positive results; they resort to the transformation of sensations, scenery, expression, creating in this way an important dimension of reality. It is the show that defines the content, such as financial resources or the product, and not vice versa. Organizations are sets of shows. At each performance answers to difficult questions are offered, questions such as: what is the problem? What is the solution? What is hierarchy? and so on. Quite often these answers are creative and dramatized. A good show should absorb the audience in order to be convincing. Just like theatrical performances, shows on a company's stage direct the audience's attention at certain characters, and let them symbolize important values and aspirations. But companies differ from theatre: in management, characters precede the actions, whereas in theatre the actions present and define the character.

John Van Maanen (1990) tells the story of his work for a company that calls its employees 'the cast' and the places where they do their services 'stages', and openly identifies with theatre. The company in question is Disneyland, a well-known amusement park and a dream destination of many children. Here, drinking alcohol, aggression or any sexual behaviour are all taboo. The park is a fantasy world offering children and their minders magical moments. Visitors may meet characters from Disney cartoons, see magic castles and go on trips into exotic lands, all in a wonderful, fairy tale-like setting. The Disney parks exude joy and cheerfulness; nothing here is to be taken seriously, everything is a fairy tale that the visitor enters for a moment. Disneyland announces itself as 'the happiest place on Earth'; happiness is the identity and the product of the park, and the employees are charged with making the visitors happy.

> The happiness trade is an interactional one. It rests partly on the symbolic resources put into place by history and park design but it also rests on an animated workforce that is more or less eager to greet the guests, pack the trams, push the buttons, deliver the food, dump the garbage, clean the streets, and, in general, marshal the will to meet and perhaps exceed customer expectations. (Van Maanen, 1990, p. 58)

Walt Disney World chooses its employees carefully, paying particular attention to their appearance, which should be stereotypically 'nice', neat, conservative and healthy. The employees joke among themselves that Walt Disney himself would not get the job because of his characteristic little moustache. The company wants its employees to look 'cheerful' and 'reassuring'. New employees are taught appropriate attitudes and behaviour in a variety of ways, such as by training courses, handbooks and billboards reminding them what positive emotions they should produce in clients. The company tries to exert as much influence as possible on the behaviour of the employees and on the emotions they stir up and show. The point is not to teach them interpersonal skills; actually, real interactions between the employees and clients are rare and strongly limited by rules and regulations. The purpose is to emanate joy and create feelings of happiness in the clients. The employees are supposed to perform the simplest tasks with enthusiasm and a contagious optimism. Employees define their own roles as 'nice props' and 'talking monuments'. The status and the salaries of employees vary depending on the kind of control, real or symbolic, that they have over the visitors. But the actors do not have any control over the content of their roles. The lines the employees say during rides and visiting the sites are scripts learned by heart. The same is true about the employees' appearance. The uniforms provided by the board cannot be modified, or adjusted to individual preferences or even to a person's characteristic traits. No ornaments or accessories can be worn, if they are not part of the uniform. Despite the limits of theatrical content, the employees quickly learn the rules of stage exchange, very much in the spirit of Erving Goffman. They learn to observe their clients and tune in to them emotionally in order to receive their positive reactions in exchange, even if they have very modest means at their disposal. They play with what they have left: feelings and the aura. When they feel the client has a positive approach, they become more witty and lively. Usually, this evokes emanation of the same feelings from the clients.

7.5   DRAMATIZING MANAGEMENT

The archetype of the Persona narratively aims at a conclusion in the form of transcendence through art. Historically, theatre was a form of religious ritual: in many ancient cultures, for example in ancient Greece, it often had a religious function. Theatre can also simply delight and daze, entertain, please, transform and, above all, express issues important to people. The Persona is a perfect tool for transmitting moods, impressions and insights, and for moving audiences. In his book *The Empty Space* ([1968] 1995) Peter Brook describes four kinds of theatre. The dead theatre is a conventional theatre, based on stereotypical means of expression, closed to new interpretations. The holy theatre tries to reach the human's spiritual dimension, it reveals and actualizes the invisible, and involves all participants, the viewers and the actors, into rites of passage beyond the materiality of the world and into transcendence. The simple theatre is close to people, unpretentious; it brings the viewer and the actor together. It shows what preoccupies people in a given time, encourages empathy and an identification with the characters, but does not promise any depth. The direct theatre is fluid, mutable, it follows experience and lets express important, though often unclear, or inexpressible, content.

The organizational theatre can behave in exactly the same ways as the other three – it can kill experience, enrich it or even sanctify. In order to use this archetype's potential and let it actualize itself in its own way, one should let it influence the sphere of imagination. The three living forms of Brook's theatre can inspire dramatization in organizations to reach the spiritual domain. They can also enlighten and provide an insight into how the actors shape reality through roleplaying (Kociatkiewicz, 2000).

In their description of theatricality of management Iain Mangham and Michael Overington (1987) show that it also has an artistic dimension. Sometimes, however, it is hidden, neglected; it is often treated in an unskilful way or manipulated, but it has a great potential which can be summoned with the help of a conscious and creative dramatization of actions. By summoning the artistic dimension of management the aesthetic qualities of organization can be brought to the fore, but the efficiency of the actions also benefits. The performance contributes something more than mere technique and mobilizes people: managers and the audience in front of which they play. The contribution consists of the capacity for connecting seemingly unconnected elements into a coherent whole.

In organizations seen as systems, consisting of elements interconnected in a complex fashion, dramatization can bring these hidden connections to light without eliminating anything of their subtlety. It can bring to the fore the enthusiasm and devotion that can be activated in people thanks to their experience.

Together with my co-authors, I investigated and developed this issue in *Three Faces of Leadership* (Hatch et al., 2005). We believe that managers should consciously adopt the roles of theatrical directors in their companies. We do not endorse the practices of those managers who tell their subordinates what they should recite. We think that they should be like imaginative theatrical directors who want to use fully the potential that the theatrical approach to business can give them: they should inspire, stimulate and motivate. The plays staged in companies should have not only a plot, but also a purpose, and the actors should have the possibility to interpret their parts creatively. Thanks to such an approach, management can inspire innovation and make people less afraid of facing the uncertainty of the environment. Theatre, when it is inspiring and inspired, has the power to provide people with the feeling of ontological safety in the face of chaos. We analysed the interviews with well-known managers, published in *Harvard Business Review*, where we found four main types of dramatic attitudes, represented by successful management practitioners. These are: morality play, modern drama, happening and global show. Morality play is based on a stable, fixed set of characters faced with a moral choice. At worst it is stereotypical, at best archetypical. In a performance of this sort there is only one desired ending, the audience knows what it is and encourages the actors to push the plot in the desired direction. Here, there is no space for ambivalence or doubts. Everything is known to the audience which, apart from jeering and passing moral judgements that agree with the director's intention, remains passive. The passivity is not devoid of creative elements, but they do not belong to the sphere of intellect but to that of emotions. The play encourages, motivates, inspires and sets an example. If it is staged well, the gist is not an imitation, but an impersonation, the entering of the character. A good example is the classical *comedia dell'arte*, the American Western or a typical contemporary TV series.

The most vivid development of modern drama took place in the Elizabethan period. The typical feature of modern drama is an ambiguous presentation of a situation or a set of characters, opening the play to various interpretations. Using Umberto Eco's terminology ([1973] 1989), one can say that such a play is an open work. The more interpretations it allows, the longer its life. Shakespeare's plays are perfect examples of good open works, as for hundreds of years great directors and actors have staged his works, playing his characters. The plays have remained fresh;

they still speak to us as vividly as they did to audiences in the Elizabethan era. In modern drama, the audience is invited to interpret the perform-ance, as a good director and a good actor do not strive to make the text more univocal or unambiguous. On the contrary, their task is to show the dilemma, express the ambivalence and encourage the viewer to think about them. The plot, however, can with advantage be clear and compre-hensible, so that it is easy to see what happens, what choices the characters make. However, it is much easier to summarize the plot of such a play than to render the moral dilemmas or the effect it has on the minds of the audience.

Happenings are plays with an unconventional, surprising structure with a preplanned outline of what has to be expressed and with what means. The characteristic of the happening is that not everything is planned and that there always is space for unexpected or new events and incidents. This kind of play depends very much on improvisation, as far as the plot is concerned. However, the performance has a fixed purpose known to the director and the actors, and the actors prepare to play their roles. The audience plays an active and purely improvisational part in the happen-ing; it cannot remain passive as it is necessary for the play to reach its aims. These include often a transformation of beliefs, a presentation of a new point of view, catharsis, or an emotional and spiritual liberation. In a happening nobody is fully in control of the events that are staged, but the director has a symbolic control over the purpose and the nature of the experience. It is a performance based on cooperation that happens anew each time, though every time its purpose stays the same.

The global show is the child of mass media. In the twentieth century the radio, and then television, made it possible to broadcast information on an unprecedented scale. Later, the so-called new media joined in, especially the Internet, and changed our planet into a global cafe. The media make it possible to advertise such events as concerts or theatrical performances on a global scale. The concerts of groups such as Led Zeppelin or Nirvana attracted enormous crowds. In our global world it is technically possible to reach almost all of the inhabitants of the Earth – the main problem is to adjust the message to 'everybody'. There are artists who indeed made an attempt at this endeavour, such as the King of Pop, Michael Jackson, or more recently Lady Gaga. At worst, global artists make their message mediocre and aim at the mass market as if their art were a fizzy drink; they create art that appeals to everyone, that is, kitsch. At best, they are multidimensional and versatile, they celebrate popular culture in a way that gives a possibility for interpretation on many levels, from camp or kitsch, to intertextuality, to profound insights about being human. The global show is perfectly directed and contains the whole world; it invites everybody to take part, and promises to offer something to everyone, though not the same to each and all. It combines hyperreality with the feeling of direct and genuine presence. The audience is part of the show – or, perhaps, it is the diversity and the globality of the audience that is part of the show. It is expected that the 'viewers of the world unite', and the show has the capacity to become a feast of universality and a sign of global peace. Quite often, however, it is just a shallow show of entertainment, but one which precludes violence and antagonism. Only the Olympic Games join people to the same extent and on an equal scale; except that in the Olympic Games it is competition that is the main theme and in the global show the emphasis is on coexistence.

In the material for the *Harvard Business Review* that we analysed (Hatch et al., 2005) we found many examples of dramatization employed by managers. Usually each of the published interviews put emphasis on only one type of theatre. But there were managers who used different types of shows in different situations. In our opinion it is likely that the chief executive officers (CEOs) have more occasions and more reasons than managers of a lower level to use the theatrical approach in their everyday managerial tasks. For instance, Paul Allair from Xerox skilfully used modern drama in his approach to business. He tried to show the multifaceted structure of his company, direct people's attention to this structure and make them reflect on it:

> In fact we intend to create a company that combines the best of both worlds – the speed, flexibility, accountability and creativity that come from being a small highly focused organization and the economies of scale, the access to resources and the strategic vision that a large corporation can provide. (Howard, 1992; as quoted in Hatch et al., 2005, p. 93)

During the organization's transformation different factors and different objectives of numerous stakeholders were taken into account. The reasons for the transformation were ambiguous: 'But we were not doing it just to be perverse. The change process we have begun is extremely difficult. We have to be very diligent so that old habits, practices and behaviors don't sneak back in' (ibid., p. 94).

The changes met with some resistance, which Allair describes in terms of modern drama as well:

> My favorite example comes from the management team that designed our new architecture. Here is a group of 20 people who, more than anyone else in the company have internalized the new approach to running things. And yet, when it came to deciding to organize the business divisions, that group recommended that we start with the business division staff – the head of personnel, head of finance etc – and that the staff help each division president to choose his or her

operating people. In other words they immediately fell back into a traditional top-down functional approach. (ibid., p. 94)

Upon seeing such a response, the director-manager reacted immediately:

> I said 'Hold on. Don't we have it backwards? I thought we were trying to run this business by the line? Why would you select the staff people to help the presidents select the line? Why don't we do it just the reverse? Who are the key line managers required to run these businesses? We can help them figure that out. They don't need to hire individual staff people to do that. We can help them put their team leaders in place, then the presidents and their team leaders can decide together what kind of staff support they need.' (ibid., p. 94)

A completely different, though equally dramatic, approach to management was demonstrated by Nicolas Hayek from SMH:

> How did we launch Swatch in Germany? Did we saturate the airwave with paid advertisements? No. Anyone can do that. We built a giant Swatch. It was 500 feet high, weighed 13 tons, and actually worked. We suspended that giant Swatch outside the tallest skyscraper in Frankfurt, the headquarters of Commerzbank. It was really something to see! (Taylor, 1993, p. 103; as quoted in Hatch et al., 2005, p. 58)

Hayek invites the audience to participate in the show, he draws the passer-by into the happening; the message is enthusiastic, disorderly and provocative but, like the messages of Allaria and other managers who successfully use dramatic effects, endowed with a clear purpose. The purpose is a mobilization of different personal skills – thinking, as in the case of Allair, and experiencing, in the case of Hayek.

8. The Sage

8.1 THE ARCHETYPE OF THE SAGE

The Sage, or *Senex*, is one of the classical archetypes (Jung, [1959] 1990) referring to social role. The Sage is an older person, rich in experience, who shares their wisdom with the younger generation. The Sage can be a man (he appears in myths and stories as an old man, a prophet or a magus) or a woman (a wise old lady, a witch or an oracle) but, as the gender is not essential to the interpretation of the archetype I use here, I will use the term 'Sage' to designate a social role, regardless of the person's gender. The *Senex* can use information, experience and knowledge in a way that goes beyond their technical and rational qualities, because wisdom is more than these qualities. The Sage knows a lot about the world and human nature, and can be a mystic or a philosopher, has an open mind and a liking and understanding for everything that is human. They can be absent-minded and seem 'otherworldly', without having a negative attitude towards the world. Their estrangement from the world results from not pursuing goals the majority of people find desirable, like riches, fame or success. Sometimes the *Senex* is a stranger – which stresses their position outside the ordinary social reality, and sometimes they are presented as a borderline character, a visitor from another dimension, half-angelic, half-human, maybe a time traveller. The Sage has good advice for the young as well as, often, a tenderness that they do not translate to motherly or fatherly care, as the young must grow up and live their lives themselves. The Sage cannot live it for them, but only helps them when they need the help; they must make all their decisions for themselves. Being too much of a caring mother or father could prevent the young people from gaining their own experiences. That is why the Sage often disappears, dies or withdraws from the world in some other way in order to enable the young people to begin their own quest.

There are many well-known examples of sages in literature: the wizard Merlin from the Arthurian legends, Granny Weatherwax from Terry Pratchett's *Discworld*, Albus Dumbledore from the Harry Potter cycle, or Baba Yaga of Slavic folk tales. One of the most famous literary impersonation of the archetype is Gandalf, known mainly from J.R.R. Tolkien's

Figure 8.1   The Sage
(photo: Agnieszka Topornicka)

The Lord of the Rings ([1954–1955] 2008). Gandalf is one of the last active wizards of Middle-earth, an older person wearing grey clothes and a long beard. He is a wanderer who knows many lands and has many good friends among different inhabitants of Middle-earth. He is cheerful and kind, and he uses his wisdom to help others. He does not, however, make any important decisions for them, neither does he try to influence their actions. Gandalf is the opponent of another personification of the sage in Tolkien's world: Saruman, a wizard who used to be Gandalf's friend but went astray and began using his wisdom to gain the power to rule the world. Saruman, believing that it was only a temporary coalition that his wisdom would later help him to abandon, became completely dependent on the Dark Lord, Sauron. The key role in the trilogy is played by arte-facts – the rings that give their owners great magical powers. A long time ago Sauron gave the elves the knowledge that let them forge the magical rings, but he did it with the intention to grab the power in the future – he was an adviser in bad faith. The elves realized Sauron's intentions and stopped using the rings. Then, Sauron stole the rings with the exception of the three most powerful of them that the elves of Eregion managed to hide and give to Galadriel, Elrond and Gandalf. The mightiest of the rings, the

Ring of Power, forged by Sauron himself, was taken away from him in the battle against the united armies of elves and men. Nobody was able to destroy the ring which was necessary in order to defeat Sauron, the Dark Lord. And nobody could resist the temptations of the powers the ring gave to its owner. After a long time, the ring came into the possession of a hobbit, Bilbo, who later gave it to his relative, Frodo. From then on, the destruction of the ring becomes Frodo's life mission. Many times he meets Gandalf on his path. The wizard gives him advice, offers comfort and even defends him physically in the dramatic struggle with the demon Balrog, in which the sage dies.[45] But there was one thing Gandalf could not, and would not, do – he did not agree to take the ring from Frodo. The young hobbit tried to give it to him but Gandalf declined the offer, explaining that if he accepted it, he could not resist the temptation to use it to do good. The power of the ring was beyond anyone's capacity for control. It should be destroyed, as only in this way can the world be freed from evil. The adventure ends well: the ring is destroyed and Sauron is defeated. Saruman manages to take power in Hobbiton, which he attempts to modernize. His projects do not meet with hobbits' approval and eventually, after Frodo's return, they overturn Saruman's rule, who is in turn killed by his own servant, Grima.

Tolkien's story presents many variants of the archetype of the Sage: from the good Gandalf who has to step back in order to let the protagonists grow up and act on their own; to the Dark Lord, Saruman, who acts from a position of power, believing that his wisdom gives him the right to make decisions for others. Sages occur also outside of the domain of myth and legend – it is my belief that they have an important role to play in organizations.

Wisdom is the topic of *Vita Contemplativa*, an article by Professor Karl Weick (2004) who many researchers, including me, consider a sage in our field of study. The author lists sages from whom he learned – writers, poets, anthropologists, sociologists, management theorists and other researchers – and tells the story of what he learned. He talks of his relationship with them as complex, irregular, convoluted and full of 'hidden transformations' (ibid., p. 654). He emphasizes the crucial role of unforeseen consequences for his reflections and describes how he gradually, though chaotically, came to deepen his knowledge. He summarizes the story of his intellectual development with a quotation from the American psychologist and philosopher William James: 'Act for the best, hope for the best, and take what comes' (James, [1897] 1956, pp. 30–31; as quoted in Weick, 2004, p. 666). It is a wise way to act, and also widespread and quite commonplace. From the point of view of this chapter, two of Weick's observations are the most interesting: that a sage becomes one as a result of a long process of being involved in life and learning from other sages; and that wisdom can be seen as an affirmation of life and a good faith.

I open the archetypical tale of the Sage with a discussion of the role of consultants in organizations. I show how consultants advise: sometimes well, sometimes not so well, but always in their own interest. Then I present the topic of organizational knowledge that has become so fashionable recently in terms of the archetype of the Sage. Knowledge is seen as a resource that can be used to different ends, but this is not always good for the organization. Finally, I return to the question of genuine wisdom and consider the role it can play in organizations.

8.2   WISDOM FOR SALE, OR CONSULTANTS IN ORGANIZATIONS

One of the great precursors of consulting was the Italian Renaissance philosopher Niccolò Machiavelli. His famous treatise, *The Prince* ([1532] 2007), can be read as a consulting report for Lorenzo de Medici. The author gives advice to the young prince who wishes to ascend the throne and preserve his power, assuming that the main objective of politics is the stability of the state. All means to this end are, according to Machiavelli, justified. The prince, however, should also aim at securing at least a minimum of social approval in order not to become an object of hate. The ruler sometimes has to resort to violence, but in such a way as not to provoke retaliation. There are two most important problems for a state: good laws and the defensive potential. The prince should be an effective lawgiver, always ready for the possibility of war. Using contemporary business language, the prince should have a strategic plan in order not to be surprised by competing actors. Machiavelli also advises him to be self-sufficient: one should try not to be dependent on powerful protectors. A state ruled by an enlightened prince should cope with its main problems and needs on its own. The prince should care about his reputation, but he does not have to be perfect – nobody can boast of positive traits exclusively. The gist is to act effectively and avoid demonstrating any traits that could lead to the loss of power. The only ethics that matters is the one that applies to the state's welfare and stability. The prince should not be excessively generous, even if generosity is a trait valued in many rulers. Machiavelli advocates caution and thrift, as the state needs financial resources that come from taxes and taxes cannot be raised without risking the loss of social support. The prince should carefully select people who can be trusted. They should be loyal, intelligent and efficient. The prince should not be misled by appearances, and should be especially suspicious of flatterers. Machiavelli believed that, even though fate determines a part of our actions, we still have some influence on our destiny. The prince should be able to see fate's purposes and adjust his actions accordingly; use the chances he spots and make fate cooperate and conform with the ruler's intentions.

Machiavelli's work has long been an object of disagreement and discussion. Some consider it an example of enlightened and pragmatic political thought, and others believe that the author's pieces of advice are cynical and immoral. Machiavellism has become a synonym for insensibility towards other people, using manipulation in interpersonal relations, and the treating of people as objects. The treatise is also sometimes read as a realist work, containing a set of tools that rulers can use, depending on their preferences and conscience. While considering the moral and practical meaning of the work, it is good to keep in mind who its author was: namely, that throughout his life Machiavelli advised great politicians, in very eventful, turbulent, dramatic times. He sat down to write *The Prince* after he had been forced to withdraw from public and political life.

Steffan Furusten (2009) believes that companies hire consultants in the hope of gaining stability. He has carried out research among consultants' clients and concluded that managers hire them as external providers of knowledge about current problems of management and their solutions. The consultants, however, do not consider themselves versatile experts but, rather, they expect to become part of internal teams where they can support managers rather than work on solutions. In practice this results in adopting different roles that combine both of these perspectives. Consultants become providers of knowledge who cooperate with the managers of the companies that hire them. Furusten remarks that expertise can be bought from many different social actors in the market, from outsourcing or training companies, but that support in internal decision-making processes can only be provided by management consultants. Consultants often present their services in terms of expertise, but the most successful advisers in the market are the ones who know how to combine their expertise with the support of internal processes happening in the company. Thus, they create a new service that can only be provided by them, and the need for which is not always explicitly stated by managers. But experienced consultants know when they should play which of these roles, and they know how to combine the two when it is needed. Clients often form long-term relationships with consulting companies which makes it easier for the consultants to know their clients and their preferences. Consultants learn to read signals and react to them, offering that which the client needs at a given moment, even if it is not in the contract or has not been verbalized by managers.

Furusten calls this a unique type of improvisation that experienced consultants are proficient in. The main motif of the improvisation is the institutionalized discourse of popular consulting literature as well as the popular image of what 'consulting' is, as presented in other media. It does not mean that consultants really do what the books and interviews tell us. Rather, they translate what they do into the language and symbols known from these media. To a great extent their work is improvisation – and the media language serves to reduce the perceived uncertainty and provide a wider recognition of their actions. The effect of the consultants' work is not so much 'introducing changes' and 'solving problems', terms in which popular literature often describes their work, but reacting to clients' needs and then presenting the common effort in terms of 'changes' and 'solutions'.

Furusten's research shows that the main result of consultants' work is the stabilization of the company, an objective that is valuable though not always in fashion. Well-managed companies should survive, and that is the prerequisite for any other actions, including any innovations and restructuring fashionable at a given time. Consultants help companies attain this goal, additionally giving them an appropriate image, and providing attractive slogans whose aim is to create an impression of the company's stability in the eyes of various groups of stakeholders. With the help of the consultants' work, managers can focus on the everyday management of the company.

Tomasz Ludwicki (2008) depicts consultant–customer relationships as a key part of the consulting business. Consulting is a kind of performance with an active participation of the clients. The consultant tries both to adjust to expectations – which usually consists of a reduction of uncertainty – and to give the impression of being an expert who provides the packets of knowledge demanded by the client. In other words, the clients have to believe that what they buy from the consultant is precisely the knowledge they do not have. Consultants cannot limit themselves to selling only this kind of knowledge, as it increases uncertainty instead of reducing it. I would like to add that this may be one of the reasons why traditional consulting is not popular among academics. Instead there is a group of actors of a different type, well liked among academics, and associated with the knowledge of management practice. They are actors who popularize the ideas used later in consultancy practice, and are called management gurus.

Andrzej Huczynski ([1993] 1996) presents famous gurus, such as Taylor, Fayol and Peters, and puts their work into a historical context. Why, each in their own time and place, did they become the symbols of wisdom in management and why were their ideas bought by companies for substantial sums of money? According to the author, this results from the fact that their ideas were lucky to appear at a good moment and that their authors promoted them with an ardour typical of a religious endeavour. Ideas are perceived as wise because they are recognized as such – they are 'in', and they refer to real problems that practitioners are struggling with at a given moment. Gurus offer help based on rules that are easy to follow, and they influence the recipients' image in a positive way. Their ideas are simply packaged and sold and the sellers' purpose is the fulfilment of their own goals, which typically means gaining a profit and becoming famous as management gurus. These people promote management fashions and their own names as sages that indeed become widely recognized brand names. To make their brand last they have to be sensitive to their clients' needs and, first of all, they have to satisfy the basic need which is about offering a feeling of control to managers, in a world ridden with uncertainty and chaos. In other words, consultants can remain sages if they know how to appear to be sages, and as long as the wisdom they offer does not undermine the client's worldview and does not face the client with any serious challenges.

Consultants, then, most of all strive to uphold aims of their own, such as profit, fame or power. The development of their client's organization is not as crucial to them as, say, Frodo's success was to Gandalf. Good consultants know how to combine their personal objectives with their client's good. But there are also consultants such as the missionaries of management I described in my article 'The Modern Crusade' (Kostera, 1995). They were selling rather dubious knowledge to Polish managers, presumably for large amounts of money, in the early stages of the Polish transformation. In those days Western consultants offered easy courses in 'a market approach to management', ignoring the fact that a significant part of what they proclaimed as revelatory and new was already well known to Polish audiences and often perceived as not particularly wise. These consultants reminded me of the missionaries who joined the explorers in times of conquest and colonization to preach their truths, not in order to save the souls of the 'savages' but to facilitate the conquest. The consultants treated the Polish managers like 'management savages' who were to be dressed in well-tailored Western outfits and taught good manners at the negotiation table. The Polish chief executive officers (CEOs), among them many management veterans, very competent in both the theory and practice of management, did not protest because of the Polish idea of what good manners are about. They were taught not to interrupt speakers, and the speakers seemed to enjoy it. I should add that not much of the old managers' wisdom has survived to this day, which is a pity. Hopefully, one day their knowledge will come to be appreciated.

8.3 KNOWLEDGE MANAGEMENT, OR EVERYTHING FOR SALE

The notion of knowledge management has become one of the most popular terms in both the theoretical and practical discourses of management after Ikujiro Nonaka (1991) described it in his famous *Harvard Business Review* article as the secret behind the success of Japanese companies. According to the author, the best Japanese companies have mechanisms, in both their structures and their systems, responsible for constant innovation. This is desirable in the context of a growing uncertainty over the environment, where even good techniques and practices quickly become inadequate to the rapidly changing conditions. The source of the constant innovations is the creation of knowledge, a phenomenon characteristic of the best Japanese companies. Western companies focus on processing data, which is a mechanical activity, aimed at achieving measurable goals like increased efficiency or decreased cost. Such knowledge is operationalizable, and can be expressed and translated in abstract terms. Japanese companies approach the question of knowledge differently. For them knowledge is contained in actions, not always expressible, and reached in experience and an involvement in activities.[46] Japanese companies also know how to use accidental events in order to learn new practices and attitudes. Knowledge thus understood is subjective, often based on intuition, sudden epiphanies, the ideas invented by employees who share their thoughts with the company. The interaction is based on involvement and cannot easily be operationalized or expressed as quantitative objectives. The knowledge created by individual employees is introduced into the system of the whole organization in the course of this interaction.

The system that favours this management style is neither traditionally democratic nor autocratic, but based on the middle level of management. The task of medium-level managers is introducing knowledge into everyday practice as part of the so-called spiral of knowledge, or the process of creation and translation of different kinds of knowledge in the course of communication with other employees. Since tacit knowledge cannot be explicitly expressed, one has to rely on metaphors, images and models. In Japanese companies the middle level deals with the transfer of these images between the 'top' and the 'bottom' of the organization, as well as with the translation of the images into everyday practice. And so, the organization can turn the processes of constant knowledge creation to its advantage over competing companies as these processes will enable the company to dynamically adapt to the changing conditions and requirements of the environment.

The interest in knowledge management triggered by Nonaka's article caused a revival of many traditional ways of sharing knowledge and wisdom in companies, such as storytelling, personal mentorship relations, cooperation instead of competition, and so on. Also, it seems to have started a rapid development of interdisciplinary cooperation between scientists who want to describe knowledge-based organizations and support the creation of such entities. This is the positive side of the fascination with knowledge management. But the trend also has its dark, perhaps sinister side.

Dariusz Jemielniak and Jerzy Kociatkiewicz (2009) point out that knowledge management is far from an idea that promotes wisdom in organizations. Knowledge workers are presented by corporations as important and valuable members but at the same time they are objects of unrestrained manipulation and prone to burnout due to excess of work. Knowledge management is presented in specialist literature as either a new dynamic field or a passing fashion. A large part of publications on the subject are texts that are easy to read and tend to repeat clichés rather than provoke thought-transforming wisdom. The word 'knowledge' is used in knowledge management literature in a different way than in philosophical, theological or pedagogical writings. Its meaning in management writing is very broad and seems rather accidental. Usually, authors start with a division of knowledge into explicit knowledge and tacit knowledge (Polanyi, [1958] 1974) and use the models for knowledge transmission developed by Nonaka and Takeuchi (1995). Nevertheless, the dominant tendency in the writings on the subject is to discuss knowledge transmission with no consideration for its social, political and cultural context, as if it was another technique to be implemented and consumed. According to Jemielniak and Kociatkiewicz (2009), the phenomenon they discuss is more than a passing fashion and it deserves the attention of both scientists and practitioners. Work connected with knowledge defines and determines the contemporary era. Simultaneously, managers are trying to control knowledge and abstract it from particular people, which in the case of any work based on knowledge is not feasible. Therefore, managers must rely on their employees and their willingness to be involved in their work. Since the beginning of scientific management the employees' autonomy has been treated with great mistrust. There are attempts, then, to control the employees' work in a roundabout way, such as by controlling their social interactions. 'Thus, what the assembly line did to blue collar workers, knowledge management attempts to do to the rest (Braverman, 1974); knowledge management is the new version of scientific management, but for knowledge workers' (Jemielniak and Kociatkiewicz, 2009, p. 557).

Many publications on knowledge management are not taken seriously by intellectuals and critical readers. They may seem not serious enough, perhaps even a bit silly. However, this apparent lightness is misleading. The role of this discourse in contemporary management practice is quite serious indeed, and even sinister. Far from increasing the potential of organizational wisdom or celebrating the wisdom of the individual, professional or manager, it instead serves to assert the asymmetry of power in the organization in situations where managerial power seems threatened by an autonomous position of some of the employees. In fact it is 'used to prevent knowledge-intensive organizations from relying on the knowledge workers, and not on the managers' (ibid., p. 558).

A certain consulting company[47] that deals with outsourcing started introducing new systems that the board called the systems of knowledge management. The company, according to the board's declarations, wants 'to fully use and multiply' its knowledge potential in order to become the leader in its field in the Polish market. The work demands not only theoretical competence but also experience and the ability to negotiate solutions suited to the customer's needs. The work is then to a large extent dependent on individual employees' knowledge, skills and contacts. One of the main dangers for the company is the outflow of the most experienced employees. In the course of the last decade the company tried to bind the most valuable employees by means of various loyalty schemes, like bonuses for the years they worked for the company or employee loans. Despite these programmes some people have left the company, mainly due to the lack of prospects for promotion and career development – managers and leaders are recruited outside the company and the inside possibilities for promotion only let an employee reach the position of an independent specialist. But a specialist's status is very high. In fact, it is up to them to choose the content of their work and control their work hours. They complete many of their professional tasks outside the workplace, mainly at the client's locations.

The knowledge management project was introduced together with hidden reductions of payments (a reorganization of the bonus system, presented as 'connecting bonuses with knowledge creation') and a partial resignation from programmes seeking to bind the employee with the company. Some of the elements of the new systems are knowledge conferences, organized regularly. During every conference the management announces, according to its own 'ranking of knowledge', the names of the employees who are to be 'locomotives of success'. The conferences are meant to be platforms for knowledge transmission and a motivation for 'healthy competition' among the employees. Indeed, during the meetings some changes regarding the employees' work are made, for example the exchange of clients among the employees.

The 'mentorship' programme consists in entrusting young interns to the care of specialists who the young are supposed to help and from whom they are to learn. Actually, the interns take over some of the specialists' tasks (for considerably lower pay) and they are not expected to comprehend the whole of the project. Thus, projects that were coherent entities are broken down into parts coordinated by the interns and parts controlled by the specialists.

The time devoted to contact between specialists and clients is limited as a result of decision-making at the top. The management justified the decision by saying that similar problems should be accumulated and solved 'simultaneously'. At the same time, the older specialists are given an increasing number of projects to deals with and, after some time, they are given new projects and the old ones are transmitted to other employees. This practice is justified by the necessity of knowledge exchange. One of the effects of the new system is, as one of the employees put it, that 'everyone suddenly feels more stupid – both ourselves, and our clients'.

8.4   ORGANIZATIONS AND WISDOM

In *Apology*, Plato (1999) presented Socrates, one of the greatest philosophers of antiquity, for many generations considered one of the greatest sages in the history of mankind. The text is Socrates' speech for his own defence in a trial in which he was accused of depraving youth. He was later sentenced to death. Socrates does not consider himself a sage and he even states that the wisdom that differentiates him from other people consists in the awareness of the vastness of his ignorance. In his speech Socrates argues that genuine wisdom belongs to gods, whereas human wisdom is the knowledge of the limits of one's ignorance. In fact Socrates' public activity consisted in applying the method of asking questions and eliciting answers that made Athenians see that, even though they seem to be wise and know what they are doing, they do not really know anything. He uncovered the emptiness that lurks beneath what is universally considered wisdom; he provoked people to question widely held truths and search for true knowledge. This annoyed respected citizens who he often ridiculed, and they eventually decided to have their revenge by taking him to court under false charges and forcing him to remain silent forever.

From Socrates' words we can learn what wisdom is not: it is not what is usually considered wisdom, the appearance of wisdom, a widely held opinion; and the person who often claims to possess wisdom turns out to be ignorant. Wisdom is not made up of false beliefs shared by people; neither is wisdom the capacity for creation, as poets are guided by inspiration, not wisdom. The only wisdom available to people is, according to Socrates, the awareness of one's ignorance, a questioning of one's beliefs and the search for true knowledge. The passage by Karl Weick (2004) quoted earlier came into being into very different circumstances – Weick was not brought before a court; on the contrary, he responded to an invitation of academics who believe him to possess wisdom. But he, similarly to Socrates, does not boast of his knowledge, and stresses the fact that it came into being as a result of interactions with others – people and texts. Burkard Sievers (1994) encourages us to cherish this type of wisdom in management practice. Wisdom should be cultivated on all levels: individual, collective, organizational and in the organization's relation with its environment. Sievers connects wisdom to maturity and understands it mainly as awareness. It is only through the presence of a mature awareness in management processes that one can count on the development of organizational wisdom on other levels. Wisdom makes it easier to escape the traps and habits of the past. A large part of contemporary management techniques seem to perpetuate immaturity in human systems. The wisdom of management begins with the recognition that the human being and their actions are precisely human, that is, it begins with a 'humanization' instead of the dominating reification, which is treating people like resources, and deification, which is perceiving organizations as immortal, metaphysical beings. Wisdom is an acknowledgement of limitations and a discovery of the potential of limited human reality.

More about the techniques and methods of wise management can be found in *Three Faces of Leadership* (Hatch et al., 2005). The techniques can be derived from aesthetics, especially from stories – they facilitate the development of understanding and the Aristotelian *phronesis*, or the practical human wisdom. Stories connect everyday events and facts with universal human experience. But the tools of aesthetics, such as stories, dramatization and mythologization, can be used in management not only to develop practical wisdom. They can also provide favourable conditions for the creation of a more widely understood wisdom through catharsis, or a transformative experience of purification, in which aesthetics can be an intermediary. Aesthetics recreates real-life experiences as stories, art, music and so on, and so it influences life. Human experience, in return, inspires and gives birth to stories and other aesthetic expressions. In that way, through mimesis, management can use aesthetic methods actively to co-create reality. Finally, aesthetics refers to *ethos* – it communicates values and teaches us to distinguish good from evil. Taken together all these factors make aesthetical methods exceptionally helpful in the development of awareness, but they obviously cannot guarantee the accomplishment of organizational wisdom.

Although no one can isolate and deliver wisdom, inspiration or creativity as if they were technical skills or knowledge tools to be learned in an intellectual way, we feel that we share the obligation to train future leaders in ways that enliven their human potential . . . In particular we would like to see leadership studies embrace the aesthetic approach to business leadership we promote throughout this book. (2005, p. viii)

An excessive focus on the rational aspects, or even isolating these aspects in managerial education, is a source of numerous problems and does harm to the idea of good management that is based on the ideals of wisdom and maturity, unavailable to the purely rational mind. Peter Case (2006) also believes that a concentration just on economic aspects in management education, that dominates today, is regrettable indeed and he argues for a quick reintroduction of traditional humanist and intellectual education in managerial curricula. He rejects the idea of Machiavelli's 'wise ruler' who can preserve the appearance of credibility, honesty and dignity. Such a ruler is not wise – but a liar and a hypocrite. Real moral dilemmas that managers have to deal with should be honestly taken into account in their education. Case does not believe in 'business ethics' and observes that using it as rhetoric accompanies a fall, rather than a rise, in moral standards. He believes that a restoration of the simple, human search for virtues, values and morality in everyday conversations on management can give hope to those who care about the reinstatement of wisdom in management. In particular, management can profit from Stoic philosophy based on three pillars:

(1) maintain moment-to-moment vigilance and restraint with respect to one's thoughts; (2) consent to events imposed by destiny; and (3) act in the service of the human community in accordance with justice. (ibid., p. 287)

Ancient texts, if they are to be useful to managers today, demand a radical reinterpretation and this is an urgent task for managerial education (Case and Gosling, 2007). Education curricula for managers are terribly hollow – not only has the word 'wisdom' disappeared from them many dozens of years ago, but also any content to which this word referred is absent from them. This content cannot be automatically transferred from antiquity, nor can it be grafted from other spheres of life with the hope they will be accepted. The authors observe that notions such as 'wise action' or 'a wise opinion' are greeted by practitioners with nostalgia but they are also perceived as pieces of language coming from another world. The problem lies not only in the lack of an appropriate contemporary context for these words and the lack of their use, but also in the functional division of work and in specialization. Wisdom demands a holistic approach to life which is unfamiliar to the majority of contemporary managers. But wisdom as such is not unfamiliar to management – classics of management such as by Chester Barnard who believed it was of utmost importance, come to mind.

Case and Gosling believe that we do have a connection to this kind of wisdom, we only need to update it. To support their claim they refer to ancient philosophy, a way of life and a path through life. Today people tend to think about philosophy in terms of intellectual categories, as a discipline of humanist studies, a type of knowledge. But for the ancients, especially for the Stoics, philosophy was also practice, action. The practice had its roots in a deep involvement in the search for wisdom; literally, the word 'philosophy' means in Greek 'love and wisdom'. Wisdom encompasses, apart from knowledge, ethics, experience and approach to life. In Stoic philosophy there is to be found content perfectly suited to the situation of contemporary managers. The content can be summarized in the principle of the three pillars quoted above (Case, 2006) and they can be updated with the help of empirical research; for example, ethnography is particularly well suited for this aim, as it shows practices in their natural context. Case and Gosling present notes from their ethnographic observation, where the actions of a chief executive officer can be easily translated into the language of Stoic philosophy and can be discussed in this language. The classic virtues are still present in management practice today; they are only absent from the discourse, and not from the managers' professional lives. Philosophy offers us language to express many vital problems, mainly moral and experiential, that cannot be expressed in the technical language available to contemporary managers. In other words, philosophy opens the possibility of talking about many important elements of a manager's life that cannot be talked about in another language. It does so on the condition that management students will be shown examples relating to their practice, instead of examples taken from the discourse of classical philosophy.

In contemporary organizations practising wisdom is possible in many contexts, including knowledge management. An example of such practice has been described by Vidar Hepso (2008), an anthropologist working for the research department of Statoil. Hepso has carried out ethnographic studies of the everyday work of Statoil's undersea operations coordinators. The employees were trained as engineers and their work consists in installing sophisticated equipment undersea for oil digging. Each platform demands an individual approach and a systematic making of difficult decisions, in cooperation with several of the most powerful people involved in the project. They work both on land and at sea, they communicate with both sea and land workers, and many of these interactions are interventions requiring the use of advanced technology. The coordinators' purpose is to accomplish their task – the company expects them to find the right resources and work out the appropriate methods. Their work, then, consists mainly in a constant transgression of the boundaries of what is familiar and organized, and in taming new areas and situations. In their daily work Statoil's engineers pass judgements that exceed their technical expertise. Their task is to cope systematically with paradoxes, and their intuition and experience proves immensely helpful in the process. The paradoxes refer to basic moral dilemmas, such as the necessity of building trust versus power that is based on manipulation undermining trust, or the dilemma of universalism versus particularism in communication. The engineers are given the autonomy necessary to deal with these and similar paradoxes in their work. Perhaps, thanks to the autonomy, the company is facilitating the development of wisdom in this employee group.

9. The King

9.1 THE ARCHETYPE OF THE KING

The King[48] is one of the classical personality archetypes (as opposed to the archetypes of transformation; Jung, [1951] 1977, [1959] 1990) that have accompanied humankind since time immemorial. The King symbolizes authority, power and the ability of the spirit to guide others towards lofty goals. A good King is anointed by higher powers, he or she exudes energy that the followers can recognize and which does not come from this world. Kings seek to establish order and laws using their uniqueness and the authority that issues from it. The King knows how to distinguish good from evil and uses his or her authority to introduce a new, better order. The King knows how to transmit to others the blessings that come from higher forces. The power of the blessings gives people energy to act and to bring them good luck. The King is an example and a personification of righteousness, dignity, generosity, and purposefulness. He or she is also human and human weaknesses may interfere with the right accomplishment of their mission or even undermine it completely, and lead them onto the paths of tyranny and violence. Ruling without empathy, an excess of ambition or a lack of maturity in other spheres can be very dangerous for a person embracing power. An ordinary person can learn by their own mistakes. The King is devoid of this possibility, as his or her mistakes always have consequences for others. In all, the King is a highly ambiguous archetype – an object of hope, on the one hand, and a source of great fear, on the other. He or she can liberate himself or herself and others, but also enslave people and inflict terrible pain.

The archetype of the King is present in many myths and tales, like the Mesopotamian *Gilgamesh* epic, Hippolyta, Queen of the Amazons, daughter of the god of war, Ares, the Biblical stories of King Solomon the Wise, the mighty Queen of Sheba, or the stories of King Arthur. In particular, Arthur is a rich and very well-known personification of this archetype.[49] Arthur was a legendary British king who defended the country against the invasion of the Saxons. He was the son of King Uther Pendragon and Igraine, born out of wedlock. Uther entrusted the baby to the care of Merlin, who was supposed to guard the secret of Arthur's birth.

Arthur was raised in the family of the knight Ector, ignorant of his real genealogy. When Uther died heirless, Arthur was put to a test. Merlin announced that the person who managed to take at the sword Excalibur from the stone would be the king. Arthur managed to do it and became the King of England. In one of his battles the sword was broken, which was a bad omen. Supernatural powers come to the rescue – Nimue, the Lady of the Lake, gave Arthur an intact sword. From then on Arthur was invincible. His kingdom entered its Golden Age. Arthur married Guinevere who gave him what is probably the most famous piece of furniture in Europe – the Round Table. The

Figure 9.1   The King
(photo: Monika Kostera)

king turned it into an archetypical institution for sharing power; he ruled well and justly, and did many glorious deeds.

But he also had his dark side, which can be seen in the shape of Sir Mordred, a vile traitor and Arthur's illegitimate son. Mordred was the fruit of Arthur's incestuous relationship with his sister Morgause. When he was born, the oracle prophesied that he would become a patricide and a traitor of his kingdom. Having heard the prophecy Arthur ordered the drowning of all the children born on the fatal day. The only child who survived was Mordred, who lived to fulfil the prophecy. Arthur and Mordred both died in the battle of Camlann, delivering deadly blows to each other.

Arthur was a natural-born leader anointed to be King. The motif of formal and informal leadership which is the dominant aspect of the archetype of the King was discussed by many management researchers. Barbara Czarniawska-Joerges and Rolf Wolff (1991) contrast three characters associated with exercising power in organizations to show their importance for the organizations: the manager, the leader and the entrepreneur. The authors believe that the three roles are archetypical, which means that they are eternal and will never be out of fashion. They are an expression of significant expectations included in the organization's cultural context in the past and today, of human hopes and fears; they are the main symbols that enable people to make sense of organizational events. The entrepreneur will be discussed in one of the following chapters.[50] Here, I will concentrate on the two remaining characters, and in particular on the common ground between them. Czarniawska-Joerges and Wolff argue that the leader is a symbolic figure who seems to control fate. The leader is believed to have causative powers that are in fact distributed among many people and artefacts; the leader lends their face to different events and processes; '*Leaders serve as symbols representing the personal causation of social events*' (ibid., p. 535).

The manager fulfils their role through coordination of people and resources to attain the organization's goals. The manager's domain is everyday work, ordering, looking after the organization. The role is less spectacular but very useful. Often the manager does the same things as the leader, only on a smaller scale and in front of a less enthusiastic audience – that is, they protect the organization from the perils of a violent environment. The manager and the leader can also part ways and play two different roles: the Miser and Moses. Leaders and managers together influence one sphere of the company's reality – they exercise symbolic control over the company's destiny. This sphere, its bright and dark varieties, is discussed further on in this chapter. I will close the story about the King letting the archetypical tale fulfil itself according to its internal dynamics. Two different conclusions follow. Accepting one or the other depends on whether the archetype's bright or dark tendencies will prevail: the monarch's enlightenment and just reign, or the overthrowing of the tyrant and the rule of the people.

9.2   LEADERS AND FOLLOWERS

Plato (2007) believed that societies need leaders just like a boat needs a steersman. In his *Republic* he describes an ideal leader – a philosopher king, lover of truth and wisdom. He can see true ideas, the matrix of all things that are hidden from the eyes of most of us who pass our lives chasing shadows. The world resembles a cave where the unfortunates, chained to the walls, observe only moving shadows, without any means of seeing the objects that project them. The leader, however, perceives the world in a different way than other mortals and finds different pleasures – one who has seen true beauty and good will never look for them in the world of appearances.

The ancient Far East philosopher Sun Tzu (2008) has famously considered the nature of leadership and, like Plato, also believed that the leader should be morally superior to the subjects. The leader's moral perfection makes it easier for him or her to influence fate and, therefore, it is more likely that the leader will be successful. The leader should have a cheerful disposition and communicative talent but his or her way of thinking is not always accessible to others. The leader pursues loftier aims than ordinary mortals, does not desire fame, is not afraid to retire – his or her real purpose is to defend the country. He or she knows how to interpret the position and the intentions of the enemy and to adjust the army to these predictions. Despite having superhuman features such as a perfect morality and the gift of foreseeing the future, the leader is not condescending to others but is understanding towards them. In return for his or her trust the leader demands obedience. Similarly to Plato's leader, the leader in Sun Tzu's writing is a thinker and a sage – an enlightened Taoist master. Are these skills inborn or can they be learned? This is a question that has been troubling philosophers and thinkers since Plato and Sun Tzu.

For many years the dominant belief in organization theory was that the characteristics of leader are inborn, one is simply born a leader. Among the features listed were the following (Stogdill, 1974): the capacity for adjustment, a sensibility to social situations and behaviour, assertiveness, willingness to cooperate, credibility, perseverance, self-confidence, resistance to stress. It was also believed that the leader should be characterized by intelligence, tact, the ability to express their opinions and convince others, organizational skills, and so on. The main task of such leaders was to make their subordinates attain the organization's goals. An exceptionally valuable skill was the creation of structures useful for the initiation of purposeful interactions. The hereditary nature of leadership traits is considered today to be at least highly debatable. The usefulness of the traits theory is also problematic. No one knows how to make sure whether a person possesses such traits. Tests differ in usefulness and credibility, and the so-called leadership traits tend to change depending on the stage in a person's life and on the situation.

Many researchers studying leadership in management believe that leadership can be taught, or that leadership skills are acquired and lost depending on the situation. The conditions that influence these features may be connected to the organization's environment, to the group of people that is managed or simply to the situation. One of the most famous models of situational leadership is the one proposed by Kurt Lewin (Lewin et al., 1939) who distinguishes three styles of leadership: autocratic, democratic and laissez-faire. Autocratic leaders have clear expectations vis-à-vis their subordinates and what they should do, in what manner and in what time. In an organization governed by an autocrat there is a hierarchy and a division of both responsibility and authority which often has a clearly centralized character. Autocrats make decisions on their own, without consulting their subordinates.

For example,[51] one of the managers of a branch of Poczta Polska (the Polish Post Office) who took part in a training course in leadership in the early 1990s held such a leadership style. He wanted to make all the decisions on his own, saying that he did not like wasting time on unnecessary discussions. He believed that the company paid him for decision-making and other employees did not have as wide a perspective as he did and, besides, they did not carry the responsibility for the welfare of the whole organization, and had their own particular aims that blurred their perception of the situation. In a team there are always some conflicts; people always have different expectations and different points of view. The person who is supposed to rise over the perspective of particular individuals and reconcile the partial visions is the manager. He did not believe that leadership traits are inborn; he tended to think that one's viewpoint depended on the perspective and that a person develops the traits that the situation demands. He agreed, though, that not everyone in his place would behave identically.

The second characteristic leadership style is the democratic style that consists in involving the subordinates in decision processes. The leaders who choose this style ask others' opinions but reserve to themselves the right to make the final decision. They often support their subordinates, help them in getting to know the situation. People feel more responsible for what they do and often they feel responsible for the success of the entire organization. The research conducted by Lewin and his co-authors showed that in the long run this style was the most effective, even though the members of a team led by a democrat were less productive than the subordinates of an autocrat.

An example of a democratic leader on the training course for Poczta Polska was a manager of one of the branches who believed that it is better to discuss decisions with employees, even if it takes much more time, than to risk that they will be implemented without proper care, which can happen if the decisions are taken quickly and by one person only. She claimed that from her experience she could see that a team that is well informed copes better in unexpected situations and, what is more, it can efficiently monitor itself. The manager does not have to waste her time keeping an eye on people and can concentrate on more important matters such as modernizing the services or consultations with clients in order to ameliorate the quality of the company's services. She was also convinced that people responsible for their company are more satisfied, and that it shows in their everyday work: 'they simply smile more often at the clients'. She believed that 'every boss has a different idea of leadership' and there can be no monopoly on good ideas. She also believed that one can learn to be a good manager but everyone has different predilections, for example, she could not be an autocratic leader 'as she just does not like it'.

The last of the main leadership styles is laissez-faire, that is, the style that delegates authority and responsibility. Such a leader leaves as much as possible to be decided by subordinates; they are made responsible for decision-making, which is not always coupled with their knowledge of the company's purposes and potential. The leader leaves it to the subordinates to gather information, find decision criteria and make choices. Lewin's research showed that this style was the least effective – others were not willing to cooperate with such leaders and complained about their treatment of them.

During the training for Poczta Polska a manager who led a small team that got on very well admitted to this leadership style. He believed that one should not 'improve something that works well' and that his team was a group of mature people who had known one another for years. Furthermore, the clients' expectations were constant and known to everybody. His task, as manager, was to provide good work conditions and ensure a good opinion of the office in the eyes of the central management and, most of all, not to 'spoil a well-functioning office'. To attain this goal one should, in his opinion, give people the maximum of freedom as they know very well what to do and expect such independence.

I chose my three examples for the management styles from among well-managed offices. In other words, the managers all did well in their job, regardless of the differences in leadership styles, or perhaps precisely thanks to them. According to a popular theory of leadership, known as the situational theory, the effectiveness of different leadership styles is relative and depends on factors such as the qualities of the team in question, the sort of environment, the type of tasks, and so on (see e.g. Hersey et al., 1996/2007). All these models emphasize the unique role and position of the leader, a bigger awareness of the needs and purposes of the entire organization and a greater recognizability outside.

There are numerous leadership theories of leadership and many theories explaining the social and effectual conditions and consequences of various attitudes.[52] My aim is not to present a comprehensive survey of all of them, or even of a fair sample, but to show how business leadership interacts with the archetype of the anointed King. Therefore, I limit the story here to quite basic issues and instead concentrate on showing how closely linked contemporary business leadership is with the archetype of the King, whether born a leader or introduced to the secrets of his or her role, or perhaps both.

Manfred Kets de Vries (2003) views this link quite literally. According to him the example of Alexander the Great, the Macedonian king, provides lessons that could be directly applied to contemporary business. Alexander is one of the most famous rulers in our part of the world. In the course of his life he created a gigantic empire and gained an almost divine status; he changed the history of civilization and the power relations in the world of his times, he became familiar with places and people previously unavailable to his fellow citizens and managed to achieve more than anyone else before him. He gained control over nearly all of the world known in his times, from the Greek islands to the Indian subcontinent. Alexander was a student of Aristotle who taught him to admire Greek culture and civilization. Since he was a little boy Alexander had dreamed of greatness and his role models were, among others, the Persian ruler Cyrus II, the demigod Heracles and two Olympian gods: Zeus and Dionysus. After his father was murdered, the young Alexander became King and started his conquest of the world. The Macedonian army owed its successes not so much to their technique, the number of their soldiers or fame but to the strategic genius of the young King. Alexander, however, was not satisfied with military success. His aim was to promote Greek culture and to learn about the cultures and customs of the conquered people. Alexander was not only intelligent but also magnanimous, loyal and brave. But he could also be violent, cruel and vindictive. His main vice was a growing self-satisfaction that changed into self-adoration. He expected others to admire and worship him. Eventually, he lost touch with reality and succumbed to paranoia coupled with the conviction about his uniqueness. He became completely obsessed about himself, increasingly surrounded only by a world he himself had created, out of contact with other people. Finally he plunged into a darkness of a solitude in the midst of people. In the end, the dark side of his personality prevailed over the light one. It is certain, however, that thanks to the light side he achieved much in his life and the history of the world took the shape we know from our history books.

Kets de Vries, not ignoring the dangers of Alexander's attitude, shows what contemporary managers can learn from Alexander the Great. First of all, they can learn how to become visionaries, seeing further than anyone else. A leader should have a strategy, an idea, and know how to react to rivals' weaknesses. Also, they should create a convincing set of social roles, and a set of roles for their followers. It is important to know how to cooperate with others and to enjoy cooperation and solidarity. Alexander's fall began with the collapse of his relations with other people, and this should be a warning to all leaders, including the contemporary ones. Going back to the positive lessons, a leader should be open to innovation and dare always to be creative. Just like Alexander, a contemporary business leader should know how to manage meanings and how to be not afraid of the so-called soft elements. The manager should know that myths, metaphors and stories can serve to create a common identity. It is important for the leader to help and support those who believe in him or her. Such people are the leader's greatest assets and it is a grave mistake not show them gratitude and encouragement. This brings us back to Alexander's faults, as he clearly lost his ability to take care of his supporters and instead became mistrustful and paranoid toward them. So, empathy has to be cultivated, even if it consumes a lot of energy and seems to disagree with leadership principles. Only compassion keeps us mentally healthy and gives us a sense of equilibrium in the world. Furthermore, the leader should plan and provide good succession for the organization. Alexander did not secure an heir for himself; also, he could not consolidate his successes. In terms of the ideas of Czarniawska-Joerges and Wolff (1991), perhaps he was a brilliant leader but did not know to be a less spectacular manager. Finally, Alexander lacked one more crucial managerial skill – he did not know how to create self-governing mechanisms at the lower levels of the organization. Delegating authority is crucial as well as providing means and maintaining subsystems in the state of balance.

Kets de Vries (2003) observes that the main problem for Alexander, and for many other leaders, was the addiction to power. The same author (1998) provides us with profiles of two outstanding figures of contemporary business: Richard Branson from Virgin and Percy Barnevik from ABB. De Vries notices their common characteristic (also present in Alexander the Great): their ability to transform systems and their environment. Barnevik and Branson not only turned their organizations into business empires, but they also irrevocably changed their environment, redefined the fields they work in and made their companies models to be followed by others. The characteristic that gives them the power to change reality is not in fact a single trait but a set of dreams, visions and expectations coming from others – it is charisma. The word comes from the Greek and means 'a gift of gods'; a charismatic leader is literally an anointed leader. The metaphor was first used in reference to leaders by Max Weber

(1947/1964). It was taken to mean the source of power resulting from a unique bond between the leader and their subordinates, thanks to which people are willing to follow the leader as they believe the leader will lead them towards great goals or because they consider them to be a person of unique traits and virtues.

9.3 TYRANTS AND THEIR SUBORDINATES

The King is anointed by a higher force but is still just a human being. His or her special mission may silence the voice of conscience, make them dependent on and even addicted to power. Then the King compromises his or her humanity, and metamorphoses into a tyrant. Immoral and degenerate, they enslave people and in the process themselves become slaves. But why do we allow for such an enslavement, we leaders, and we followers? Erich Fromm (1941/1994) ponders this question in his famous book *Escape from Freedom*. Why does a person need a leader if the leader is toxic or simply a murderer? Why do people find enslavement attractive? Fromm shows different ways of escape from freedom, one of which is authoritarianism. It consists in building one's life around power, both as rulers and as ruled. Becoming part of an authoritarian society and succumbing to other people's power, people escape from their identity. They relinquish responsibility and get rid of dilemmas posed by their conscience, choosing passive submission. Similarly, the ruler, relinquishing their human freedom of choice, is only apparently free, but is becoming enslaved just much as the subordinates. This position makes all the choices in the decision-maker's stead, and they can avoid moral or spiritual dilemmas, or in fact any existential questions. Freedom is the true human nature – it makes us human. Freedom forces us to face life dilemmas on our own. Getting rid of freedom, we are no longer alone and become parts of something larger and more important than ourselves; we get rid of the pain of existence and dispose of the burden of responsibility for our lives. But we also relinquish our humanity.

Man is born as a freak of nature, being within nature and yet transcending it. He has to find principles of action and decision-making which replace the principles of instincts. He has to have a frame of orientation which permits him to organize a consistent picture of the world as a condition for consistent actions. He has to fight not only against the dangers of dying, starving and being hurt, but also against another danger which is specifically human: that of becoming insane. In other words, he has to protect himself not only against the danger of losing his life but also against the danger of losing his mind (Fromm, [1968] 2001, p. 69).

Giving themselves up to authority, the human being tries to avoid fear; he or she believes that this will help them to avoid losing their mind but, on the contrary, it is often the excess of power that makes people lose their minds. In exchange for one's freedom, one gets the sense of security resulting from muffling the pain of existence that is often associated with madness – but in fact, the pain is a natural companion of our being human. Genuine psychological health can only be born out of a free self, the path towards balance and happiness leads through suffering and there are no shortcuts to happiness. 'Power and reason cannot coexist peacefully, and reason is always the loser' (Kets de Vries, 2006a, p. 212).

Manfred Kets de Vries points out, following Plato, that at first the tyrant always seems a protector. Totalitarian regimes and murderous rulers have always been present in the history of mankind. They continue to be such a threat because everyone of us has the seeds of evil that make them possible. Tyranny consists in the ruler's forcing people by means of fear and terror to do things in keeping with the tyrant's will. A tyrant will not let anything limit their power – laws or compassion are obstacles that need to be got rid of. For a tyrant the most desired political system is totalitarianism as it gives them unlimited control over the members of society. The repressions are directed not only against people's deeds but also against their thinking. A tyrant in a totalitarian system eliminates all resistance, they keep identifying and liquidating new enemies, often using very weak evidence, not more than a suspicion. Other systems, such as authoritarianism, give the tyrant somewhat less direct power and so are less invasive. But even in these cases all the dynamics of authority concentrates on keeping the power and securing comfortable lives for the tyrant and their family. Other purposes, such as the satisfaction of social needs, become less important. The tyrant usually perceives opposition as a dark force that has to be eliminated. Such regimes tend to dehumanize their antagonists. They are presented as less than human, and so unworthy of human rights (Arendt, [1958] 1999). Such a perspective facilitates resorting to violence – the objects of violence are not entirely human beings and so the ethical rules that culture is founded on do not apply to them. Outside observers and the perpetrators of violence are more willing to accept what they do to others. In the end it is the victims of violence that are to blame. Kets de Vries (2006a) argues that, even though one can sometimes hear voices saying that some societies are not ready for democracy or that democracy is not effective enough, it is democracy that we need most.

Humans have a dark side that becomes dangerous when they acquire power. It is a characteristic of all leaders and their followers, subjects who make their rule possible. 'What makes despots so dangerous for the world community is not so much their tendency toward violence as the ease with which that tendency can be indulged' (ibid., p. 213). The dark side has to be controlled and only democracy can provide mechanisms for such control. Besides, it is not true that the totalitarian system is more effective – supporting the administrative system and the apparatus of violence costs much more than the 'waste' of means on the doubling of functions and the means of control that prolong the decision-making process typical of democratic systems. The totalitarian system is less mature and cannot learn; therefore, even after the tyrant has been overturned, the system cannot resume healthy functioning.

Societies afflicted by totalitarianism lose the balance of mind. Similar dangers for the wholeness of mind in organizations develop due to toxic leadership and authority (Kets de Vries, 2006b). The most typical phenomenon today, but also a classic one, is of narcissistic leaders who aim at setting their accounts straight with the world. Devoid of empathy and concentrated exclusively on themselves, they create an increasingly idealized image of themselves and adjust to it an equally untrue image of the world, losing touch with the reality in which other people live. They may have great achievements but they are not gained through experience. Experience takes too much time and is not effective enough in their eyes; moreover, it exposes them to factors that could be dangerous to their image, such as feelings and concerns. A narcissistic leader loses the sense of his or her boundaries; for them other people are extensions of their own ego and body. For narcissists, it seems only natural that others should carry out their orders, regardless of their own needs. A narcissistic person does not understand that others have their own needs and that he or she is not the centre of their universe. Moreover, the leader does not differentiate between themself and the organization and treats the organization as if it were an extension of their body. Narcissists close themselves to all signals that ruin this point of view, especially to any bad news. They hate opposition and cannot cope with criticism. Indeed, they deal rather badly with all kinds of signs that the other person may have own needs or thoughts and thus they cannot take care of other people or, even less, lead them through a difficult path.

Why are there so many narcissistic managers? The answer is partly because they look impressive, just like 'a manager should look like', not only in terms of external appearance, but also in regard to attitudes, education and accomplishments. Often nobody makes as good an impression as a narcissistic person: they are the only ones who devote all their lives, all their energy, to creating a favourable image of themselves. Others dedicate much of their time to other things, such as learning, caring about other people and relaxing, and so they cannot reach such perfection in producing a good impression as a narcissist does. Also, one of the factors that may lead to the formation of narcissism is charisma (Kets de Vries, 2006b). People project their expectations onto the leader and only very mature and balanced persons can resist those expectations, which make them more than human. They can also accept these expectations are guided by a sense of duty: 'If people believe in me, I cannot let them down and I must become a superhuman for the good of the people and the organization.' Such an attitude may eventually turn out for the good anyway, because it does make the manager deaf to others. He or she can use those expectations as a good source of energy and see themselves as serving other people. The hero turns into a villain when they start believing in their idealized image, get carried away by pride, consider themself better than other people and stop learning from experience.

Whole organizations take on the characteristics of their leaders; they come to resemble them in their pathologies as well. At the end of the day organizations lose due to their leader's despotism. The employees are more willing to leave a despotically managed company, and the ones who stay are less satisfied with their work, less loyal and feel less responsible for the collective good than they would in a democratically managed company (Tepper, 2000).

In a certain Polish company[53] situated in the Poznań area, the manager, who is also one of the company's founders, concentrated all of the power in the company in his hands. He had the final say in all the decisions, both the crucial ones and the less important. The employees believed that he indeed was the company, which was named after him, and the employees believed that he was able to ensure security of employment, even in difficult times. His friends were always impressed by his knowledge, experience, intelligence and material status, even before 1989 when he worked in the sector that was then called in Poland 'private initiative'. While others drove their little locally produced Fiat 126s, he drove a Western BMW; while others were cramped in tiny flats with their in-laws and cousins, he had a villa on the outskirts of Poznań. He also had class and was generous, which was not then regarded as always typical of people with such income. He did not forget about his old friends and was willing to befriend new people. After the shift of 1989 he was among the first who started building the new economy. The company he set up developed fast. After 2000 it was already competing in international markets. He was a really talented businessman.

Simultaneously, however . . . it is hard to say whether he had always been like that or whether he changed over the course of time. Some people recall his fits of anger from when he was much younger, when he lost control and offended people by verbally attacking them. Such fits became even more common in the company he created after 1989. From time to time he would choose a victim, somebody who reacted in a 'suitable' way, such as being visibly petrified, lost for words, terrified or alarmed. Whenever he lost control, the manager did not care about who witnessed these scenes. He seemed completely oblivious to others' reactions; insulting the chosen object and using the most vulgar expressions, he yelled and his face turned red. Virtually everyone was afraid of him. The boss, usually a brilliant and charming person, became really terrifying in such moments. The people who were the objects of his fits of rage said that they felt attacked physically, they felt faint, sick, they were shivering and experienced a strange weakness in their legs and especially in the knees. As this happened in the presence of others, including guests and even clients, there was often a sensation of profound shame as well. Sometimes the verbal attacks were accompanied by throwing objects. Although the manager had never actually raised his hand at any of his employees, they often felt as if they were hit psychologically, not only told off but stripped of their dignity or, as one of the target of one of such fit of rage put it, 'psychologically degraded'.

The manager sometimes apologized for his fits, especially at the beginning of the company's existence, but always in private. Publicly, he has never admitted that something bad had happened. He acted as if what he did was normal. If anyone was concerned about his behaviour, he talked about them as abnormal, hysterical persons. He once said of a person who reacted to his attack with shock, and then depression, that she was not quite right in the head and should consider leaving the company, as she was not suited to normal social situations. However, most often the boss physically avoided the people who he had offended the most. His personnel division reallocated such people to posts that would not demand any interaction with him. The researcher was struck by the understanding and acceptance that the employees showed for the despotic behaviour of the boss. No one chose to accuse him or talk about him in negative terms. Many quite shocking stories about the manager's aggressive behaviour were verbalized but the interviewee either did not comment at all, or explained the boss's behaviour. Sometimes they even blamed the person who was attacked. 'Everybody knew' that 'some people' were told off more often than others, whereas the smart ones never got told off. Nobody came to the defence of the person who was being attacked.

Only ex-employees, who had left the company, were willing to be more definite and also to evaluate the manager's behaviour in negative terms. One of these ex-employees said that at a certain point she could not stand it any more and spoke up in the defence of a young secretary who was being attacked by the owner. In her story it was not a moral choice or an act of bravery but a manifestation of her own human weakness – she could 'no longer take it', as opposed to others who were more 'relaxed' and 'could take it'. According to the researcher's knowledge many people in the company had problems with insomnia, and suffered from depression and other problems. Many key employees chose to leave the company, but it is still a leader in its area. The employees worry about the future as the boss is not young any more and will have to leave one day. What will then become of the company?

9.4 ENLIGHTENMENT OR FALL

The archetype of the King gravitates narratively towards one of two endings. The first is the monarch's enlightenment, where the King regains his or her humanity. The second is the overthrowing of the King, then an interregnum follows: there is no King and the people rule the empire. We shall have a look at both variants.

Henry Mintzberg, one of the greatest contemporary thinkers in the field of management, published his article 'Managing Quietly' (1999) which provoked some interesting discussions. Mintzberg criticized mass culture for glorifying business leaders who present themselves as celebrities and are shown as stars of management, brilliant strategists 'introducing massive changes'. But good management is silent, with no publicity – perhaps even a little boring. So many 'great' leaders of the past later turned out to be failures and their fame was all too often a result of a collective infatuation. The façade of greatness was often covering an interior of blandness and shallowness. Their 'great changes' did not stand the test of time and were often simply harmful due to enormous social and material costs. Fashionable terms used to glorify the heroes, such as globalization or change management, are in fact nothing more than slogans designating quite worn-out truths. Good managers have always acted globally and introduced changes – but they have done it quietly, bearing in mind the company's good and not their gigantic egos. Managers should not 'improve' companies on their own – instead, they should assume responsibility for the companies' long-term development. Noise interferes with thoughtful management. But good leaders who manage silently have always existed. Such an approach to management requires respect for people, the organization and real time: for the past and the future. A concentration on flashy leadership shifts the focus to the present and narrows vision to what is fashionable here and now. Such managers are busy making grand gestures, 'turning their organizations around', regardless of their long-term good. 'Might not the white knight of management be the black hole of organizations?' (ibid., p. 27).

But companies thoughtlessly turned around collapse. Companies that continue going strong are the ones nobody 'turns around' – instead, they are managed quietly and their leaders do not make it to the headlines. Quiet managers are inspiring; they do not empower their employees but they take their rights and power for granted. They make their employees' development possible and give their employees energy. The employees are not treated as human 'resources' but as the members of the team. Quiet managers care about their people and organization. They devote more time to preventing problems than to fixing them. Instead of managing invasively such as, for example, introducing ever new structural solutions to solve problems, quiet managers manage by becoming as if permeated with the problem; they let solutions enter the whole of organizations, pervade its culture, structure, all its systems. It is not spectacular but it is sustainable. These solutions last. Quiet managers do not sign their names at every spectacular change programme, but rather they initiate processes, set an example, form the avant-garde and show how certain tasks should be executed.

Quiet management is about thoughtfulness rooted in experience. Words like 'wisdom', 'trust', 'dedication' and 'judgement' apply. Leadership works because it is legitimate, meaning that it is an integral part of the organization and so has the respect of everyone there. Tomorrow is appreciated because yesterday is honoured. That makes today a pleasure (ibid., p. 30).

Quiet management is about letting people to manage on their own, without the leader. But is that not what a good manager is for? Jean Lipton-Blumen (2005) shows how important a role the leader plays in strengthening the employees' self-governance. People are often full of fears of uncertainty and that is why they so easily fall prey to toxic leaders. A good leader is not one who promises to change the reality completely but one who helps employees to face reality without fear. A noble leader never actualizes visions that assume doing harm to others. They always show respect to people and their organization. Their leadership consists in supporting 'the leader inside' each of the organization's employees; good managers are often not interested in assuming the roles of leaders. I agree with the author that offering managerial positions to people unwilling to be leaders may be a good idea. It may very well be so that they have, paradoxically, the greatest chances of becoming good managers. But there are other ways of developing healthy leadership.

Ann Cunliffe and Matthew Eriksen (2011) present relational leadership as a way of engaging with others to which the leader remains morally accountable. A relational ontology makes us reconsider the role of various social actors as it proposes that the origin of experience is intersubjective.

Seen this way, organizations are systems of communication and people who the leader is in relationships with. It is a way of being-in-the-world, based on recognition and respect of the others' otherness where the relations are founded on trust and responsibility. The main mode of realizing the leadership role is by dialogue and 'recognizing the heteroglossic nature of dialogue and the potentiality that lies within the interplay of voices within dialogic or conversational spaces' (ibid., pp. 1436–7). A relational leader should become attuned to the situation while keeping their integrity. This is a kind of leadership that employs and develops practical wisdom, an experiential knowledge that is deeply rooted in values and the ability to make judgements.

Another proposition concerning graceful management is based on hope and beauty, as put forward by Nancy Adler (2011). Adler argues that the contemporary world, full of ugliness, consisting of injustice, abuse and pollution, is in need of beauty. Beautiful management can make the difference by providing solutions worthy of humanity. What is needed first and foremost is creativity, as well as repositioning businesses as part of a bigger whole: society, and the planet. Leaders should be courageous: to see both ugliness and beauty, to create beauty when possible and to inspire people. Leadership artistry is based on seeing ourselves, in the first place, as human and making the most of our humanity.

An example[54] of a relationally sensible leader is a long-time employee of a high-tech company who became the CEO after the former glamorous CEO had initiated a 'turnaround' of the company. The turnaround proved very expensive and caused severe financial difficulties, and it also proved toxic to the culture: people felt burnt out, many highly qualified employees left and the morale was exceptionally low. The company used to carry out a yearly survey on work satisfaction but now this was cancelled with the official justification that it 'cost too much'. However, the glamorous CEO did not think that his huge bonuses cost too much. When this became known to the trade unions, they intervened and demanded a survey. The average level of satisfaction turned out to be between 1 and 2 on a 5-point scale, where 1 was the lowest note and 5 the highest. However, the human resources (HR) department did not reveal the results and they were kept secret. Employees could only hear rumours that the situation was 'really bad'. This was confirmed by worsening economic performance. At this point the glamorous CEO was encouraged to leave by the company owners. After a period of uncertainty, one of the long-term employees, then about to retire, was asked to take over the control of the company. He protested, arguing that he would not make a good CEO and that he, anyway, was about to leave. Faced with emotional blackmail – 'If you do not agree, the company will collapse' – he gave his assent on the condition that he would be allowed to leave in two years' time, no matter what the situation at that time.

The two ensuing years were good for the company. The yearly work satisfaction surveys showed an increase in satisfaction and a growing trust for the management. The average results had never been so high before and reached an incredible 4.88. The quiet manager was an invisible leader but he was available to others. The employees made use of this extensively, especially in the beginning. They used to come to his office and to pour out their troubles or ask about things happening in the company. The manager was softly spoken and gentle; he always made use of the knowledge and judgement of each of the employees, and he liked to consider the pros and cons of different solutions with the employees who came to him with. Finally, people stopped coming to him with all their problems but they acquired more faith in their own strength and possibilities. The company gained momentum, its financial results regained balance and after the two years of the quiet manager's leadership they reached the level of before the unfortunate reorganization by the glamorous CEO. After two years the manager, in keeping with his earlier declarations, asked the shareholders for their permission to retire. They were reluctant to grant their permission but were bound by the arrangements they had made earlier. The staff, upon his leaving, thanked him for the two best years in the company's history. 'You should not thank me; you did it yourselves and you will manage very well without me', the quiet manager said as he, very touched, accepted a goodbye present from the employees: 'I have not done anything unusual.'

A different kind of conclusion is the overthrowing of the tyrant and the setting up of self-management. Manfred Kets de Vries (2009) describes the moment when Romanian citizens lost patience. Nicolae Ceausescu, who up to then held all the power in his hands, was caught and executed. Regardless of the mechanisms and games of authorities that led to the bloody ending of his rule, it is often the case that particularly cruel despots are often killed by the people or by their closest supporters. The tyrant's wife and several of his cooperators faced a similar fate. For years Ceausescu had been worshipped as a genius, an unerring, superhuman leader. He brutally suppressed the opposition, led the country to extreme poverty, and the standard of living dropped drastically during his rule. During his regime people died in prison because they were accused of 'inappropriate' views or 'wrong' attitudes; many died of hunger or because of untreated illnesses. In 1989 the Romanian people took to the streets. About 1000 people were killed by the regime's secret police. Finally, the dictator and his wife were caught and their government ended in tragic bloodshed – they were quickly executed. A tragic fate befell the tyrant who had himself been the cause of tragedy for a whole society. What happens next? Many scenarios are possible, from a new tyranny to the rule of the people.

The great American linguist Noam Chomsky (2005) believes that all authority is in fact illegitimate. Those who are in a position of power have a duty to justify their position, and only if their justification is accepted can their power be temporarily deemed legitimate. The legitimization of power is an ongoing process as the situation alters and the needs change. For example, an adult looking after a minor exercises legitimate power when they prevent the child from hurting itself. The situation changes when the child comes of age and can make his or her own choices. Grown-up people should have the possibility to decide about their lives. An organized form may be helpful if people want to make such choices together. Chomsky believes that the form of self-government that used to work in kibbutzim has many interesting lessons for us even now. In these organic organizations all workers had the obligation to participate in the decision-making process and all power had to be justified constantly. Self-government and self-governing bodies are not fashionable in management theory and practice at the moment but they used to work quite well for many people in various times and places, not only kibbutzim, but in the former Yugoslavia in manufacturing and education, in Swedish industrial enterprises, in Polish pre-World War II housing cooperatives, and others. Self-managed work teams are democratic organizational structures, independent and based on the members' responsibility for the organization and the control of work (Sexton, 1994). People, like ants, are capable of organizing themselves on their own, which creates an interesting potential that can be used by organizations on the condition that the latter are willing to give up central leadership to a greater extent (Anderson and McMillan, 2005). Self-management and self-leadership can be understood as an elimination of a special organizational function that consisted in controlling, planning, task distribution, and so on. And, consequently, it eliminates the costs connected with this function. The self-managed team continuously corrects deviations from the assumed norm and motivates itself. That is why in order for self-management to function, people must be mature enough to be guided by internal motivation. The teams of employees should have appropriate education and preparation, a common vision, shared values and beliefs as well as the trust of the head of the board. The structure called adhocracy is based on similar principles as self-managed teams and can be a good starting point for the development of self-governance in contemporary organizations.

A famous example[55] of self-managed work was the teams at the Volvo plant in Kalmar, in the east of Sweden. Volvo had the ambition to become known as the opposite of Fordism. In 1974 a new factory was opened that was to rely on production in work centres (as opposed to assembly lines). Such an organization of the production process required a high degree of self-control by the workers' teams. A natural consequence was implementing a fully self-managed system in the factory, with wide autonomy for the employees, similar to the autonomy characteristic of professions. Hierarchy was abolished, together with the former labelling of the various posts. Instead, each employee was prepared to do all the tasks required in the production process. The employees swapped places in work centres and so everyone participated in the production of the whole automobile. The teams, comprised of 10–25 people, were responsible for completing a given task in a particular amount of time. It was up to the team to decide who completed which task and when. In 1987 the teams managed to lower the fault rate by 90 per cent and raise work satisfaction to an unprecedented level, which also explained a lower incidence of illnesses among the employees. In the 1990s the factory was closed because of the new commitment to highest possible profits in Western industry, which in practice meant an abandonment of all projects that could be replaced with lower-cost ones. Ironically, at the end of the 1990s the factory was bought by Ford. According to theoreticians such as Jeffery Nielsen (2004), the story of self-management is not over yet. He argues that there may be an interesting future ahead for the idea of leaderless organizations. The need for leadership results from thinking in terms of positions, posts and hierarchies. This favours the development of unhealthy elements of the human psyche. If such organizational cultures were replaced by ones based on reciprocity and cooperation, making use of the healthy aspects of the psyche, there would be room for the development of skills and attitudes such as creativity, responsibility, respect for others, and so on. Organizations could dispose of leaders forever.

10. The Adventurer

10.1 THE ARCHETYPE OF THE ADVENTURER

The Adventurer is one of Jung's personality archetypes (Jung, [1959] 1990). An adventure is a risky enterprise that stimulates the protagonist mentally and physically. It is about the overcoming of difficulties and the accumulating of new experiences. For some people adventure is the main content of their lives; nothing else seems as irresistible to them as facing new challenges. Joseph Campbell ([1949] 1993) describes a typical protagonist of myth in terms of adventure. The hero leaves his or her familiar environment to explore the unknown, and visits places where he or she will be subjected to numerous tests. Heroes are aided by supernatural forces and characters, learn new things and begin to see the world in a new way. Having learned a valuable lesson, they may go back home. The reward that is gained from the lesson not only enriches the protagonist but is often very valuable to others: it helps the hero to save the world and to help fellow human beings.

The same pattern is repeated in many myths. For the protagonist the adventure is an initiation, it makes transformation possible -- an Adventurer then is also a character associated with the archetypes of transformation. Transformation is the ultimate, metaphysical purpose of experiencing adventures. Fairy tales and folk tales have a similar, characteristic structure (Propp, [1928] 1968): in the beginning the protagonist leaves their family home to travel and experience many adventures which they face bravely, and returns home in glory. The adventure may consist in a journey, or a test for the intellect; it can require coping on one's own in a new situation, meeting new people, accomplishing new tasks, and so on. The common features of all these elements of an adventure are novelty, something the protagonist had not have to deal with before, as well as the necessity to take risks, to become involved in actions the result of which is unknown and very uncertain.

One can say that an adventure means facing uncertainty and an adventurer is someone who actively seeks such challenges, someone who is not satisfied with ordinary building of culture which consists in creating islands of certainty, or rather of sense and predictability, on the ocean of chaos

Figure 10.1   The Adventurer
(photo: Jerzy Kociatkiewicz)

that is human life. In our culture ambiguity is perceived as something outrageous, something to be avoided at all costs (Bauman, [1991] 1993). An Adventurer actively transgresses this dogma, leaving safe domains of culture behind and seeking out the unknown. Some well-known legendary and real examples of Adventurers are Hua Mulan, a legendary female soldier from ancient China who fought many success-ful battles dressed as a man; the demi-god Herakles who accom-plished 12 heroic labours; Atalanta, the fearless huntress raised by Artemis who con-quered male heroes in the Calydonian Boar hunt and drew first blood from the beast; and Amelia Earhart, the United States avia-tion pioneer who set many records and became an icon during her lifetime.

A famous contemporary example of a hero who actively seeks risk and adventure is the fictional Indiana Jones, the main protagonist of a series of films directed by Steven Spielberg, based on the story by George Lucas, with actor Harrison Ford starring as the eponymous character. Doctor Henry Walton Jones, also known as Indiana or Indy, is an archaeology professor. The stories are set in the 1930s to 1950s. Unlike many scientists Indiana Jones is not satisfied with only reading and writing – he is drawn into the unknown out there, where danger and improbable events await him. The most famous of the protagonist's adventures is narrated in *Raiders of the Lost Ark* (1981). Indiana Jones encounters secret agents of the US military intelligence who tell him that the Nazis plan to find the Ark of the Covenant and use it to gain absolute power over the whole world. The protagonist is entrusted with the task of regaining the Ark. The agents promise to exhibit the Ark in a museum, if Indiana manages to bring it to the USA. With the help of his ex-girlfriend Marion, Indiana, equipped with an artefact necessary for further proceedings, arrives in Cairo where the Nazis have already started their excavations. The Nazis are assisted by Indiana's main scientific rival, the Frenchman Belloq.

Indiana and Marion manage to outsmart the Nazis who turn out not to have the right data (Belloq made a mistake in his calculations). After many dangerous adventures the couple find the Ark but this time they are out-smarted by their enemies, who take the precious object away from them and throw them into a dungeon full of poisonous snakes. The protagonists manage a daring and close escape – they traverse the dark dungeons, climb out to the surface and manage to prevent the Ark being sent to Germany. With the Ark they board a steamer going to the USA. The Nazis do not give up and continue chasing them. The villains manage once more to regain the artefact; this time they also kidnap Marion. Another turning point ensues – now it is Indiana who is chasing the Nazis.

Finally, the ultimate confrontation takes place. Indiana and Marion, bound and unable to move, versus Belloq and the Nazis who have the Ark and are much more numerous. The situation does not look promising for our protagonists. Still, they manage to escape almost unscathed. The villains are lost by virtue of their greed and pride. The Ark turns out to be a powerful, supernatural artefact; its power exceeds the Nazis' expecta-tions, but the Ark will not let itself be controlled by them. Knowing this, Indiana and Marion close their eyes when the Nazis open the Ark. They adopt an attitude of humility towards the Unknown, an attitude alien to their enemies. As a result the Nazis and their collaborator Belloq die and our protagonists manage to survive and get back home safely where US intelligence agents are already waiting to tell them that the Ark is hidden in a safe place. The adventure ends with the hero's triumph and the saving of humanity and the planet from a disaster. But the promise that the Ark was going to be made available to the public, so important for Indiana, was not kept. This is a setback for the hero but that is not all. The audi-ence has a feeling that this is not the end of the adventure – and they are right. Indiana Jones does not create systems, he is not a faithful fiancé, and I suspect that he may not be a persevering and patient scientist. I also have the impression that he is not particularly responsible. Indiana keeps moving, he is restless, reckless even – adventure is the essence of his life. An adventurer never has enough of adventures, there is no adventure that they would consider the ultimate one, even if, due to human mortality, it could prove to be the last one.

Stefan Kwiatkowski (2001) characterizes the intellectual entrepreneur in terms reminiscent of Dr Jones. He or she is someone not satisfied with success, not deterred by failure, nor focused on competition. Such an entrepreneur is not interested in learning in a traditional way, through adjustment to an existing context or an intelligent use of that context to change the existing standards. Intellectual entrepreneurs go beyond the existing frameworks and create new ones. They look for risk, happily accept instability, and regard change as their daily bread and not a state of emergency that we have to go through quickly to return to a more stable and ordinary state of affairs. The intellectual entrepreneur's work consists in taming chaos: 'They learn a need of constant change. They seldom destruct and seldom tame people. They manage chaos and thrive on opportunities it opens to the knowledgeable and the courageous' (ibid., p. 6).

Richard Branson, the legendary boss of the Virgin Group, characterizes his work in similar terms (Branson, 2009). The joy of acting in business consists in taking risks and crossing borders that seem impossible to cross. Simultaneously, unlike many mainstream management texts, Branson's book does not focus on success. For him business is an endless chain of successes and failures in a continuous game with fate. Just like Indiana Jones, Branson does not seem a person who would be ready to call any ending a 'happy ending' – or an ultimate defeat, for that matter. These two states are there only to make possible what is in between them – a great, never-ending adventure. In the end only the adventure counts.

In this chapter I first talk about adventures available to ordinary business people, that is, about fashions in management. Then I present the character of the troublemaker, a darker embodiment of an Adventurer. Finally I let the archetypical story run to its narrative conclusion with the story of organizing seen as pure adventure: of entrepreneurship and entrepreneurs.

10.2   AN ADVENTURE FOR THE CAUTIOUS, OR FASHIONS IN THE WORLD OF ORGANIZATIONS

Edward Sapir famously characterizes fashion as a 'custom in the guise of departure from custom' (1931, p. 140). People often feel the need to experience something extraordinary, an adventure that consists in breaking with current habits and customs. Fashion offers such a possibility without the risks of rebellion. Small changes in external appearance and behaviour give the satisfaction of trying something new, as well as the certitude that other people will do exactly the same, in a similar way. This gives people a sense of both adventure and safety. Sapir observes that people promoting new fashions may be particularly aware of the need to reconcile conformism and individuality that is the very essence of the phenomenon of fashion. Fashion is born out of the need of breaking with habitual patterns, and the curiosity and unease that lurk in most of us. 'This general desire to escape from the trammels of a too regularized existence is powerfully reinforced by a ceaseless desire to add to the attractiveness of the self and all other objects of love and friendship' (ibid., p. 140). According to Sapir fashion is a path that gives a person an opportunity for a rediscovery of themself. Or, perhaps, it gives the impression of such a possibility, an impression that may be illusory.

And so it works as well for managers, who just like other people feel the need for change and exploration but also want to preserve the conventions that grant them recognition and acceptance. Fashion in management seems to be an answer to this dilemma, it enables managers to feel revolutionary and conservative at the same time. Barbara Czarniawska (2005) writes that fashion in management means both change and tradition, especially in the long run. It is a symbol of both conformism and nonconformism. Fashion is paradoxical, as it consists in innovation and imitation, standing out and adapting, evolution and revolution.

Czarniawska quotes examples from the sphere of public management: cities, just like people, want to be fashionable, or rather the cities' governments desire it for them. The authorities of three cities – Warsaw, Stockholm and Rome – were striving to make their cities fashionable. For example, trams have become fashionable again and many cities which have abolished tram lines, like Stockholm and Rome, are building them again even if they already have a satisfactory public transport system, as in the case of Stockholm. With no clear need, except for the need to follow fashion, Stockholm's authorities decided to open a tram line on the outskirts of town. Managers in both the public and business sectors can be divided into those who follow fashion and those who promote it, but the division is only clear in retrospect. As a result they form temporary milieus comprised of those who accepted a certain fashion or those who rejected it. In all, '[i]t is important to admit that the world of management can learn from the world of fashion, by the way of analogy, not metaphor. Management is as fashion-prone as clothing industry, interior design, science and everything else' (Czarniawska, 2005, p. 146).

Stephen Barley and Gideon Kunda (1992) present waves of fashions in management regarding the role and ways of control. The authors disagree with the popular view that sees the changes in approaches to control as continuous progress – from enforcing control to relying on norms and rules. Instead, they believe that we are dealing with cycles. For a certain time the discourse style that dominates is one based on introducing procedures that make the employees, by virtue of their rationality, act in accordance with the management's purposes. The organizational effectiveness is understood as a result of implementing the systems and methods that serve achieving clearly defined purposes. Organizations are viewed as mechanisms, more or less complex, mechanical or electronic. Then a new period begins when, instead of rational procedures, mainstream management discourse introduces normative rhetoric that, through referring to norms and cultural values, is supposed to force the employees to confirm and act in the 'proper' way. According to this approach, organizations are societies based on the collective values and moral involvement of the participants. The leaders are to inspire, set the example, encourage involvement and care about the employees' good. Control in such organization begins with the selection of people equipped with traits considered desirable. Once part of the workforce, they are subject to personnel management systems which are based on shaping their personalities, attitudes and identities. Literature emphasizing the advantages of rational respectively normative aspects tends to concur: in a given period most publications concentrate on one or the other. The periods are cyclical: after a normative period, a rational period follows, and so on. Subsequent new waves bring some new ideas but some key issues tend to return. During the time analysed in their article, beginning in the 1870s and ending with the publication of their article, Barley and Kunda spotted five clear cycles. Regardless of wave, people are always assumed to be fluent in the logic dominant in the cycle: managers are experts in interpersonal relations or in rational systems, employees make decisions calculating the financial profits and losses or on moral grounds, and so on. Barley and Kunda argue that waves of fashion are concurrent with business cycles. During times of expansion rational waves dominate; during recession, normative. Similar links between fashion and economy have been observed with regard to skirts: during expansion periods skirts become shorter, and in times of crisis they get longer (Gaffen, 2007).

Eric Abrahamson (1996) presents some of the great creators of management fashion. These are: consulting companies; the so-called management gurus, or famous people from the world of business, consulting, and less often academia, who often talk in public about current issues connected with management and business; and business schools. These 'management trendsetters' compete with one another to gain the leading position and to be top fashion innovators. Therefore they try to investigate practitioners' attitudes to know what ideas might interest them in subsequent seasons. They work to present their portfolio of ideas in an interesting manner so that their clients will like it. The right rhetoric is important, it has to present the promoted techniques as both something absolutely new and a manifestation of rationality and progress. They have to get to the practitioners before their competitors, so they also fight for the access to clients. In the time when Abrahamson was writing his article, some of the trendsetters seemed not to be able to catch up with the others. This was mainly true for business schools and the academic celebrities. Their competitors were trying to present them as old-fashioned and unattractive to practitioners. Abrahamson proposes counteraction, believing that a more significant contribution of academia to business fashion would be favourable to all parties. It is important to keep in mind that promoting fashions requires a knowledge of specific techniques and consists in a struggle with powerful competitors. Also, one has to know how to get close to the client. The clients – managers – are by no means a passive audience for these energetic actors. They make active choices, they have their own preferences. Thanks to the new promoted fashions they want to learn something new and test new ideas and solutions without any risk. The loss of interest in a novelty that has become unfashionable does not have to result from the irrationality or frivolity of manager-dandies but may be a consequence of the need for adventure. They may be well aware that the new solution is not the ultimate cure for all the company's all ailments but instead a test, a quick adventure with a new idea. When the novelty is no longer new, one has to look for a fresh novelty.

In the beginning of the 1990s, together with a colleague experienced in management consulting, I took part in several interesting consulting projects connected with the privatization of selected Polish strategic management companies. Together we carried out research among the managers of the privatized companies to get to know and describe in terms of cultural change the process of structural and strategic changes in Polish companies (Obłój and Kostera, 1994). We noticed many changes that seemed superficial, as they consisted in replacing old slogans with new ones while all the deeper norms and values remained unchanged. Sometimes this seemed both cynical in an almost refreshing way and hilariously absurd at the same time – new slogans promoting capitalism were literally pasted into the places where the old ones propagating the Communist Party used to hang. They were painted on similar billboards and contained similar catchphrases, such as 'The market is leading us towards a better future', replacing 'The Party is leading us towards a better future'. 'You know', our contact in the company said, 'we've seen many things here and there are many more to be seen.' Such simple imitation was regarded by the Polish mass media at the time as pure unrestrained conformism and a lack of dedication to the changes. But it can, in fact, hide many other attitudes, such as the desire to keep the 'evil eye' of the authorities away, create the right appearance, and safeguard the survival of the company and employment for the people. This simple trick could just divert the attention of future reformers, as it has proved to have done successfully many times until then.

I observed such attitudes later during my research among the managers of Polish companies in the early stages of transformation in Poland (Kostera, 1996). My interlocutors talked about their tactics for protecting their companies from the destructive urges of successive reformers in the pre-1989 era, usually energetically enforced initiatives of the authorities, the Party, the administration or the federations.[56] For these managers the change of façade was not an occasion to experience a controlled adventure. On the contrary, it was an attempt to prevent an uncontrolled adventure, to prevent drifting in the rough ocean of system changes that were taking place in Poland at the time.

But these managers were not adventure-adverse if they got a good chance. In contexts that the managers perceived as safe for their companies they enjoyed experimenting and testing novelties, including the 'Western' ones. For some of them management training could provide such safe context.[57] Very open attitudes could be observed in postgraduate students of a management school where I have been working. The students demanded novelties, they were eager to read texts and discuss them, adopting different attitudes towards the theories they analysed. They impersonated various characters in our case studies with energy and enthusiasm. We had very animated discussions in the classroom which did not, however, give rise to any animosities outside the classroom. Years later one of my students wrote to me in an email: 'I finally could play with different ideas – live through a real adventure in modern management, an intellectual mountain climbing. I should add that it was a climbing with safety measures, without any potentially disastrous effects for the company.'

10.3   THE ORGANIZATIONAL TROUBLEMAKER

Mary Douglas (1966) pointed out that societies have a tendency to link threats such as natural calamities or illnesses with behaviour that consists in breaking cultural norms and taboos. Societies can be divided according to the types of behaviour-control mechanisms dominating in the culture. Generally, the aim is always to make individuals refrain from actions that consist in breaking norms and, therefore, are considered dangerous. Simultaneously, all societies need risky behaviour to function. For example, nomadic tribes relied on individuals willing to test new types of food or to search for new areas for settlements. Culture promotes such behaviour when the environment is full of threats and the need for risk-taking is vital (Douglas, [1985] 2004). Douglas contrasts two cultures: the settlers from Virginia whose survival depended to a large extent on the situation in sea trade, and the East Coast Puritans who could feed themselves independently. The first group created a culture accepting of risky behaviour such as gambling and horse races, and it even enjoyed engaging in them. The other group avoided risk and condemned gambling. Still, Douglas thinks that there may be individuals who have a natural tendency for risky behaviour, just as there are people who are naturally blond or have the AB blood type, but believes that this thesis cannot be proved or disproved in a satisfactory way. However, sociologists can only describe the social consequences of such behaviour.

Before we go on to discuss the business world, let us look at recklessness from the perspective of a sports anthropologist. Catherine Palmer (2002) presents sportspeople who do extreme sports. Among others she describes mountain climbers of both genders. The press presents them either as heroes or as obsessive fanatics and mountain climbing is depicted as either an example of great bravery (especially when the climber is a man) or a symptom of neurosis (usually when the climber is a woman). But all of these sportspeople were quite similar: they felt an irresistible need to climb mountains even if they were never to return. This does happen, and not so seldom: having many friends who engage in this sport I have seen too many early funerals. This does not, however, discourage others. All kinds of people try to climb Mount Everest: women, men, the young and the old; recently, Mount Everest was climbed by a blind person. It seems we will never see a day when mountain climbers could be satisfied with exercising on an indoor climbing wall.

There are also no reasons to believe that reckless attitudes will completely disappear from the business world. Some individuals are perhaps prone to risky and troublesome behaviour and some business climates may particularly encourage them. Sometimes the troublemakers act in a reckless way without any consideration for the consequences their deeds may have for other people and for their own companies. Such behaviour is also exhibited by people in managerial positions. There are managers who have no qualms about making decisions that could prove potentially destructive; they even seem to enjoy making such decisions. Situations of this kind give them the sense of broadening the borders of their selves, and their personal value systems do not dissuade them from exposing their companies to danger (Illies and Reiter-Palmon, 2008). Such value systems make their holders focus only on themselves, the striving for success, and on achievement, facing challenges. Other people are outside of these value systems. According to the research carried out by Jody Illies and Roni Reiter-Palmon, the managers most prone to destructive behaviour were those for whom power was a crucial value; the least likely to behave in a destructive way were those who valued universality. What is more, power as a value correlated negatively with satisfaction, whereas universalism correlated with it positively. The researchers did not observe a relationship between risk-taking and effectiveness: some risky decisions were beneficial to the company, and some, quite the contrary.

Although risk-taking in business may have some positive consequences, there are organizational troublemakers whose actions in the long run have only negative effects on other people and whose attitudes seem almost psychopathic. Such people feel no fear and they are never held back by empathy – and that is perhaps why they often make it to the top, to the highest managerial posts. Clive Roland Boddy (2006) has analysed the implications of the actions of such managers for organizations and corpo- rations. The author's research shows that such managers are responsible for a more than average number of organizational problems. The effects of their actions include: crises and collapses of organizations that leave people without employment and make investors lose their money; environmental pollution; and negative consequences for the stock exchange. This does not mean that the actions of more careful managers are never negative, but it is less common. People with the characteristics of troublemakers are not common. People who have such characteristics can be classified as psychopaths – the lack of empathy combined with a complete or nearly complete lack of fear and a high level of resistance to stress are the main features of the psychopathic personality. Conscience does not interfere with their actions as they do not use a conscience. Organizational psycho- paths may make a very good impression on their superiors as they have no qualms about playing the roles that will secure them a promotion. Unlike criminal psychopaths, they are not always inclined to do physical harm to others and they have better control over themselves as well as better manners; they are intelligent and seem well socialized. They do not have to be asocial or antisocial – they do not feel compelled to break social habits and laws but, similarly to asocial individuals, they become bored easily and have a strong tendency to take reckless action. They do not display higher feelings but can act them out in order to make a good impression on others. Their charm and ability to make appropriate connections help them in getting promoted. When they occupy positions of power, they use their authority to play for high stakes with no regard for the good of the people, the company, the environment or the stakeholders. For them, social responsibility is only an empty slogan. Usually, soon after control over an organization has been gained by organizational psychopaths, a small group is formed that gains all the profits, whereas all the others lose their work and income. Psychopaths do not feel attached to anyone or anything and everything is to them just a stake in the game or the pool they want to scoop. It is an endless adventure – they never feel fully satisfied, each success is only temporary, they have to continue playing. Therefore, paradoxically, they never end up as rich pensioners. The only feeling they actually can experience is the excitement from playing for high stakes, and they aim at feeling it as often as possible and as intensely as possible.

As a result, organizations ruled by psychopaths gain psychopathic traits themselves – rich and devoid of conscience, they function in their environment in a way that no responsible person would accept. Why do organizations become heartless so easily? Daniel Pink (2009), a management guru, believes that it results from anachronistic motivation systems that function in the majority of organizations. The systems, based on the so-called carrot-and-stick approach, were invented over a century ago and their scientific foundations were questioned a long time ago. The recent crisis in the banking system is one of the effects of this outdated approach on contemporary business. Normal human motivation is based on different principles. In order to promote pro-social behaviour, characteristic of normal personalities, we should give people the safety of employment and the possibility to experience work satisfaction thanks to internal motivation. A modern motivating system should contain three crucial elements: autonomy, mastery and purposefulness. The anachronistic motivation systems reward results, especially short-time results, and encourage involvement in games and behaviour that is socially irresponsible.

A famous example of a troublemaker company that ended its existence causing serious loss to its stakeholders, or even a synonym of irresponsible management in our times, is Enron. Philip Linsley and Philip Shrives (2009) characterize it as an extremely individualistic project. The company's motivating system generously rewarded the employees who performed well and severely punished those whose performance was weaker. The company was focused on gaining as much money as possible. This resulted in rivalry, enmity and petty fraud such as giving wrong fuel prices by one of the department in order to increase income, and other harmful organizational games. Such incidents occur in many companies and are, at the moment, the rule rather than the exception, even if they are counterproductive and create a negative aura at the workplace. However,

Enron was special because there such behaviours began to constitute the foundation, define the culture as such, through a lack of any mechanisms that could put a stop to negative incidents of this type, and through the existence of systems that even enhanced them, such as the company's assessment system which promoted the most determined and unscrupulous people and eliminated those unfitted to this predatory culture. This made the entire organization into a troublemaker culture.

Linsley and Shrives show how the unusually high organizational cohesion and the homogeneity of the employees, on the one hand gave Enron great power to act, and on the other hand how this force was used to play for increasingly high stakes. Nobody tried to stop the progressively more unethical and illegal actions of the company. And so Enron openly used its political connections to negotiate lucrative contracts; the organization manipulated the market to profit from the energy crisis in California, and engaged in other irregular and even illegal games. Such games were also played inside the company, as employees played against one another, often to the disadvantage of the company.

The scandal regarding Enron's accounting fraud opened the stakeholders' eyes to other improprieties and offences committed by the company, such as misleading accounts, dishonest transactions, putting debts and losses into fictitious market actors, extremely risky finance management and feigning disturbances in energy delivery to fuel the market. The scandal ended in Enron's bankruptcy, and resulted in the loss of the good name of the consulting company, Arthur Andersen, which was responsible for Enron's bookkeeping. A total of 21 people, including two of Enron's key managers, were found guilty of different offences. Enron's CEO, Jeffrey Skilling, was a manager with no inhibitions, a model organizational troublemaker. He crafted his outlook just as carefully as he assembled his team: when he became CEO he changed his appearance to make a good impression on the stakeholders and he selected only those who were willing to act like him for his closest co-workers. He did showed no interest to the feelings of others, nor in social norms and the law. In his spare time, he engaged in extreme sports.[58]

10.4   ENTREPRENEUR AS ADVENTURER

Joseph Schumpeter (1949) uses Bakunin's (1842)[59] idea of creative destruction to describe the entrepreneurship process. An entrepreneur is someone who builds a new order while simultaneously destroying the old one, who is the driving force of progress and transformation as they look for solutions outside the existing structures. The entrepreneur revolutionizes markets and the economy, shatters the balance of forces, and introduces innovations in the place of old-fashioned solutions. Societies owe innovations and changes to entrepreneurs – restless spirits (*Unternehmergeisters*) who are always waiting at the economy's margins ready go beyond the familiar and universally accepted. Usually, they are not inventors themselves but they know how to use novelties to develop new types of entrepreneurship. According to Schumpeter, innovation may consist in introducing a new product, implementing new production methods, gaining new markets or new supply lines, or new manners of production organization. Peter Drucker defines an entrepreneur in a similar way, as a radical creator of novelties: 'people who need certainty are unlikely to make good entrepreneurs' (Drucker, [1985] 1993, p. 26). The reason for this is that the work of an entrepreneur consists mainly in taking risky, innovative actions, in paving the way for others: 'Entrepreneurs innovate. Innovation is the specific instrument of entrepreneurship. It is the act that endows resources with a new capacity to create wealth. Innovation, indeed, creates a resource' (ibid., p. 30).

Bengt Johannisson (1987, 2005), an author famously passionate about entrepreneurship, narrates how entrepreneurship is not about managing resources but creating them when needed. He claims that an entrepreneur's work is the opposite of what a manager does – an entrepreneur does not try to preserve the fragile balance but derives new forms out of chaos. Instead of eliminating, 'cost-cutting', reducing and consolidating, he or she thrives on excess. In a sense, entrepreneurship is an art and the entrepreneur an artist. Just as a sculptor creates in the medium of stone, and a painter in light, an entrepreneur creates in social and economic material. The purpose is the process itself, it is endless and does not lead to any given satisfactory result. There is no measure for entrepreneurship and no definite scale to describe it. It is often measured according to financial results but this is a very superficial assessment, like categorizing works of art according to their financial value. One may look at entrepreneurship in this way but such an approach will reveal one, very superficial aspect of this activity, without explaining neither the purpose nor the source of entrepreneurship. Entrepreneurship is complex, multilayered, baroque: it reconciles oppositions such as anarchy with order, revolutionary and evolutionary tendencies, vision with action, experience with reflection. It cannot be classified easily and the attempts at describing entrepreneurship usually focus on just two extremes. The core of entrepreneurship, however, consists in a simultaneous intensive coexistence of the opposites, in combining them into a meaningful whole by the entrepreneur, in going beyond conventional acting and thinking.

Entrepreneurship means undermining and changing old institutions,

abandoning old models, crossing boundaries, discovering new possibilities, exploring new territories and, finally, creating new institutions.
An entrepreneur is an independent and untamable spirit but also a person
who can cooperate with other people, as entrepreneurship is a collective
phenomenon. According to Johannisson, entrepreneurship is a way of life,
both work and play, a passion consisting in organizational transcendence,
an active creation of reality.

In an article already mentioned[60] about the three organizational archetypes – managers, leaders and entrepreneurs – Barbara Czarniawska-
Joerges and Rolf Wolff (1991) characterized the latter, emphasizing in
particular one aspect of the entrepreneur's activity: their willpower, better
known in management literature as initiative. An entrepreneur never
succumbs to habit but cannot draw exclusively on their experience; the
core of their activity is creating a new being, which is always difficult and
requires great determination. Before an entrepreneur has convinced others
of the rightness of their vision, they must bear alone the burden of creating reality and this is a 'heavy burden to bear. What seem to be anecdotal
stories of mad inventors and innovators might be actually quite true, in
the sense that the unsuccessful inventors are people whose reality did not
become socially confirmed. Those who succeeded, though, are the makers
of our worlds' (ibid., p. 534).

Creativity is a universal phenomenon, every normal human being is
creative (Maslow, [1962] 1968), but not everyone expresses their creativity
as an entrepreneur. Chris Steyaert (2004) points to the fact that very often
even people predestined to entrepreneurship cannot use their talent in the
conditions artificially devoid of excess that dominate in the cultural systems
of today's organizations that prefer order, economizing, calculation, and
so on. Analysing the Polish cultural context for entrepreneurship, Beata
Glinka (2008) demonstrates how context can encourage or discourage the
willingness to face challenges and how it can be connected with a stronger
or weaker social acceptance of entrepreneurial attitudes. The author has
conducted deep cultural research into Polish entrepreneurship, analysing it
from the angle of several cultural spheres such as the family, education, mass
media, literature and film. She believes that Polish culture does not support
entrepreneurship, is inconsistent and 'difficult to describe – it undergoes
continuous transformation while at the same time it is made up of permanent values and behaviour patterns, it is full of paradoxes; in it the sense of
agency and laying claims, activity and passiveness all coexist' (p. 249).

Culture seems to favour small business owners, who are perceived as
hard-working people who barely manage to keep their heads above the
water, and do not have much to do with the archetype of the Adventurer.
A more restless soul, searching, paving the way, is suspected of dishon-

esty, trickery, unreliability and oddity. I think that this can discourage a sensitive and creative Adventurer but will not stop a psychopathic trouble-maker who does not care about other people's opinions and feelings but only cares about creating the 'right' impression and raise their chances of winning in their uncompromising life game.

Despite unfavourable conditions there are many talented entrepreneurs in Poland. Sometimes they manage to speak to the media. Then they try to describe their work, which is qualitatively different from the work of a manager or an administrator. 'Financial success is important in that it gives some degree of freedom. One can actualize one's passions that were too risky earlier', Grzegorz Hajdarowicz said. 'On the other hand, the fact that we work 16 hours a day does not mean that we are overworked', Orfinger explained. 'In the end we do what we really enjoy' (Piłat, 2009).

Entrepreneurs emphasize the fact that their work includes both suc-cesses and failures; it is not a continuous stretch of victories. Also, financial success is not an aim in itself. It is confirmed by Andrzej Blikle (2009), a great Polish entrepreneur, professor of mathematics and an heir to a family tradition of entrepreneurship. Blikle's company is well known throughout Poland – for over 50 years it has been offering delicious Polish-style doughnuts and other confectionery. According to Blikle, profit is only a condition for the company's existence, not its purpose. Just as food makes human life possible, so profit nourishes the business. Eating is rarely a person's purpose and meaning of life and, if it is so, this does not speak well of such a person's state of health. Exactly the same is true about business, according to the entrepreneur.

In numerous interviews Blikle presents himself as a business Adventurer who keeps searching for something new, and his search is for him a source of joy. He is both a scientist and an entrepreneur, interested in such diverse fields as quality management and information technology (IT). For him, crisis is a threat and a chance; he believes that during a crisis one should one should prepare for growth, learn and employ the best people dismissed by competitors. It is also the time to look at oneself critically in the mirror and invent oneself anew. In the speech quoted above the entrepreneur talks about his moral sensibility: 'Who else can be happy than the person who knows he does not do any harm to other people' (ibid.). In interviews Blikle emphasizes the role of loyalty to the employees and his trust in his company. Money can only satisfy basic needs. Blikle believes that an employer should enable their employees to satisfy higher needs, like the sense of belonging and self-actualization. Although Blike is certainly an Adventurer, he is not a troublemaker. He says that practising values such as tolerance, justice and diligence gives happiness – a lasting happiness that does not bring a sense of repletion.

11. The Trickster

11.1 THE ARCHETYPE OF THE TRICKSTER

The Trickster is one of Jung's classic archetypes (Jung, [1959] 1990). A Trickster is a rebel and a nonconformist who uses paradox and irony; often, is a person who possesses wisdom, but they can also be an ordinary clown or a rebellious jester. Even if the Trickster is not wise, his or her action can stimulate reflection and amaze, which in turn can create new ways of viewing reality; the Trickster can also uncover new realms of reality that were covered under common truths and habitual interpretations. The archetype of the Trickster appears often in mythologies – usually in the shape of a wanton spirit or a powerful supernatural creature who plays tricks on deities and people. Tricksters are not depicted as an evil spirit though they may be perverse, transgress accepted norms and break habits. By doing so they may open people's eyes, but will not offer any new truths or appearances to replace the shattered illusions. The Tricksters like to change shape, impersonates others, becomes an epitome of transformation. Sometimes they are just a swindler. Tricksters lie with abandon, and often cannot see the difference between the truth and a lie, or at least no moral difference.

An example of a deity who helps people to see a new dimension of reality but sometimes is simply malicious is the Scandinavian Loki, who will never miss an opportunity to play a trick on others, be they gods or mortals. Lilith is a powerful trickster, an ambivalent and untamable spirit, known for her wisdom but also for her scorn for humankind, who she enjoys to seduce, vex and deprave. A more kindly Trickster is the Greek Hermes, who usually has good intentions but likes to play tricks on people and enjoys stealing sometimes, especially from fellow Olympians. He is also the only Greek god who can travel freely between the three worlds: Olympus, Hades and the human world; therefore, he is often depicted as a patron of communication.

The Trickster is ambiguous morally and geographically, but also personally. Their gender is unclear: they can be a hermaphrodite, a bisexual person, or change their gender according to need, mood and perhaps whim; not unlike the protagonist of a sketch by the Polish cabaret group

Figure 11.1   The Trickster
(photo: Monika Kostera)

Barbie Girls, where a woman cross-dresses as a man, cross-dressing as a woman, who cross-dresses as a man ... (Goll, 2009). The Trickster's age is also indefinite; though often young in spirit, not infrequently they enjoy taking on the shape of an old person, or indeed, vice versa. Nothing is straightforward or clear-cut about this character. He or she is not an innocent eternal child – if the Trickster appears in the guise of a child or a youth, they are precociously mature, full of a cynicism typical of a much older person. The Trickster also appears in legends, fairy tales, folk tales and jokes as a person more cunning than others, a con man or woman, a joker but always more perceptive than others, somebody who can provoke a turning point, who in the worst possible situation can see the solution the others cannot see. In folk tales the Trickster always takes the side of the oppressed, defends them and supports them, and has no qualms about using his or her exceptional skills to cheat the strong, rich and privileged. In this way the Trickster not only helps the poor but also shows the powerful that they are just people and have their limitations. Tricksters give hope to the the oppressed that a change is possible.

An example of a Trickster in contemporary literature is Charles Nancy from Neil Gaiman's novel *Anansi Boys* ([2005] 2006). Unexpectedly, Charles learns that his father, the remarkable Mr Nancy, has died of a heart attack in Florida. Charlie is a silent, unassuming person, a prudent bookkeeper, as opposed to his father who liked to impress people, shock and break social conventions. The young man goes to the United States for the funeral. There he learns that his father was an incarnation of the African deity Anansi, a patron of spiders and a personification of the trickster archetype. Apparently he transmitted his divine traits to Charlie's brother, the existence of whom the latter had not known about. It turns out that in the search for his brother Charlie is to be assisted by a spider. Charlie will not believe it and decides to go back home. Once, when drunk, he asks a spider to help him find his lost brother and this is how a sequence of incredible adventures begins, starting with the appearance of the brother, Spider.

Their acquaintance starts with a curious mourning of their father which consists in their getting completely drunk. Spider impersonates his brother, seduces his fiancée and discovers the frauds that the company his brother works for commits on its clients. In exchange for keeping this information secret the manager of the company grants him a long leave and a large amount of money. It proves to be a trap – while he is absent the boss tries to put the blame for all the irregularities on him. The manager is visited by one of the company's clients and the boss, in panic, kills her and hides the body. The client cannot find her peace in the afterworld and asks for help with her mission to take revenge (one of the people she asks is Anansi). In the meantime Charlie, who desires to get rid of Spider, goes to Florida where he uses the help of his father's friends. He is sent to the beginnings of the world where he meets other deities: Tiger, the Bird Woman and others. The Bird Woman is supposed to help him in getting rid of the troublesome brother. After he comes back home, he becomes involved in many unexpected events – for instance, he is interrogated by the police, while his fraudulent boss flees the country. Spider does not disappear but his life turns into hell – he is constantly assaulted by birds. Eventually the Spider Woman helps Tiger kidnap him and the latter takes away Spider's magical powers.

The revenge on Spider, however, is simultaneously a revenge on Charlie as they both originate from the same line. Charlie begins to realize his connection to Spider and he even learns that he and his brother used to be one person and were magically divided into the good and the evil halves. Charlie seeks out the Bird Woman and convinces her to abandon her revenge. Spider is saved and he regains his magical powers. The protagonists live through several more adventures, in the course of which they save Charlie's ex-fiancée, imprisoned by his ex-boss. Eventually, Spider is married to his brother's ex-fiancée and becomes a restaurant owner and Charlie becomes a musician and gets married to a policewoman with whom he has a son. In this literary interpretation the figure of the trickster is morally ambiguous and this ambiguity is stressed by the division of the protagonist into two characters who, unlike in the case of the Self and its Shadow, are ambiguous as well and, what is more, they swap their roles in the end.

Jerzy Kociatkiewicz (2007) presents various perspectives on information technology (IT), derived from the stories told by users belonging to several professions and employed by different types of organizations. The author does not focus on structures but on processes in which he looks for dynamic patterns and not correlations valid at a given moment. From this perspective the narratives of the professionals' cooperation with computers recalls myths: technology took the place of various archetypes, including the Demon, the Angel and the Trickster. In these stories computers are intelligent, even smart, they have an incredible capacity for data processing. At the same time they can be fussy, difficult to handle, unpredictable. The effects of computerization on people are both salutary and destructive. In a longer perspective, the latter begins to dominate, as is often the case when we deal with Tricksters. According to the author the computer's role is ambiguous, although certainly IT technology has a great potential for enabling more intelligent organization processes. Spiteful computers' tricks always consist in showing the users their limitations and weaknesses. For example, when the hard drive breaks down, the user loses all their files and has a serious problem. In fact, the breakdown only shows how lazy and incautious we are; if we made backup copies, our loss would not be that painful. Still, many people neglect it. Also, computers adopt some of our traits and vice versa – the users adopt some of the traits of the technologies they use. Just as in many stories about Tricksters, such mingling of personalities can be troublesome but also enriching for the person in question.

Martin Parker (2009) presents the figure of the pirate on the basis of classic stories and contemporary business representations. In the old days a pirate was a Trickster, a rebel assaulting the mighty and powerful and defending the poor and ordinary people. He or she was an ambiguous figure – a bandit or a liberator, at times worshipped and at times reviled. But pirates were always perceived as strong characters posing challenges to authority. In their communities pirates introduced forms of government based on social justice; they were a varied group, in their nationality, gender, race and sexual orientation. Our Hollywood representations changed the pirate into somebody resembling a troublemaker. Recently, the famous series introduced us to Captain Jack Sparrow, a typical pirate-trickster, a character who is ingenious, actually almost mad, and also very lucky. His actions show the utter arbitrariness of the boundaries and conventions created by human authorities. Simultaneously, the film version of the story is toned down by a set of stereotypes and clichés that are supposed to help the movie in becoming a blockbuster. After the film became a success, Jack Sparrow and other pirates became a marketing tool: products, icons that were to encourage people to buy different articles, such as, for example, lunch boxes. Still, Jack Sparrow remains a Trickster because he manages to tell a story that can be used for purposes the seller did not foresee – it can be used to question, undermine and challenge the establishment and, in the first place, to mock the self-satisfaction of the power-holding elites. Captain Jack Sparrow questions such fundamental issues as identity, the relation of an individual to the state, and business morality.[61]

I will now tell a story of organizations who operate on the borders of the law or outside them but still abide by certain ethical norms, mainly those advocating the protection of the weak and oppressed. Then I present the phenomenon of organizational lie, in a broad sense, as an omnipresent and everyday activity undertaken by different groups, including the management. Finally, I characterize lateral thinking as an exceptional and creative manifestation of the archetype of the Trickster, a kind of thinking that has positive social and economic consequences.

11.2   ORGANIZATIONS OUTSIDE THE LAW

The American journalist Hunter Thompson is considered by many to be an honorary anthropologist, mainly due to his famous book on the motorcycle gang, *Hell's Angels* (Thompson, [1966] 2003). The author devoted a year to a participant observation of the gang, he conducted interviews, spent time with the gang members and tried to understand their point of view. He could access the gang thanks to his acquaintance with a former gang member, who was Thompson's friend, and a journalist as well. Thompson's adventure ended when he was beaten by gang members; these came, however, from a different part of the gang than that he was focused on. The relations with the gang members he studied remained friendly and his description of the gang's habits is lively and enables the reader to understand the motorcyclists' culture. When Thompson decided to investigate the gang from the inside, it had a very bad reputation and a bad press. Some of the rumours turned out to be true – the motorcyclists drank heavily and did not shun violence, they would sometimes steal and they did not have any respect for official authorities. Thompson, however, portrays them as people, not monsters. They share a passion for motorcycles, they love adventure, they like to joke and have fun. Not all of them are or have to be criminals; they live on the border of the law but respect certain rules of social coexistence. Their dark image is the result of the black legend created by the media and the society which is perceived by the gang members as a crowd of cowards and bores. Besides, the motor-cyclists are an underprivileged group, with a low social status and scarce possibilities – for them, membership in the gang is a way of life, a way to gain human dignity and freedom, unavailable to them because of the poor financial conditions and the low social status which fix a person spatially and culturally.

> Most Angels understand where they are, but not why, and they are well enough grounded in the eternal verities to know that very few of the toads in this world are Charming Princes in disguise. Most are simply toads, and no matter how many magic maidens they kiss or rape, they are going to stay that way ... Toads don't make laws or change any basic structures, but one or two rooty insights can work powerful changes in the way they get through life. (ibid., p. 267)

The gang's culture is antisocial but not anti-human. The Angels do not hold any grudges against people; on the contrary, their casual attitudes to social structures show a way out of the alienation and claustrophobic hierarchy. The Angels mock social norms and values; it is true, though, that they often do it in a brutal and vulgar way.

Mocking the law is neither the only way nor the necessary form of distancing oneself from existing social structures that are practised by such organizations. In his famous ethnographic work on a poor Italian quarter of Boston, MA, which the author chooses to call Cornerville, William Foote Whyte ([1943] 1993) describes examples of organized fraud and racketeering. The research was carried out in the United States in the economically difficult time between 1936 and 1940. His aim was to understand the poor people better and to tell their story to others in a way that would make it easier to understand their perspective. Foote Whyte socialized with the local people, and for some time he lived in the quarter he examined in order to carry out participating observation. He had many contacts who helped him become involved in the life of the neighbourhood, most notably a young man named Doc who was his main contact. Thanks to him he learned about many aspects of the community's life unavailable to a person from the outside, such as the life of gangs and various illegal or semi-legal activities. He also took part, though reluctantly, in an election scam in the beginning of his participating observation.[62]

In the course of his research, he met some prominent local gangsters including Tony Cataldo, who was involved in various illegal businesses, mainly smuggling and gambling, and also had a significant political influence on the community. Cataldo explained to the researcher how a gangster business is run, emphasizing the importance of proper organization. All employees are remunerated. A just and credible system should be in operation; this is what people in Cornerville expect. Sometimes it is necessary to use the services of the 'protective association'. Usually a warning from people dealing in smuggling or gambling is enough; if that does not help, they beat the person in question, as a warning. Ultimate solutions are used only in exceptional cases. A 'protective association' is necessary because '[i]llegal businesses do not inspire men with respect for property rights, nor do they have the same legal protection which serves legitimate businessman' (ibid., p. 121).

But crime, violence and illegal business were not popular among Cornerville gangsters. They preferred to function at the border of the law, in a grey area, as long as it did not conflict with their conscience. The most popular and socially accepted type of illegal business was gambling. In the Cornerville inhabitants' original countries, such as Italy, this was considered neither a crime nor a sin, while in the Puritan United States of the 1930s it was both. The immigrants had no qualms about getting involved in this business, which proved a good source of income. They themselves enjoyed gambling as well. Such illegal business was mainly based on trust and an observance of internal cultural norms. Violence should not be aimed at your 'own folks' – and it usually was not. The gangsters liked to spend the money they gained in local shops and restaurants, trying to support local companies and legal businessmen. Gangsters forcing legitimate businessmen to pay for 'protection' were rare in the district. Sometimes gangs provided funds for legitimate investors. The author quotes an example of a local small firm that had no chance of getting credit and decided to ask several gangsters. They complied with his request, thanks to which the entrepreneur could buy the appliances he needed. The investment paid off economically – the company developed, although from this time on it only apparently dealt with legal business. It also paid for other reasons: it enabled the gangs to launder dirty money and gain a fictitious, but actually legitimately functioning, source of income. Foote Whyte has even heard the story about a gangster who, thanks to a similar investment, joined 'the light side', or became a respected businessman. The police cooperated with gangsters to a certain extent, if the gang curbed violence and took care of 'order' on its own.

Sometimes grey zone organizations are agents of change in a longer perspective; sometimes they manage to undermine the whole economic and social system in which they function. Alf Rehn and Saara Taalas (2004) describe Russian *blat'* as the basis for contemporary entrepreneurship and a phenomenon dating back to the times of tsarism. It developed intensively in the USSR as an answer to the lack of goods and the official production system's inability to satisfy people's needs. The black market offered what could not be bought officially. Illegal agreements, old-boy networks, acquaintances and connections were all organizational tools in the black market. Sometimes clearly illegal methods were used, such as bribery or intimidation, but usually the black market entrepreneurs operated on the edge of the law, somewhere between legal business and crime. Cheating the system was even seen, in a sense, as virtuous. Rehn and Taalas state that such practices were both common and efficient, and that 'the Soviet Union was the most entrepreneurial country and economy that the world has ever seen' (ibid., p. 150), because its structures forced the citizens into entrepreneurial mindsets. Drugs were not sold in the black market – it was the domain of strictly criminal organizations, like the mafia. The authors remark that the mafia's activity can also be seen as entrepreneurial as it uses modern marketing techniques and introduces innovations.

Blat' is not a criminal organization as it does not look for its space outside the law but rather in the grey area. It also refers to the domain of the market – *blat'* moves on the borders of market institutions, using the traditional gift economy that consists in building the participants' social status through an exchange of gifts that the whole community automatically, and as if accidentally, profits from. *Blat'* functions in a broad and interesting social space, in the intersection of culture, economy, politics and management. Similarly to gift economy, *blat'* is based on the principle of imbalance which is a source of the dynamics of goods and services turnover, alternative to the market mechanism. It looks for possibilities of provoking an imbalance by doing other participants favours, which leads to the accumulation of the cultural potential and a higher status. Incidentally, organized crime works in similar ways; it strives to provoke an imbalance. It does so, however, in a different way – by using other participants in the transaction or by taking from them more than one is allowed to. In both cases, resources are created where they have not existed before. Rehn and Taalas argue that both forms of activity are species of entrepreneurship. But whereas *blat'* can be productive, crime can only be destructive.

An example of an organization that is quite straightforwardly negative from a legal point of view, but not from a moral one, at least in its own eyes, is the gang called the Black Kings that operates in the US suburbs inhabited by poor Afro-Americans. It has been described by the US sociologist Sudhir Venkatesh (2008). For seven years the author carried out ethnographic research of this criminal organization which mainly focuses on drug selling. He observed the grey area and criminal milieus and tried to understand how they worked. Thanks to good relations with his contact, who was the head of the organization, he even became the leader of gang for a day. He was not involved in illegal actions but contacted people and tried to understand the organization's social dynamics.

The result is an ethnography which is understanding but multifaceted and distanced from the organization's functioning. The organization is a response to the social marginalization of Afro-American inhabitants of the suburbs, and a way to evade the structures where the chances for personal development and good work are nil. The gang members gain money, respect and a sense of dignity, simultaneously creating their own rules which they always follow. In a way the gang establishes its own law on the basis of its own justice principles. Venkatesh describes how the organization defends the weak, punishes those who break the organization's laws (for example, it punishes a drug addict who beat a woman on the territory under the gang's 'protection'), and fights with competing gangs who are presented as devoid of moral principles and only interested in gaining money. The gang's leader, J.T., presents his organization as a body that acts in the inhabitants' self-defence, in the style of Robin Hood; he even talks about it as the only effective means of social care. According to J.T. only the gang protects the poor and ensures that there is order in the neighbourhood; they always take care to pay attention to the inhabitants' needs. The police and the healthcare services keep away from the neighbourhood and one can never count on their help. The rich do not care about the poor black people who only exist for them as numbers in the crime statistics. The gangster's arguments seem sincere. His organization devotes much time and energy to 'care' for the inhabitants – but this is a strange kind of 'caring'.

The other side of the story about this organization is that it is based on violence, it does not refrain from killing, it profits from other people's misery, by extortion of money for 'protection' from everyone who has a legal or illegal business in the neighbourhood. The inhabitants do not perceive the gangsters as saviours but are afraid of them and try to avoid them. On the other hand, it is also true that nobody counts on the official authorities' help either. Instead, everyone tries to solve their problems through self-organization and cooperation, without the help of either the police or the Black Kings.

11.3   LIE AND BLUFF

In his latest, provocative book *The Economics of Innocent Fraud*, John Kenneth Galbraith (2004) argues that contemporary economy is based on numerous fundamental lies, more or less innocent. The great economist states that the rift between reality and conventional wisdom is broadening, which makes theory and ideology increasingly detached from practice and, in consequence, increasingly normative. At best, the theory and ideology consists in an innocent deluding of oneself; at worst, it becomes a sophisticated fraud.

In the first place a change in terminology has occurred which has not been followed by any changes in practices or in any basic phenomena. Today, instead of saying 'capitalism', the term 'market economy' is used, even though the mechanisms are the same. The market suggests that the consumer has power, but it turns out to be illusory. The real power today is in the hands of the boards of gigantic corporations and the most important aspects of economic life are controlled by management and not by market mechanisms. The owners have only symbolic or illusory control but no one talks about this openly. The boards care mostly about themselves, granting themselves bonuses regardless of their companies' performance, and invest in creating the image of 'market position' or in developing the needs of statistical consumers. The belief in the existence of a two-sector economy is also a lie: often many of the public sector's missions are taken over by the private sector in the name of enlivening the former. We also deceive ourselves as far as our understanding of work is concerned. Work can mean a painful necessity, hard work demanding great sacrifice or a nice way to spend our time, according to our interests and needs. What is more, the latter understanding of work is nowadays more valued morally and financially. Such an approach to work leads to the disappearance of the ethos of work for the society's benefit, which is replaced by an ethics that promotes the self-satisfaction of the well-paid and a condemnation of people willing to work hard for low pay. Yet another lie is the assumption that in their approach to management, market organizations follow different rules than do public bureaucracies. As much as market companies take over the mission of the public sector, they also change into hierarchical bureaucracies. It does not make them more effective than public sector organizations in the same role, but it gives them more power. Another lie is connected with the possibility of foreseeing and influencing business cycles. These possibilities are illusory and, at best, the illusion is an innocent lie making people feel better but, usually, it is a fraud that brings huge profits to financial advisors and banks. The economic axioms we adopt are misleading, they distract us from searching for functional solutions and give more power to only one type of social actors – the boards who have become so powerful that they can elude responsibility for their deeds. Ineffective managers are hired to manage new companies; and sometimes the protagonists of major scandals and the perpetrators of evident misappropriations are given managerial positions in different organizations. The first condition for introducing meaningful changes is, according to Galbraith, accepting the truth and building new solutions on its basis.

Apart from these serious falsehoods, one also encounters numerous smaller organizational lies, everyday fabrications and distortions, also more or less innocent. Abhijit Patwardhan, Stephanie Noble and Ceri Nishihara (2009) present an example of misinforming clients by call centres which the authors call strategic dishonesty. It consists in influencing the consumer's conceptions through an overt lie or a suggestion on the border of the truth, and lying in such a way as to persuade the client to make a purchase. It is not always a premeditated action; it may be undertaken in good faith and its moral judgement is not always morally unambiguous. The researchers' interlocutors, employees of call centres in India, told them about many dishonest or not completely honest methods of talking with clients. The methods included: changing their accent to the same as the client's; introducing themselves as foreign students working in the client's country and not abroad; adjusting their conversation style to local customs, such as asking a British client before Christmas about their Christmas cake; changing their names to make them sound more local; and so on. Many of these methods were openly supported by the management; there are even taboo topics, such as the real localization of the centre, about which the managers tell the employees to lie.

Tuomo Takala and Jaana Uripainen (1999) have conducted ethnographic research that included long-term contact with two high-level managers. The managers answered questions regarding ethics and lies. Both managers declared high ethical standards. In their responses, however, they indicated that sometimes lies are not morally despicable, because in some situations they do not count as untruth. While they absolutely valued the truth value of acquired information, they did not always think it right to be completely open with all their stakeholders. Sometimes you have to hide the truth for some time so that your competitors will not use it against your company. Also, a lot depends on relations with other people: cooperators, shareholders, employees. Lying destroys relationships and causes loss of trust which is so crucial for balanced management. Sometimes, however, it is necessary to use white lies, to modify the truth – when it does no harm to anyone. And sometimes one should directly conceal and protect information, for example when negotiations are in progress and one does not know their outcome.

Employees and potential employees lie as well. Jennifer Wood, James Schmidtke and Diane Decker (2007) have examined untrue and not fully true work applications from the angle of their effectiveness; that is, they were interested in to what extent human resources employees were willing to hire a person who provided inaccurate information in their documents. Glaring lies, that is giving information that was false, were classified as explicitly negative. An interesting outcome of the research was the observation that experienced employees paid less attention to false information that was not a glaring deceit, such as using hyperboles or omitting some facts, and did not treat it as a lie. As a result, they were more willing to hire a person who gave such information in their application form. Ying Wang and Brian Kleiner (2005) quote a whole set of examples of employees' dishonest behaviour including theft, lying and neglecting the company's good, and note that US business loses about 6 per cent of profit every day as a result of such actions. Employees lie to their superiors, clients and to one another; they do it impudently, or subtly, but usually unconsciously and innocently, if the questions of ethics and morality are not discussed in the company and they have no example from their superiors. According to Wang and Kleiner, education helps in raising ethical standards – some employees really do not know that they act wrongly. In order to maintain high ethical standards one should pay attention to the selection of employees, reject candidates with a history of dishonesty and regularly control the employees' work. Also, it is important to stimulate honest behaviour positively by commending honest workers and showing them respect.

Another common form of lying is financial and accounting frauds. Austin Mitchell, Tony Puxty, Prem Sikka and Hugh Willmott (1994) portray British accountancy companies as falling short of their official ambitious ethical declarations. The declarations are a smokescreen for negligence, irregularities and distortions. Professional organizations that control ethical standards through auditing do not fulfil our expectations and do not always react as quickly and as firmly as they should. In view of these facts, the authors state that accountancy should not be treated as a profession as its ethical standards and the care in maintaining them are too low. Accountants do not put the social interest or the interest of their profession before their own private interests and do not have a strong moral backbone. Instead, one should talk of the accountancy business, and submit it to strict outside control, like all types of business. One cannot rely on accountants' self-control. The belief in the bookkeepers' professionalism has made them evade responsibility to society for too long.

The adequacy of self-regulation, as demonstrated in the failure to discipline auditing firms and the inaction in response to sustained questioning about conflicts of interest, should be problematised rather than taken-for-granted (Wilding, 1982). Such a project is fraught with difficulty not just because the

accountancy industry is highly secretive but also because it is so 'grey' and virtually invisible. In this, its boring, technical image has perhaps been its greatest
asset. (Mitchell et al., 1994, pp. 49–50)

Managers are not protected in this way, they are too visible. In pre-1989
Poland chief executive officers (CEOs) were a visible professional group
and they had to plot, while constantly being watched by authorities and
various supervising instances. They manoeuvered between the independence of their companies and their submission to central bureaucracy.
An example of a morally ambiguous organizational lie in the Polish
context was the attempt to shift the balance towards a greater autonomy
of companies by skilfully using untrue information. In the course of my
field studies (Kostera, 1996), I encountered many descriptions of such an
organized white lying.

The CEOs tried to present their companies' performance, and the
degree to which they had accomplished their plan,[63] in such a way as to
avoid major interference by other bodies with their companies' management. The other bodies included the party and the unions, as well as the
secret service. Everybody knew that the secret service was present in the
company, but sometimes even the CEOs did not know who the agent was.
It was also perceived important by the managers to keep at a distance the
local and central state administration, such as the people's council and
ministries, bureaus and other institutions which tried to gain access to
the resources or broaden their power. In order for their organizations to
emerge from such a struggle unscathed, the managers had to prove in their
reports that the plans imposed by authorities have been accomplished or
that the results had even been a little better than the average: not too good
but not too poor either. The managers also had to be careful not to direct
too much attention to themselves, whether positive or negative. Both
could mean limiting of the company's autonomy which was seen, unofficially by the managers, as the real failure of management. Therefore, they
had to be wary of political actions, they had to avoid too frequent appearances in the media, be careful not to employ troublesome people, and so
on. Reality rarely adapts to wishes, so the results had to be somewhat
'stretched'. The managers relied on their talent and their trusted people
to do this. They could not take it too far – they could not be caught lying
openly. A good poker player bluffs but will not be caught and manages to
win until they are able to preserve the balance between the truth of their
cards and the façade they present. I borrowed the poker metaphor from
one of my interlocutors who added that he did not play all these tricks for
fun or for his own benefit, but for the good of his company that had to be
protected against the central bureaucracy that would otherwise destroy it.

11.4 LATERAL THINKING

Edward De Bono ([1967] 2007) uses the term 'lateral thinking' to refer to the kind of creative thinking that is free of the bonds of logic and criticism. Lateral thinking is not directly goal-oriented; instead, it follows unknown paths. It is especially helpful when we are faced with a problem that seems impossible to solve or when we want to discover something new or see something familiar in a new light. De Bono believes that thanks to such thinking one can break with old thinking habits and face the most difficult intellectual challenges. Ordinary thinking, which de Bono calls 'vertical thinking', only uses common lines of thought and, as a result, arrives at predictable and not really original solutions. Looking for novel answers and eurekas, it is better to adopt another perspective. Chance is a good ally of lateral thinking – sometimes the best solutions appear in the form of associations seemingly unconnected with the main topic. In lateral thinking there is also space for a sense of humour, especially the kind of humour that combines seemingly disparate notions and things. The basic difference between lateral and vertical thinking comes down to the non-linear nature of the former and the linear and ordered nature of the latter. Lateral thinking consists in searching for many alternatives before drawing the line of reasoning. One of lateral thinking's crucial characteristics is its non-sequentiality, or thinking about several aspects of a problem simultaneously, outside an ordinary frame of reference. In order to think laterally, the person should refrain from selection processes, that is, not give up on paths of thought that seem wrong. Finally, the lateral thinker has to be ready to concentrate completely on the thinking. Lateral thinking is not unlike contemplation in that respect but its outcomes are different. Neither is it identical with creative thinking, even though it has many common points. The difference between them is, primarily, that creativity is subjective while lateral thinking strives to attain an objectively set goal. De Bono believes that everyone can learn lateral thinking, although not everyone is naturally predisposed to this kind of intellectual procedure.

> Some people will have an inherent propensity to creative thinking. It is all about motivation. It is the difference between enjoying possibilities and only being happy with certainties. Our methods and message are uncomfortable for some people, whereas a creative person loves exploring possibilities – it can be an emotional experience. (Powell, 2007, p. 1062)

As it is a skill as useful as mathematics, de Bono supports programmes introducing teaching lateral thinking in schools. Such systematic solutions were accepted in schools in many countries including India and China (Powell, ibid.).

Lateral thinking may also be useful in management. Stephen Butler (2010) argues that basing managerial decisions on experience often proves reasonable but sometimes blocks novel solutions. When new ideas are needed or when a problem seems unsolvable, lateral thinking may be introduced in the decision process. The author defines lateral thinking as methods oriented on changing notions and perceptions. With these methods the past can be temporarily forgotten for the sake of creativity, so no problems are 'impossible' or 'doomed to failure'. The author argues that paying attention to the decision-maker's cognitive abilities is as important as providing the person with the necessary information. The ability to use lateral thinking can be a good idea for managers when faced with weakly structuralized problems, when the situation is complex or mutable, or when the company's success depends on introducing innovations. Lateral thinking increases the tolerance for uncertainty which can be seen as important for many managers who wish to keep up with the times. Gary Hamel (2006) believes that the management and the employees of many companies cannot think laterally, which may result from a systematic bias in favour of technical skills in the recruitment process. But linear thinking limits the number of strategic solutions and leads to wasting the company's social potential and, as a result, weakens the company's innovativeness.

John Burton and Robert Sack (1991) believe that lateral thinking is also useful in accounting. It applies to accounting methods, the institutional context and the technology used. The increasingly complex reality in which business functions demands to be reflected in the tools used, and this includes accounting tools as well. It is especially important to develop accounting by adding a broader context to it and by focusing on long-term results instead of concentrating on immediate effects. Companies would benefit from focusing on long-term and prospective actions. Financial statements produced by traditional accountancy will not support such strategies. Burton and Sack appreciate new methods and encourage continuous innovation and scientific research in accountancy.

Dean Shepherd and Evan Douglas (1998) are persuaded that lateral thinking is important for entrepreneurship. In their opinion, current educational management programmes only teach conventional thinking. The practice of entrepreneurship demands the knowledge of both the 'science' and the 'art' of management, and the latter is the essence of entrepreneurship. The art of entrepreneurship is its masterly level where a person creatively uses their knowledge and is able to take the initiative, not waiting until they are forced to act. It is about both reflection and acting, creating new directions for operations; provocative, non-sequential thinking, thinking that does not demand exactness at every stage; it consists in using what is unexpected and unconnected with the mainstream of our operation. All these traits make lateral thinking so valuable for those entrepreneurs who conceive of themselves as practitioners of art.

Shepherd and Douglas are convinced that many business schools, instead of teaching lateral thinking, actively discourage their students from this approach. Success is presented as the goal that one sets before oneself and then the way to attain this goal is analysed. The element of chance is treated as mere noise or not considered at all. This approach presents entrepreneurship as a controlled process which stands in sharp contradiction to all entrepreneurship practice. Thinking in these terms may sometimes be useful in management but it is limiting or harmful when applied to entrepreneurship. Business schools seek to present entrepreneurship as an activity that can be planned, which is only partly true. Some entrepreneurial operations can be planned but the very essence of entrepreneurship – innovation – by definition eludes all attempts at planning. At best, business schools can provide a technical basis for entrepreneurial actions through teaching marketing, finance and other techniques. These approaches, however, also have a side to them that actually restrains entrepreneurship. If they are used as the starting point for students, they can easily forget that entrepreneurship creates markets, builds relations with clients and contributes a new quality. Therefore, market research is not helpful in the introductory stages of a process and, most importantly, the entrepreneur should not be guided by the results of such research. The gist of innovation is that it is a product, a market, a need, and so on, that does not yet exist.

A famous example of a company that many believe to be actively using lateral thinking is Google, first and foremost known for its search engine of the same name. It started as the novel research project of two Stanford University PhD students. The company survived the dot-com crash and entered the stock market in 2004. Today it is one of the giants in the Internet business but continues to be innovative as far as its products and its functioning are concerned. The company is famous for providing its employees with conditions that facilitate creativity: no uniforms and no tendency for homogenization, social benefits including health care, good food, access to sport facilities, and so on. Gary Hamel (2006) considers Google one of the most prominent examples of lateral thinking in business.

Its top team does not spend a lot of time trying to cook up grand strategies. Instead, it works to create an environment that spawns lots of 'Googlettes': small, grassroots projects that may one day grow into valuable new products and services. Google looks for recruits who have off-the-wall hobbies and unconventional interests – people who aren't afraid to defy conventional wisdom – and, after it hires them, encourages them to spend up to 20 per cent of their time working on whatever they feel will benefit Google's users and advertisers (ibid., pp. 9–10).

Google's structure is based on small hetararchical[64] teams with the minimum of management and the maximum of horizontal communication. It even makes an effort to include the clients, as users who wish to test the company's new products in the test phase are invited to cooperate. Gary Hamel thinks that Google is so successful thanks to the fact that it neglects conventions and ignores truths that are deeply rooted in managerial wisdom, such as the belief that the CEO is the company's main strategist. Overturning the old truths creates space for innovation. Clive Wilkinson, the chief architect of the Google premises, said that his aim in designing the buildings was to create a space for both logical and lateral thinking (Campbell, 2006). Favourable conditions for logical thinking include silence, a space enabling concentration. Lateral thinking can develop in dynamic, non-schematic surroundings. The right conditions should be provided for people preferring either of the two styles of thinking; but the close distance between them may perhaps also encourage them to change surroundings. Apart from small work rooms, the architect designed meeting places, such as cafés and common rooms. According to Campbell, such dynamics stimulates continuous learning and prevents intellectual fatigue.

A final remark: the Trickster can be very innovative, he or she can be a defender of the poor and the oppressed. However, he or she should not be trusted, especially when he or she begins to preach ethics authoritatively. The discrepancy between declarations and life lie at the heart of this archetype. Therefore, the Trickster's real and declared ethics do not have to go together, as the other side of the provided examples also shows.

12. The Eternal Child

12.1 THE ETERNAL CHILD ARCHETYPE

The Eternal Child is one of Jung's personality archetypes (Jung, [1959] 1990). It appears in two variants as *puer aeternus*, the eternal boy, or as *puella aeterna*, the eternal girl, though the gender is not crucial in my organizational reading of this archetype. The Eternal Child is full of enthusiasm and energy, open and sensitive, full of inventiveness and often has beginner's luck, as the fortune is on their side. It is the embodiment of the potential, the sum of possibilities, a personification of becoming and optimism. Perhaps it is lucky precisely because they it accept luck, have no prejudices and are not burdened by memories and complexes. The archetype is a symbol of hope and rebirth. The dark side of the Eternal Child is its dislike of changes and especially, its reluctance to grow up. It avoids commitments, cannot, and does not like to be responsible, and tries to evade the powers that can limit them. In some legends the Eternal Child is the opposite of death and mortality, an embodiment of the will to live and faith in life's potential. In mythology this archetype appears in the shape of Kore, returning every spring to her mother, Ganymede, the beautiful eternal youth who serves as the cup-bearer of the gods, and in Iacchus, the child incarnation of Dionysus.

In literature, it is represented by Peter Pan, a magical character associated with eternal childhood, and Pippi Longstocking, a character I will present in greater detail as she perfectly fits the story of the Eternal Child in organizations. Pippi is a character created by the Swedish writer Astrid Lindgren who told the stories about an extraordinary girl to her daughter when the girl was ill (Lindgren, [1945] 2003). Her daughter and her friends liked the stories so much that Lindgren decided to write them down and publish them. In the beginning publishers rejected her manuscript but she finally managed to find a publishing house who issued the book. The publication of the book turned to be the beginning of Lindgren's great literary career and a turning point in Swedish children's literature. And so, the book was itself a beginning and a result of a series of chance events (Pedersen, 2007).

Pippi is a girl who lives on her own in a cottage called Villekulla. She has a monkey and a horse and a big bag full of money. Her father is a sailor and is rarely home, and her mother is dead; as Pippi says – she is 'an angel in heaven'. She takes care of herself, which she enjoys very much. The girl does not want adults to interfere with her life, and especially she avoids Mrs Prysselius who wants to send her to a children's home. She does not go to school though she likes learning new things and she likes other children – she simply cannot understand the sense of school discipline and is unable to comply with it. Pippi has many friends and with the two closest of them, Tommy and Annika, she lives through amazing adventures. Pippi looks different from others – she has red hair tied in thin plaits, wears clothes in vibrant colours that do not match, and enjoys wearing big man's shoes. She acts in an unconventional and spontaneous fashion; the effect of her joy in life and a positive attitude to the world. She sleeps with her feet on the pillow, changes cleaning into play, and hands out presents on her own birthday. Her everyday life is unusual and fascinating. She can see something remarkable in the most common things. For instance, once, when she decides to become a 'thing-searcher', she finds a rusty can that turns out to be a wonderful discovery – you can put cookies into it and thus make it into a great cookie can. One day she invents a new word, 'spink', but does not know what it means, so she tries matching different things to it. Apart from her adventures in her ordinary everyday life, Pippi also experiences great adventures in exotic countries – for example, she goes with her friends to save her father who is imprisoned by pirates. Pippi does not want to grow up – in one of the stories, she swallows a 'squigglypill' which will prevent her from ever growing up. Pippi believes that adults have no fun, they only deal with the most boring matters. Thanks to the pills children will be able to stay children and play in the garden even when they are 53: 'The stars were shining above the roof of Villekulla Cottage and Pippi was inside. She would always be there. It was wonderful to remember that. The years would pass, but Pippi and Tommy and Annika would never grow up. That is, if the squigglypills were still good!' (Lindgren, [1945] 2003, p. 249).

In organization theory Luhmann's notion of social systems influenced the understanding of organizations as systems capable of continuous autopoiesis (Luhmann, [1995] 1996; Cooper, 2006). Luhmann does not mention the archetype I here describe, but focuses on what I see as one of the basic features of the Eternal Child: the capacity for regeneration and renewal. An autopoietic system is a system that reproduces its element on the basis of its own elements (Luhmann, [1995] 1996). Organizations are social systems of communication that process and create divisions that draw the boundaries of what is, and what is not, the organization (Seidl and Becker, 2006). The processes are controlled by their own systems

Figure 12.1   The Eternal Child
(photo: Monika Kostera)

logic and they should not be reduced to the actions of individual actors. Organizations are social processes with their own unique traits, among which the most important are those that differentiate organizations from other social phenomena. In other words, organizations are systems that produce and reproduce a unique type of differentiations: decisions. This is an important characteristic as it makes organizations, in the communicative sense, operationally closed systems – they do use external resources but the resources do not become part of their internal system. In other words, organizations do not communicate with the environment as such but with its internal representations. Maintaining the organization's identity is crucial to the system's survival – a continuous process that consists in a differentiation from the environment. As opposed to biological systems, the events that are part of autopoietic organizational processes are immediate and momentary. As they cannot be characterized by permanence, organizations are forced constantly to produce new elements. It is precisely this capability for constant recreation of itself that makes an organization survive as a functional whole.

The basic logic that provides the basis for an organization's functioning, according to Seidl and Becker, is complexity reduction and uncertainty absorption, or limiting the number of alternatives and elements through a set of internal points of reference. As long as the organization remains capable of reacting quickly, it has a chance to recreate itself. An organization that wishes to define everything and 'know' exactly what it is, loses the capacity for self-recreation. Robert Cooper (2006), characterizing an organization as an autopoietic system, emphasizes the element of indeterminacy and the process of continuously becoming new present in organizations. Perpetual creation is a continuously upheld promise of an appearance of new forms – it is a simultaneous appearance and disappearance. An organization is like a phoenix, reborn from ashes and constantly changing into ashes again. It is always incomplete, not completely mature, and the vision of its completion is constantly deferred in time. Paradoxically, the more an organization is capable of such constant transformation, the more permanent it is.

In this chapter I tell the story of the Eternal Child in organizations. I start with showing how organizations try to deprive Eternal Children of those features which are central for the archetype in the process of socialization. Then, I present the idea of organizations that are like Eternal Children, trying to develop traits linked with creativity. However, childishness is sometimes the same as impetuousness and a lack of responsibility. These traits can be dangerous to organizations, to employees and stakeholders, which could be seen in the crash of the dot-coms that seemed so successful in the 1990s. Finally, I let the story reach its happy archetypical ending: the Child enjoys luck and can perhaps bring more of it into organizations. This approach takes us further away from classical management and leads us, again, to the domain of entrepreneurship.

12.2 SOCIALIZATION IN THE WORKPLACE

In the 1950s William Hollingsworth Whyte provoked a heated debate after he had published *The Organization Man* ([1956] 2002) which soon became a bestseller and was translated into many languages. The author characterizes a corporate employee as a person devoid of personality, a pawn in the corporate game, a person with no will and no opinions of their own. Protestant ethics, based on individualism, were replaced by omnipresent conformism. Corporate people are fully replaceable; they do not leave their trace on reality. They are mass products, the result of schematic education that makes everyone think the same thoughts and dream the same dreams. Organizations suppress creativity and ingenuity, discourage people from cherishing originality. The process starts in school where children are taught how to be submissive and not how to develop their talents and predispositions. Cooperation becomes an end, and not a means to an end, and 'conforming to a pattern' is the main motif of socialization in an organization. The organization man is a new type of person who is not stimulated to act by inventiveness but by the thought of conforming to the group, becoming mediocre, adjusting. Inventiveness is not even supported by universities, which strive to conform to the expectations of business. Universities design curricula with the purpose of preparing their students to play organizational roles. Colleges teach students how to become conformists ready to complete specific tasks instead of developing their creative potential and teaching them to blaze new trails. Whyte believes that the consequences of such attitudes will in the end prove disastrous, both for individual people and for organizations. Organizations are too much afraid of freedom to respect individuality, and without individuality one cannot create original values.

> Management has tried to adjust the scientist to The Organization rather than The Organization to the scientist. It can do this with the mediocre and still have a harmonies group. It cannot do it with the brilliant; only freedom will make them harmonious. Most corporations sense this but, unfortunately, the moral they draw is something else again. A well known corporation recently passed up the opportunity to hire one of the most brilliant chemists of the country. They wanted brilliance but they were afraid that he might 'disrupt the organization'. (ibid., p. 213)

Even though more than 50 years have passed since the publication of Whyte's book, and moral rhetoric has changed radically – from the social ethics criticized by Whyte to the 'liquid' individuality (Bauman, 2000) – and even though the management fashions have changed several times and the pendulum has swung several times from collectivism to individualism, his argument still seems valid to many a reader. Socialization in organizations, including schools, comes down to teaching conformism. It results from the desire to make the participants' behaviour more predictable, and the participants themselves perhaps wish for more maturity in the organization's culture. But the price of this process is a curbing of inventiveness, individuality and organizational creativity. Obviously Whyte did not believe in the effectiveness of such a lesson of conformism that 'does not produce maturity. It produces a sort of permanent prematurity, and this is true not only of the child being taught life adjustment but of the organization man being taught well-roundedness' (Whyte [1956] 2002, pp. 396–7).

According to the theory of autopoietic organization, socialization is always in fact a self-socialization as it brings the individual face to face with constant choices: conformism or non-conformism, attraction or rejection, involvement or deviation (Vanderstraeten, 2000). These constant choices produce bifurcations, or the possibilities for the occurrence of various scenarios. In contemporary society deviation is often valued more highly as non-conformism gives the individual more freedom and enables originality. According to Vanderstraeten, socialization understood in terms of autopoiesis takes into consideration the whole scope of deviation and makes it a social communication system that can function as a frame of reference for socialization. This attitude enables us to view socialization in organizations differently. Socialization is after all a process in which the socialized individuals are active too – or, perhaps, they are the most active ones in the process. Thus, the process of socialization may provide an opportunity for a renewal of both the individual and the organization. The question is whether contemporary organizations use this potential.

John Van Maanen's articles, the result of his field studies in various organizations, show what socialization looks like in practice. He states that in a police department that he examined new policemen were enthusiastic and full of internal motivation to work (Van Maanen, 1975). In the process of socialization their idealism ebbed and gave way to quieter satisfaction and keeping a low profile, characteristic of well-socialized police officers. Still, the level of involvement in work in the police force was higher than in other organizations. The organization rewarded those new policemen who declared a weaker motivation. New recruits quickly realized that attracting too much attention brought more trouble than benefits. The signals from the environment suggesting that society disapproves of the police also had an influence on the socialization process. The superiors most of all valued obedience, which also curbed the enthusiasm of new police officers. The researcher noticed that the metamorphosis usually happened after six months' working for the police.

The strongest influence on the socialization process is exerted by the position a person occupies in the organization. If it is a position formally distinguished from the 'ordinary' structure, the organization always wants the new person to adopt the organization's viewpoint. If the new person's role is too far removed from the organizational context, they find it difficult to transmit the learned attitudes and skills from this special socialization sphere to their everyday work inside the organization. Therefore, such formalized organizations place more emphasis on transmitting attitudes than work methods. Whether new employees are socialized individually or in groups is also of considerable importance. Group socialization leads to a greater averaging of results and a better conforming to group norms. Management's expectations do not always match group standards so it does not have to lead to vertical conformism, that is, to conforming to the expectations of people who are higher in the hierarchy.

Another factor influencing organizational socialization is its nature: socialization can be serial or disjunctive. Serial socialization is about experienced members, who are role models, preparing new employees to assume similar roles. Disjunctive processes are where there are no role models and the new participants make their own way into the organization's culture. Serial socialization leads to a greater homogenization of attitudes in time and, consequently, a lower innovativeness and the tendency to keep the status quo. The duration of socialization is also important: the longer the socialization, the more average the attitudes. Group processes develop solidarity and facilitate a greater intimacy in the socialized groups. Finally, the question of the presence and availability of a mentor or a teacher is valid. The bond with a mentor will always be stronger than the bond with an abstract 'organization'.

Another study by the same author (Van Maanen, 1978) shows that different methods of transmitting knowledge and teaching skills indispensable at work do not result from the differences between people but from the differences in organizations' socialization strategies. The homogenization effect is in fact not always an intended side effect. The newcomers submit themselves to socialization as the state of temporariness is extremely stress-inducing. People actively search for answers about how to cope in a new situation. Socialization strategies provide them with full sets of such answers which they often accept in their entirety, 'just in case'. And the organization is interested in socializing new members as the company's stability and productivity depend on the results of socialization and, more precisely, on whether the company succeeds in transmitting its mode of operation to new generations of participants.

Sometimes adopting a new organizational role results in a dramatic change of an individual's identity. Van Maanen lists the most popular socialization strategies of organizations and concludes that some of them have a particularly strong and destructive influence on people's identity. This is especially true of the strategy of investiture and divestiture that consists in a purposeful interference with an individual's personality by supporting and reinforcing some of the traits the individual already has, and divesting the person of other traits. Investiture is confirming an individual's traits which the organization considers positive by promoting the person, which strengthens the desired features in the course of promotion. An example of divestiture or dismantling of characteristics is subjecting a recruit to cultural influences that deprive the person of a sense of dignity or the willingness to resist. As a result, these characteristics are eliminated and replaced by a growing acceptance of organizational collaborators. Investiture reinforces and confirms the status quo; divestiture provokes the levelling down of standards and an advanced homogenization.

An example of destructive socialization is provided by Krzysztof Konecki in a story that comes from his field studies where he used the method of covert participant observation (Konecki, [2003] 2007). He was employed as an unqualified worker in a factory and focused on investigating socialization processes. His co-workers in the field did not know that he was in fact an academic conducting ethnographic research. He was treated in the same way as all the other new unqualified workers. As a 'newbie' he found himself at the very bottom of the hierarchy. The socialization strategies he was subjected to were informal and prolonged in time, and consisted mainly in various degradation rituals applied by other workers. They included mainly mocking and practical jokes. These practices differ from ordinary factory humour in that they are completely one-sided: the person who is mocked cannot react to the jokes and if they do, nobody laughs (regardless of the 'objective funniness' of the jokes). Apart from the jokes, other practices consisted in using epithets to remind the new person about his place in the hierarchy, for example: '"he's the guy from the scrapyard", "if you keep on working like that, we'll send you back to the scrapyard", "you'd be better off sweeping the floor", or "you're not good enough to be a cleaner", and so on' (ibid., p. 57).

The researcher did not succumb to the destructive force of this socialization as he was aware that he was not a real participant in the organization. The experience, however, was quite intense and he realized how destructive it can be for a person who is really employed in the factory.

12.3　WORK OR PLAY?

In his famous book entitled *Homo Ludens*,[65] Johan Huizinga ([1938] 2003) focused on the role of play in culture. The play element has a creative influence on the formation of culture; one can even say that culture comes into being as a result of play. Children know how to play without being taught, they have a need to play, and they enjoy it immensely. Adults like playing too, it gives them satisfaction and helps in actualizing many creative ideas, but '[r]eally to play, a man must play like a child' (ibid., p. 199). Creative adults can, like children, let themselves be carried away by play, they can immerse themselves in imagination without losing the sense of difference between play and reality.

Huizinga formulates five defining features of play. The foremost one is freedom – play is freedom, it can be based on principles accepted willingly. Any play that is forced or goal-oriented stops being play. Play happens outside ordinary reality, is not a part of it, but the players can be intensely absorbed by it until they lose the sense of play. When the boundary between play and reality is crossed, play becomes serious. Play is distinguished from ordinary reality in a spatio-temporal sense, it is physically located outside ordinary life. Play has its beginning and ending; after it has ended, the participants go back to their ordinary occupations. It can be repeated, return to its plots and motifs, but it happens always in a world that is different from the everyday reality. Play means creating one's own order that is an absolute, ideal order, not to be encountered in ordinary life. Each detraction from this order 'spoils the game'. In this perhaps resides the beauty of play: the harmony that comes from the imagination. Moreover, play has nothing to do with material goals: 'It is an activity connected with no material interest, and no profit can be gained by it' (ibid., p. 13).

Play and culture develop simultaneously but play precedes culture:

> culture arises in the form of play . . . it is played from the very beginning. Even those activities which aim at the immediate satisfaction of vital needs – hunting, for instance – tend, in archaic society, to take on the play-form. Social life is endued with supra-biological forms, in the shape of play, which enhance its value. (ibid., p. 46)

Huizinga argues that society can be regarded as a kind of play. Art, religion, knowledge – these and other basic culture-forming spheres of life all develop thanks to play. Play can be viewed as the basic principle for society's functioning. A society devoid of a spirit of play and game is unable to develop a culture.

Contemporary research in organizations show that in their work people, and especially knowledge workers such as information technology (IT) specialists, enjoy creating their own, usually small, spatio-temporal areas for play; or they play after work, usually doing similar tasks as at work, only for free (Hunter et al., 2010). Carolyn Hunter, Dariusz Jemielniak and Agnieszka Postuła (2010) point out that IT specialists, when they play, become carefree and use their imagination almost like children, which boosts innovation. Of its own accord, play changes into work and has important (positive) consequences for it. It is also possible to look at work as a kind of game and play, although it is possible that Huizinga would not have accepted such a line of thinking, as he emphasized that play should bring no material profit. However, stories like the one related by Hunter and her co-authors still show some interesting aspects of the contemporary Eternal Child. Perhaps the archetype is being invoked and used by some work organizations, especially in the creative business area, such as those operating in IT business, for example.

Play and games are used to motivate people to work, as an encouragement for people to share their knowledge. Some corporations use it to

manage organizational knowledge[66] (Qi and Meloche, 2009). IT specialists are more willing to learn new tasks when they are presented as 'play'
(Webster and Martocchio, 1993). Managers are encouraged to play as
well. For example, strategic marketing can be viewed as a sort of game and
play that constitutes a productive supplement to serious planning work
(Jacobs and Heracleous, 2007). Bogdan Costea, Norman Crump and John
Holm (2007) believe that such attempts at using play to boost the effects
of work are an appropriation of play by managerialism. For many people
the workplace has become a place to work not just with a task, but also
with oneself. Human souls become managed and work should yield results
not only in the shape of a product or a service but also in the shape of
well-being or even happiness. Involving play in work may be an attempt to
invade the private domains of life of the employees, which until now have
usually been unreachable by attempts at 'motivation' and productivity-
enhancing programmes:

> The sequence of the argument was as follows: 'business excellence' is generated
> by 'strong organizational cultures'; in turn, strong cultures require commit-
> ment; commitment can only be engendered through participation; and one of
> the most effective contexts for creating participation is the representation of
> work as play. Play is the ultimate effortless mediator of intense involvement in
> work. (Costea et al., 2007, p. 158)

The results of this approach are remarkable: for a whole new generation of
Western managers, forging a connection between a 'decent job' and 'good
fun' is an obvious feature of corporate culture management. However, this
is not accompanied by talk about responsibilities:

> The new ethos of work finds a central place for 'having fun' (leading, by impli-
> cation, to new levels of liberation). Perhaps, more fundamental is the indication
> contained in these uses of play that a new understanding of the horizon of life
> is on the brink of emergence: the anticipation of life with no foreseeable end,
> or, at least, promising endless youth through a perpetually preserved and active
> 'inner child'. (ibid., p. 163)

One of the most famous examples of childish and happy-go-lucky management is the so-called dot-com bubble from the turn of the century. In
the 1990s the stock prices of companies operating on the Internet were
rapidly increasing. Many of the companies were set up to absorb the free
venture capital, and the growth in stock prices was the result of specula-
tion in stocks. Some of the new dot-com companies had no well-thought-
out development plans, and their strategy was simple: rapid growth and
taking a leading position in the market. Then the company was profitably
sold. The idea of setting up dot-coms was not without chances to succeed,

which can be seen in the examples of companies from that time that are still operating in the Internet. They are good platforms for advertising and selling. The use of the new medium could be quite helpful for business: Internet companies have unprecedented scope for direct contact with the customer, which gives great possibilities for positioning and niche activities. What proved fatal for dot-coms was their approach to management: the lack of a business plan; and unreal operational models, not always motivated by the will to make a quick profit but often resulting from an excessive optimism and a lack of responsibility. These companies' Internet sites attracted attention with their imagery, colours, inventive presentations and games, but the interest did not translate into sales that would bring real profits to the companies. The companies counted on their luck instead of trying to learn from their markets and potential clients. Often this resulted from the expectation of quick and impressive action, as well as their often being innovative and ahead of their time, together with a reluctance to find and analyse their niche. The bubble burst at the turn of 1999 and 2000 – stock prices plummeted and many companies collapsed, often without ever making any profit. However, the companies which, apart from good ideas, also had sound accountancy and marketing management, still prosper today.[67]

One of the most famous examples of an ephemeral company is boo.com, a company that dealt with e-commerce, founded by three young Swedes with no previous experience in managing a company. Boo.com was a marketing giant, and all its actions were immediately made famous. The company had branches and employees in many countries. The founders made contact with the best banks and investors. They also had much fun, especially the entrepreneurs themselves. Gunnar Lindstedt (2001) writes about the enthusiasm and carelessness of the management, which was manifested in their optimism, and their unwillingness to control anything or do any 'boring stuff' in general. Lindstedt describes how one of the company's founders suddenly left the room in the course of a job interview in Madrid because he felt bored. The company's website was not perfect but it contained some then innovative ideas. A massive advertising campaign caused numerous clients to visit the site in hopes of seeing something interesting. Here the first disappointment awaited them – the site was especially dissatisfying for those people whose modems were slow (and in those days this was true of the majority of Internet users). And Apple computers users could not access the site at all. The company's offer was equally disappointing. Boo.com sold sports clothes. The company did not offer any discount to make the clothes cheaper than those in traditional retail shops, it only promised free shipping. After some time, the company started offering discounts when its financial situation was really bad. The biggest disappointment was the sales: they only reached 1 per cent of the planned level. Investors were not willing to spend any more money on the company. Several months of intense partying and marketing fever were followed by the company's spectacular collapse.

12.4   LUCK LIKES TO BE LIKED

Luck, also known as serendipity, plays an important part in scientific discoveries and other spheres of life. It appears as lucky chance, a sudden enlightenment that comes when one is searching for something else. The trick is to know how to receive such an unexpected gift and use it in an appropriate way. 'Luck likes to be liked', as a lucky friend of mine says. A too strong orientation on goals, rationality or too much determination interfere with following luck. In order to see and receive luck a person has to be a bit like a child, they need an open mind, the desire to experiment, and a respectful approach to the uncertain and uncontrollable. In their study *The Travels and Adventures of Serendipity*, Robert Merton and Elinor Barber ([1958] 2004) write about the role of lucky chance in science. By that they do not mean 'randomness' or happy-go-lucky approaches. On the contrary, reliability and the use of existing theories are part and parcel of their ideas, perhaps best demonstrated in Merton's other famous book, *On the Shoulders of Giants* ([1965] 1993). For Merton and Barber serendipity is the ability to see what is in front of our eyes, the ability to be happily surprised, just like Pippi when she was a thing-searcher. Merton and Barber describe serendipity as encounters with sudden enlightenment. Scientist, writers, artists and other creators often have such illuminations that point them in directions they would not have considered otherwise. Serendipity goes hand in hand with inspiration, a flash of understanding; it is about life and liveliness and not at all about chaotic Brownian motions of the mind. Although it is the antithesis of a traditional, rational acquisition of knowledge, it leads to wisdom. What is harmful to science (and to other spheres of life where discoveries and novelties are essential) is too strict management and control of research, too much emphasis put on procedures and rules, and not enough space for luck, chance and serendipity. Meeting luck and being able to receive it is what makes many discoveries and creative acts possible. It does not have to be about any particular talent for chance discoveries but of a property common to all humans that makes them possible, or according to Merton and Barber, due to an inherent quality of the system. And, indeed, everyone has been a child once. Therefore, this archetype is close to most of us. Perhaps it is easiest to invoke it not by gaining something, but by getting rid of things:

learned truths and layers of acculturation, barriers between a spontaneous perception of the world and the conscious self.

In organizations serendipity is especially valued by entrepreneurs and researchers involved in studying entrepreneurship. Nicholas Dew (2009) believes that the ability to use serendipity is one of the most important traits of entrepreneurship. An entrepreneur is, in many ways, similar to a discoverer, an artist or a scientist. It is known that discoverers often discovered places or truths other than the ones they had set out to find in the beginning, and the example of Columbus is a case in point. Artists as well discover new territories by chance, like Picasso whose famous Blue Period began because he once was forced to use blue paint as he had run out of other colours. Scientists sometimes make their discoveries by pure accident – the discovery of penicillin is a good example. Fleming was lucky when he saw in his laboratory that his experiment was ruined by mould. The success of many entrepreneurs is also the result of serendipity and the ability to use it. A good example of a lucky entrepreneur is Thomas Stemberg, the founder of Staples, the office supply chain store. When he was still a salaried employee, he ran out of printer tape and could not buy it anywhere and so he came up with his own business idea. Honda's discovery of an American market for small motorcycles was equally accidental, not a result of market research. Honda's employees imported small motorcycles for themselves when staying in the United States, where they lacked good means of transport.

Dew believes that for an entrepreneur it is essential that several elements occur together: the resource that is the combination of the entrepreneur's prior knowledge; contingency; and the search of the entrepreneur. An entrepreneur's knowledge does not have to rely on education, especially formal schooling. Experience and common sense are equally or even more important. Contingency has to be seen and grasped. Of course, it is impossible to foresee and cannot be translated into points in a business plan. Nonetheless, it constitutes a key element of the entrepreneur's business. Apart from knowledge and contingency, the search is the third element necessary for a serendipitous discovery. Some people seem to be more gifted for such searches than others. Maybe this is due to the fact that the search is an activity more suited to the Adventurer than the Eternal Child, an archetype not readily available to everyone. The three domains overlap creating spaces in which lucky chances may come into being. At the intersection of search and knowledge is systematic exploration. In the common area of searching and contingency there occur pre-discoveries that may lead to later discoveries. In the space where contingency intersects with knowledge appear moments of spontaneous recognition, moments of spontaneous astonishment that can also lead to later discoveries. The area where the three domains coincide is the space of serendipitous discovery. Entrepreneurs are active in all of the three areas; their creative work consists in provoking situations where at least two of the model's elements overlap, that is, knowledge and search. The majority of their efforts, however, may prove ineffective as the element of chance, contingency, is of vital importance. Still, in favourable circumstances a contingency may appear and help to materialize a serendipitous discovery that may become the basis of a new entrepreneurial activity:

> Enduring entrepreneurial firms are often products of contingencies. Their structure, culture, core competence and endurance are all residuals of particular human beings striving to forge and fulfil particular aspirations through interactions with the space, time and technologies they live in. (Sarasvathy, 2008, p. 90)

An entrepreneur has to be open to surprises, instead of trying at all costs to control everything in the organization and in the environment. A great help in developing that ability comes from within the human psyche: imagination enables accepting the unforeseen and joining it with resources already possessed.

Some authors, like Göran Svensson and Greg Wood (2005), believe that the ability to use lucky chances is an important characteristic of a good manager, a trait very helpful in managing people. A too rational and systematic approach to leadership does not yield such positive results as manuals promise. Leadership often fails due to an excessive urge for control and a reluctance to use serendipity. Michael Eriksson and Mats Sundgren (2005) argue that an openness to lucky chance can prove vital in strategic management. On the basis of their ethnographic research carried out in two big pharmaceutical companies undergoing a merger, the authors show the advantages that may result from writing the element of chance into the strategy for organizational change. This does not mean leaving the important decisions to blind fate, but rather using lucky coincidences to one's advantage. The companies let their strategies have indeterminate boundary areas which were tested against each other as they went, and adjusted to situations in the environment by the managers. Thanks to this strategy, satisfactory synergetic effects have been reached and the merger of the two companies proved exceptionally successful. The value of the shares rose, new jobs were created and valuable innovations were introduced.

Alexander Styhre (2008) describes the case of a research and development unit of an international pharmaceutical company where openness to chance, lucky coincidence and permission for employees to play during their work hours resulted in many valuable innovations. However, there were also other forces at work, leading in the opposite direction. The strategy of the organization is a constant balancing of two tendencies: innovation and rationalization. While more traditional operating methods are used in other units, the research and development unit functions according to different rules. Innovations are mainly play that involves individual and collective skills. One of the groups of employees working for the unit are researchers with scientific, university experience. The management believes in introducing innovation because they assume that is an indispensable condition for gaining an advantage over competitors. Some managers, but not all, realize that innovation depends on luck and that it cannot be as precisely planned as the work in other units. From time to time a member of management attempts to eliminate the chance factor and to 'isolate' the work processes from chance. Rules and regulations that aim at ordering the 'chaotic' work of the department are implemented. But this does not make the organization immune to the unpredictable; it only eliminates innovativeness. So these attempts are usually quickly abandoned and the research and development unit can continue its creative work.

13. Gaia

13.1 THE ARCHETYPE OF GAIA

Gaia, the archetype of Mother Earth, is not one of the classic Jungian archetypes,[68] but I consider it to be one of the central archetypes in our times. Gaia is a personification of our planet, most notably of its life-giving forces; it is often seen as the symbol of life and nature. In the Greek pantheon Gaia was one of the primordial deities, *Prôtogenoi*, the first creatures in the history of the world that gave birth to all creation.[69] She was worshipped as the mother goddess, omnipotent, not always caring and protective, but imperious or even cruel. As Mother Nature she appears in mythologies and folk tales, including Slavic, Nordic, Babylonian and many Indian mythologies. She also appeared in medieval legends, in a metaphorical shape, though she was not worshipped in this epoch as a goddess. Today we tend to think in terms of broader ecosystems or even to view the whole planet as a system supporting the rise and development of life, subject to evolution, self-regulating, and striving for survival as a whole. The planet's sum of its ecosystems is the biosphere, or the system joining all living organisms and their mutual relations, including the atmosphere (air), the hydrosphere (water) and lithosphere (earth). The archetype of Gaia draws attention to the importance of the biosphere in our value systems and to the primordial nature of life on Earth. It also shows the precedence of nature over culture and civilization. Gaia is the goddess of fertility, diversity, growth, bloom, symbiosis and intelligent forms of life – but also of decay, the struggle for survival, deadly micro-organisms and predators. Gaia does not favour any forms of life over others, is infinitely tolerant and also infinitely cruel; she makes no exceptions and loves the prey as much as she loves the predator.

A contemporary representation of Gaia is the movie entitled *Koyaanisqatsi* (Reggio, 1982). In the language of the Hopi Indians the title means 'life thrown out of balance'. The film has no typical narrative plot, there are no protagonists in the ordinary sense. It is a poetic vision made of images and music.[70] First, images of a prehistoric cave painting are shown. These pictures were discovered in a national park in Utah, in the United States of America and they depict people. The next image is the launch of the Apollo rocket. Then the film presents nature scenes: landscapes from a bird's eye view, floating clouds, sea waves. The shots are long, harmonious; nature runs its course, changes slowly, floats.

At a certain point the viewer is presented images that show human interference – it is still nature but ordered, with an enforced structure and symmetry. These are no longer wild areas, but fields, nature still flourishing but organized by humans. Its beauty is different, its harmonies are based on different rhythms. Then, the film's pace becomes faster. Human civilizations emerge, big cities, buildings; the tempo increases, the pulse quickens, patterns and repetitions appear. The most famous sequences of the film show, from a bird's eye view, the traffic in a big US city at rush hour and people using public transport. Everything is enormously accelerated, tiny cars and human figures move on the screen in surprisingly neat columns. The film also shows, in acceleration, assembly lines, people doing repetitive work, manufacturing TV sets, sausages, clothes. At some point the film moves to the level of the individual: the faces of passers-by become visible, the pace slows down, the faces seem distant and mysterious. The last scene shows an explosion of a space shuttle. The machine goes up and then explodes suddenly, black ashes fall down to the ground. The film is usually interpreted, in accordance with its title, as a criticism of the contemporary lifestyle that is in conflict with nature. It can also be read in a different way – as a story about various types of harmonies, beginning with the eternal ones for which time passes very slowly as they are subject to the forces of nature, and ending with human-made rhythms that agree with the pace of life of human civilization. The latter harmony is an expression of human aspirations and dreams as well as a consequence of how short human life is, especially when compared with the cycles of nature, such as mountain formation or the evolution of species.[71] On Earth there is space for everyone and everything: for oceans, clouds, mountains, people and their travels, even though these seem incomprehensible from the point of view of nature. Only in the scene of the exploding space shuttle is there a violent imbalance presented: humans try to leave their planet and go to space, and they become separated from their Mother Earth.

Elisabeth Ryland (2000) uses the archetype of Gaia to reflect on ecological awareness in contemporary management. The author points to the gap between the individual and organizational awareness on the one hand, and ecology on the other, and proposes to bridge the gap by resorting to the Gaia archetype. People are aware of how harmful for the natural environment and, consequently, for life on Earth the activity of industrial organizations can be. But it is difficult to counteract this destruction of the natural environment in a way that would be equally systematic to the destruction. Industry and the global corporations that are responsible for most of the

Figure 13.1   Gaia
(photo: Jerzy Kociatkiewicz)

pollution have much more power than any actor that is aiming at stopping them. This makes people worry about survival, about the future, and experience a collective sense of guilt. Contemporary culture seems simultaneously entangled in guilt and a denial of how bad things are, which make it look irrational, bizarre at times, characterized by seemingly groundless, collective fits of depression, frustration and panic. In the meantime Mother Earth, the force that is able to restore balance to her living creatures, needs balance herself. It is a reciprocal relation: humans have to restore to Gaia the balance she needs and then they will get back in return the balance they strive after. Ryland argues that sustainable growth organizations can be a link or a tool in such contacts as they are beings located between the individual and the environment. A single person may feel overwhelmed and helpless in the face of nature – and in the past, humans usually stood no chance in a confrontation, such as drought, flood, tempest or earthquake. An organization which, apart from financial goals, also has other aspirations, including social aims and the care for the natural environment, can more effectively represent human needs vis-à-vis the power of nature. It can also better cooperate with the ecosystem, and search for symbiosis. The Gaia archetype helps to restore a broader perspective to management; it reminds us that the planet provides organizations with resources but also demands respect and attention, not only to its financial and other human-made dimensions, but also to its living, organismic side. An organization that can cooperate with its environment becomes more sustainable:

> Leading proponents of the environmental value system advocate a new and sustainable industrial revolution. The sustainable approach is intended to counteract the widespread poverty, social crises, global instability, and general habitat

destruction resulting from the untenable assumption of current economic principles.

The goal for sustainable business activity is one of stable global biosystems rather than unlimited material prosperity of the few. (Ryland, 2000, p. 397)

Ryland adds that this attitude demands, among other things, the development of a new type of accountancy as well as taking into consideration managerial purposes other than financial ones, which is a common practice today. The periods of accounting for business should be prolonged and become adapted to a long-term perspective in management. In this way the frame of reference for managerial decisions can include future generations and the organization's environment in the broadest sense.

First I present postcolonial theory applied to organizations and management. The theory makes us look at our contemporary world as one whole, with no centre and no peripheries, where various places and cultures constitute equally important parts and may help to generate a multitude of local management models. Then I present the idea of management for sustainable growth, or management that actualizes a set of purposes, the most important purpose being a harmonious combination of economic and ecological goals.

13.2 THE EARTH IS ROUND: A WORLD WITHOUT CENTRE OR PERIPHERY

Edward Said's *Orientalism* (1978) is one of the books that has had a major influence on academic discourse on globalization and culture in the last 30 years. The author argues that the Western countries' attitudes vis-à-vis the Middle East are based on completely erroneous assumptions. The eponymous orientalism consists in, on the one hand, a romanticization of the life and culture of the Arabic countries that distorts the true picture, and, on the other, in the imperialistic tendency of the West that strives to subdue the lands inhabited by Arabic people. Both tendencies are combined in the discourse that legitimizes the Western attitudes as historically, economically and politically justified. Said argues that the gist of this discourse is not the fact that it distorts the image of the Middle East – all unfamiliar cultures are considered exotic and interesting – but that it legitimizes colonialism. The otherness of Arabic cultures is presented as inextricably linked with inferiority. Orientalism permeates all Western notions of the Middle East: scientific, literary and popular. Such images were also included in the educational curricula in the Middle East. As a result, it led to the shaping of a postcolonial mentality among the Middle

Eastern elites. Said's *Orientalism* is considered one of the founding works of the field of social sciences called postcolonialism. Postcolonialism is the study of the effects of colonialism on culture. Postcolonial studies aim at broadening the understanding of and provoking respect for cultural diversity, the identities of various peoples and societies, as well as enabling the creation of a full cultural polyphony. Postcolonial theorists also aim at fighting racism, revealing latent motifs of accepted ideologies, presenting alternative ideologies and outlooks on cultural phenomena, overturning the roots of colonialism[72] which is viewed as a system of cultural values that functions in countries politically and economically subordinated to more powerful states.

Postcolonialism in management is about 'conducting empirical research in geographically postcolonial contexts [and in] the attempts at developing management theories complying with postcolonial ideas present in other fields of study' (Kostera and Śliwa, 2010, p. 55). The conditions for an understanding of globalization processes and the adoption of a constructively sustainable approach to globalization in management demand our knowledge about colonial influences in different parts of the world. There is a growing tendency to respect various cultural contexts and to deprive 'growth' of its culturally unambiguous colouring which still permeates the theory and practice of management. Sustainable growth means taking various identities into consideration and not adopting only one dominating perspective. Obviously, wishful thinking or the publication of texts encouraging a greater openness to others is not enough. Postcolonial management is about encouraging people, including management students, to think critically and not to accept univocality as the 'normal' state of affairs. Postcolonial theory can help us to understand our practices and the theories of others and, as a consequence, also one's own perspective as one among many, as Kostera and Śliwa point out.

Bobby Banerjee and Anshuman Prasad (2008) describe the development in postcolonial theory in the last decade. They have observed a rise in the number of papers and scientific magazines, and a growing interest in the subject visible in scientific conferences. The voice that can be heard most often is that which talks about the necessity of a decolonization of minds; in other words, it questions the restricted scope of business thinking and the absolute hegemony of Western models. Postcolonial theory is particularly useful in international management, where it helps in identifying neocolonial assumptions underlying practical and theoretical solutions. The authors define neocolonialism as 'a continuation of direct Western colonialism without the traditional mechanism of expanding frontiers and territorial control, but with elements of political, economic and cultural control' (ibid., p. 91).

Banerjee and Prasad argue that the awareness of the role of neocolonialism in contemporary management is important for both Western people and the people who come from underprivileged cultures. The prefix 'post' can be misleading: postcolonialism does not mean historical studies, though the knowledge of history can help us to understand the present. Colonialism is a phenomenon that still exerts influence on contemporary life. Today, it usually takes on a different shape and does not have to mean the attempt of one culture to influence another; it can also be a mindless attitude to the world consisting in the interpretation of certain phenomena with the help of culturally foreign categories. It can result in self-marginalization or a resignation from one's sense of dignity and the care for one's identity. Quite often it is the effect of the conviction that there is only one possible way leading to progress, development and success. As the main aim of postcolonialism is to direct attention to diversity and coexistence of various possibilities, theories and practices, the very field itself is characterized by an advanced heterogeneity and includes diverse and incompatible theories and intellectual stances, from neo-Marxism to deconstruction, liberalism, poststructuralism, alterglobalism and ecology. The subject of study is also more diverse than the mere study of the social and economic situation in former colonies. In this field one can find studies dealing with the transformation from a planned economy to capitalism, the oligopolization of business in India, or the relations between aboriginal people and the businesses functioning in their territory.

For instance, Martyna Śliwa and George Cairns (2009) have explored how international management textbooks copy neocolonial attitudes and apply them to management, even when they try to take into account the diversity of perspectives and broaden the spectrum of managerial practices by adding new, more 'local' methods. Śliwa and Cairns point to the fact that in the textbooks they analysed the amount of historical knowledge that is presented is very small. The concentration on the present leaves students ignorant of the origins and development of the theories they study. Students cannot achieve a historical perspective on the theories they are taught and can easily become convinced of the theories' inevitability.

But in social sciences there are no absolute truths, and even the illusion that they exist is dangerous, which postcolonial studies (along with other theoretical stances) clearly show. Absolute truths limit the imagination and the scope for activity, not for ethical or practical reasons but because of unquestioned assumptions.

The very idea that management studies serve the purpose of organizations that employ the graduates, and the resulting concentration on methods and techniques, are in fact elements of a new ideology that has stealthily entered the curricula. From the perspective of this ideology, ethical or ecological questions seem secondary. Textbooks present global corporations as examples of good practices, stressing the fact that they are completely separated from cultural contexts. They promote the model of an international company's employee, single and childless, self-reliant, but not necessarily speaking the language of the country they work in. In marketing they propose fully decontextualized categories, including the analysis of demographic segments of the market, such as age and race, without any knowledge of the subject and with no problematizing of the issue, as if the categories were arbitrary and random, without any cultural or political roots. Some textbooks demonstrate a somewhat greater sensibility. For example, one of them analyses the growing role of the black middle class in Brazil, but even this text does not discuss any of the political, social or cultural consequences of this tendency. These publications present accounting as a field that should be globally homogenized, and US standards and practices are more or less directly presented as superior. Similarly to other areas of business, accounting is taken out of its cultural, historical and political context. Standardization understood in this fashion is in fact an instance of open neocolonialism. The analysed books do not favour the growth of diversity or even the growth of the importance of sustainable growth in contemporary business. Instead of developing in students the ability to think independently, they discourage them from individual thinking and this remains the dominant paradigm of higher education.

13.3   ECOLOGICAL AWARENESS

Gaia, the famous book by James Lovelock ([1979] 2000), proposes a fundamentally different approach to our planet than the materialistic and mechanistic outlook adopted in the previous century. The author presents the Earth as a complex living system that consists of the biosphere, the atmosphere, the lithosphere and the hydrosphere. The Earth actively searches for the optimal living conditions, striving for balance in the processes of homeostasis. It constitutes a sort of an enormous organism or, rather, a context for all life. The regulatory system that controls the parameters vital for life includes the temperature of the surface, the structure of the atmosphere and the oceans' salinity. It can be said that life strives to provide the condition for its continuation. In his more recent book on the Gaia hypothesis ([2006] 2007), Lovelock argues that the only way to prevent ecological calamity is through the wise use of science and technology and not a rejection thereof. Life on Earth is in great danger; the system desperately tries to defend itself but cannot restore the balance on its own. The mechanisms of self-regulation have been disrupted as a result of destructive human activities. Only people can undo the damage they have done, leading to the point where we are now with regard to pollution and climate change. The author believes that it is too late for a 'return to nature'. Now is the time to use modern technology to help Gaia recover.

The Gaia hypothesis also has some pertinent implications for management. Marius de Geus (2002) considers the question of the extent to which ecological utopias, or ecotopias, can provide inspiration for specific business activities. The author believes that such utopias can have a navigating function in management. Visions of a future society based on the principles of sustainable growth can provide a frame of reference for the assessment of companies' activities; they can serve as a kind of ethical system. They can also motivate managers to create new methods and models of management even if these visions will not provide them with straightforward answers. It should be kept in mind that great utopias have become devalued as impractical, or have been compromised as the foundations of totalitarian ideologies and governments that had no respect for human beings. Therefore, the new ecological utopias should have a more modest dimension. They should not be treated as literal truths or programmes to be actualized, but instead develop ecological imagination, creating images of sustainable growth. Such images can inspire managers to formulate particular tasks and partial ecological purposes that will eventually be actualized. Recent management literature abounds in examples of such particular programmes that promote ecological purposes and values. For example, Vincent di Norcia (1996) proposes a set of planning indexes that are to help companies in including ecological purposes in their strategic management. He claims that approaching the question of ecology directly and proposing well-defined tools is more effective than an indirect approach that treats ecology as an ethical purpose that should be attained by means of a set of social or organizational aims. Reaching durable results is easier when one connects ecological purposes with technical and economic aims as 'economics and ecology should be mutually reinforcing, as sustainable development suggests' (ibid., p. 773).

Ecology can also be seen as a comfortable label or even a tool used in dishonest marketing. Vinícius Brei and Steffen Böhm (2009) cite an example of a marketing campaign that uses the slogans of ecology and sustainable growth to attract clients. A colossal growth in the amount of bottled water sold in recent years results in many phenomena unfavourable to the natural environment such as the drying up of places from which the water is drawn. The companies that sell water, however, try to convince consumers that by buying bottled water they contribute to the protection of the environment. Some campaigns are based on authentic actions. For example, Danone joined the campaign that aims at providing water in the parts of Africa that struggle with drought. Aiming to produce positive ecological associations with a product is not entirely justified, however. The associations are only meant to encourage clients – those who cherish 'green' values, in this case – to buy the product. There is no real ethics behind the façade.

One of the most constructive manifestations of ecological awareness in business is the phenomenon of ecopreneurship. It is an entrepreneurial activity that combines ecological and business purposes and where the entrepreneur's value system is oriented towards ecology. Michael Schaper (2005) characterizes the green entrepreneur as a person approaching ecological questions as an opportunity, a field for innovative action for both the company and its environment:

> The adoption of environmentally responsible business practices can conceivable open up an additional range of opportunities for entrepreneurs. The move to a sustainable business framework provides numerous niches which enterprising individuals and firms can successfully identify and service. These include the development of new products and services; improving the efficiency of existing firms; new methods of marketing; reconfiguring existing business models and practices; and so forth. (Schaper, 2005, p. 6)

Ecopreneurship is not only another form of entrepreneurship, a space for creative people and organizations, but it may also be the avant-garde of business, the beginning of a future, sustainable management. The phenomenon of ecopreneurship is new, though entrepreneurs caring for the environment have, of course, existed before. The novelty consists in the idea of a simultaneous accomplishment of business and ecological aims that appeared in management theory and practice at the end of the last century. Sharper observes that such a combination of purposes can be realized in various types of activity, from unselfish social entrepreneurial companies to firms that in the first place offer a livelihood for the entrepreneur and the employees. A combination of these purposes can also become the reason for setting up a business in the first place. Sarah Dixon and Anne Clifford (2007) demonstrate how an ecological system of values can be the driving force of entrepreneurship. For some people the possibility of fulfilling green goals becomes the motivation to become involved in business, an inspiration to create innovation. To an outside observer their actions may look like balancing between not always coherent aims. But according to ecopreneurs this is the gist of their activity and the source of energy to develop their enterprises. Dixon and Clifford stress the fact that ecopreneurs are simultaneously idealists and businesspeople, as well as, sometimes, visionaries – sustainable business starts in new innovative eco-companies.

One of the most famous examples of ecopreneurship, as well as a pioneer in this field, is The Body Shop, a company set up towards the end of the 1970s by Anita Roddick,[73] a British human rights activist and entrepreneur. The enterprise was to support her and her family as well as realize her social and ecological vision. From the beginning the company promoted recycling, natural ingredients and fair relations with clients. When it later expanded, care was taken to preserve good relation with providers, based on fair trade principles. The company's slogan led: trade not aid. It meant that the company's providers, small-scale Indian or African entrepreneurs, were paid for their goods which enabled them to survive and develop their businesses. For Anita Roddick it was particularly important that her company's actions should not only be harmless to natural environment but also supportive of nature. The consumers were also treated respectfully. The firm launched marketing campaigns that were designed to encourage people and not to beguile them. Roddick was critical of those cosmetics manufacturers who preyed on women's dreams and lied to their clients. Body Shop offered low prices, attractive scents and colours, but without provoking a sense of guilt or promoting impossible figures of beauty. A symbol of Body Shop's marketing approach was the doll Ruby, who was cute and Rubenesque, an embodiment of the joy of life, as opposed to the sad, anorexic models advertising the products of the majority of corporations.[74] Anita Roddick, with her unique entrepreneurial style, anticipated the fashion for ecology and is still celebrated as a visionary by many today (Isaak, 2007).

14. Cosmogony

14.1 COSMOGONIC ARCHETYPES

Mircea Eliade ([1932] 1961) depicts myths as stories about the beginning of history set in the times before the beginning of ordinary, secular time. Sacred time (*sacrum*) is different from secular, linear time (*profanum*). Myths continuously recreate the sacred time as they summon it and let it be experienced by next generations. This time does not proceed from the past towards the future but lets the reader or listener experience it in many directions and in many ways. Such an experience of time enables us to recreate the primal time, the moment of the creation of everything:

> The myth continually reactualizes the Great Time and in so doing raises the listener to a superhuman and suprahistorical plane; which among other things, enables him to approach a Reality that is inaccessible at the level of profane, individual existence. (Eliade, [1932] 1961, p. 59)

Myths about the beginning of the universe, cosmogonic myths, explain the creation of the world with the help of an archetypical language. Such stories are found in many mythologies, including Greek, Babylonian and Vedic. Usually cosmogonies present the events leading to the creation of the universe, as well as including its characteristics and a description of the first beings. Deities are usually treated as part of the cosmos that comes into being; they interact with it from the very beginning. The creation of the world is presented as a creative act of a deity or deities or as a long-term process of cooperation between various beings. Often the myth contains the genealogy of the first deities, with the process of creation of our familiar world inscribed into it. Humans usually appear at an advanced level of the creation process, sometimes as a crowning of the work, sometimes as a side effect or just another link in the chain of creation.

One of the most famous depictions of cosmogony in our culture is Hesiod's *Theogony* (2008). It is a story of how the gods appeared and took over control over the world that was coming into being. According to Hesiod, in the beginning there was Chaos, an emptiness that was the primeval state. Then appeared Gaia, the Mother Earth; and Eros, an embodiment of the attraction between beings, be they gods or, later, people. The primeval Eros is not equivalent to the much later deity of sensual love, depicted as a divine being of the masculine gender, often as the son of Aphrodite, the goddess of love. The primeval Eros is androgynous, she/he is the most beautiful of all deities, attracting all living beings, but having neither partner nor progeny of her/his own. Chaos gave rise to Erebos, a personification of shadow and darkness, and Nyx, Night. From Night were born Aether, or atmosphere, and Hemera, Day. Earth gave birth to Uranos and started birthing mountains (Ourea) and sea (Pontus) as well as the 12 Titans from her relationship with Uranos; among them were Kronos[75] and Rea who later became the parents of the Olympian gods, Cyclops, and Hekatonkheires. In the beginning Uranos was afraid of his monstrous offspring and hid them in the darkness. Gaia stood up for her children and encouraged them to take vengeance. Kronos resorted to deception and took revenge by castrating his father. From his blood were born new deities, including the Furies and Aphrodite, the goddess of love. In the meantime gods and Titans entered various relationships and begot new supernatural beings. Kronos gained control over the universe and from his relationship with Rea were born the Olympians, whom the father swallowed immediately after they were born, afraid of the same fate that befell his father. Rea finally rebelled and, when she gave birth to Zeus, she gave her husband a stone wrapped in nappies instead of the newborn baby. Zeus was secretly brought up in Crete. Some years later, following the advice of Gaia, Zeus made Kronos vomit all of his children. Zeus and all his siblings declared war on the Titans and managed to take over control of the world. And so, according to Hesiod, the creation of the world is accompanied by struggle and love, attraction and repulsion, as well as treason, deceit and lie.

Gaia's motherly love is not a one-sided story of happy devotion. The objects of her love are also the monsters she gave birth to, and she seems to have little mercy for her husband and her son. She also helps save her grandchildren swallowed by her son who will later become overturned by his offspring and lose his power to them. But later, when Zeus fights the Titans and pushes them down into the pits of Tartar, he loses Gaia's support. The primeval mother cares for all her children equally, regardless of their deeds and of the circumstances, though sometimes her love manifests itself as cruelty. In Hesiod's cosmogony there are no unambiguous deeds or characters. There are no gods who are only good or only evil, and all creation that is born out of their relationships is similar to them, inseparably woven into a history of love, struggle and pain.

The cosmogonic duel has also its place in organization theory. Jerzy Kociatkiewicz (2008) uses this metaphor to describe the relation between users and computer technology in organizations. The metaphor shows an important aspect of the interactions between human and technical

Figure 14.1   Cosmogony
(photo: Monika Kostera)

actants[76] from the point of view of organizations: their transforming potential. It also signals a change that has taken place in many organizations in recent years. Some decades ago computers were an uncanny and dangerous novelty, and today they are a taken-for-granted constant presence in everyday reality. The encounter of social and technical actants gave birth to a new type of organizational actant: a hybrid, a human being who uses technology to complete their everyday tasks. From the organizational viewpoint this is a qualitatively different character: a person without a computer does not behave like a person cooperating with a computer; similarly, a computer without a human being is something else than a computer that is in contact with a person and becomes an element of a physical structure (see Latour, 1987). It is a mistake to reify the computer in this relationship.

The metaphor of the cosmogonic duel enables us to see how information technology (IT) in organizations works and acts differently from 'ordinary' inanimate objects. Kociatkiewicz (2008) juxtaposed narrations on human actors' cooperation with computers that he gathered in the course of his field studies with the story of Zeus's struggle with Typhon during the war of the Titans. The field stories and the myths have similar phases. To start with, the human protagonist loses. Then they receive help from the outside, and eventually triumph over the technical actant. All the stories have in common their specific turning point where they depict the nature of the victory, which is a transformation, transporting the context to a different, higher level. Thanks to the struggle the protagonist gains authority, the power to do things that before were beyond their reach. This refers particularly to the creation of new things and creatures – as well as new artefacts that could not have been produced without the help of a computer. The prestige of computer users is growing, and also their users gain a new, higher status. These stories are not ordinary heroic adventures, tales of quest and success. The element of failure in them is almost as important as that of success. The aim of the struggle is not an ordinary victory but a familiarization of the Unknown, an overcoming of the fear of the unfamiliar. Only then can the protagonist, the computer user, benefit from the new possibilities of cooperating with the machine, which can prove beneficial for the entire organization.

In this chapter I first discuss the founding myth and its role in organization, in particular its role in organizational culture. Then I show how cosmogonic archetypes can be used to describe everyday instances of creativity in organizations and how they can provide inspiration to raise the organization to a higher, transformation level.

14.2 THE FOUNDING MYTH

Gabriel Tarde ([1903] 1962) believes that innovations are the necessary prerequisite for cultural and social changes. Thanks to innovations, societies gain the ability to adjust to the changing environmental conditions. He has in mind all types of novelties and changes, big and small, that influence people's behaviour. Inventions are rare and valuable products of human ingenuity. Apart from a flash of invention they demand human interaction; perhaps it is even true that the more mature the human relations, the higher the probability of innovation. Invention demands genius, social stability, a certain degree of liberty and well-being, and education (Tarde, 1902). An inventor is a kind of 'deviant', who breaks social habits and is unwilling to accept at face value the truths that others consider obvious. An inventor is not a well-socialized person, their invention is often preceded by moving away from their family and society. Among creators there are also entrepreneurs and other risk-takers whose actions cannot be explained by the urge for financial success. Since novelties are rare, societies single them out and promote them through imitation. Tarde ([1903] 1962) observes that the relation of an invention to an imitation is similar to the relation of a mountain to a river: inventions occur occasionally and are visible, and important points in the history of humankind; whereas the majority of cultural processes takes on the shape of flows that diffuse novelties. Not all inventions are diffused; actually, the majority are forgotten. The reason may be that they are either too complicated or too simple for a given culture. Sometimes the attitudes and preferences of key actors also play an important part in the process, for example the preference to promote innovations created by the higher social classes or other groups that enjoy social prestige. Both invention and imitation are linked to the values and beliefs of societies, and both are to a certain extent based on communication. All social changes begin with changes in beliefs and convictions.

Organizations are often also the products of invention; someone conceives of them in their imagination, creates them and brings them to life. Edgar Schein (1991) considers the role of the founder for the organizational culture. Religious movements and organizations are founded by prophets or charismatic spiritual leaders; political organizations are formed by visionaries and activists; and companies are created by entrepreneurs. The latter are Schein's main interest. He distinguishes several basic stages of a company's formation. In the beginning there is the founder and their idea for a new company. Then the founder convinces other people about the idea and together they invest their time, money and energy in its realization. The next stage is the actualization of the idea in structures, patents, physical space, and so on. Finally, other people become involved in the firm's activities, as employees or partners. In this stage the group starts sharing their experiences and the organization's culture is being created. One of the most important roles of culture is the offering of meaning to the lives of the people involved in the organization, as well as providing a defence against the fear of uncertainty. The foundations of culture are a set of assumptions, often unconscious, about what the organization and the environment are and what the participants are like. The shape of these assumptions is influenced by the person of the founder and the original idea that is the basis for the organization. The influence is to a large extent unconscious and not fully intentional – the founder comes from a particular background, has certain attitudes and views the world in a definite way. All these factors influence the way the original idea is put into practice and the shape the organization's culture is going to take in the beginning. As the company grows and develops the founder's influence is increasingly modified by the actions and attitudes of other people. It remains there as part of the organization's cultural foundation in the shape of several basic assumptions. The processes of hiring new employees are a continuation of the firm's culture creation and can bring the company closer to the founding idea or take it further away. And this leads us to the question of where employees come from, or how entrepreneurs recruit their first cooperators.

Bartosz Sławecki (2010) presents the results of his research on small businesses in the Poznań region in Western Poland. He is particularly interested in the practices of hiring employees by the founders. It turned out that founders rarely use employment agencies or other formal channels to find recruits. Instead, they prefer to employ people they know, preferably family members. This practice makes it possible for them actively to influence the culture of their companies. Small business founders consider their closest family to be the guarantee of the efficiency of employment processes. Family members are involved in the firm's fate and willing to show consideration for the founder's ideas for the company's development. The small business owners think in terms of the family's and the company's continuity and identity. Employing a close family member means, to them, the company's survival. Close family members enter organizational structures according to different principles than other employees. This practice changes the dynamics of micro companies' structure and culture, opening them to conflicts and inequality. This does not apply to employment of distant relatives; the founder has fewer bonds and regards them as pretty much the same as any other employee. The division line lies, then, between close family and 'the others'. Family becomes for the owner not only an element of the company's identity but also a source of capital, which shapes the dynamics of investment management. One way of avoiding conflicts while not losing this core identity is to rely solely on close family members. This is seen by founders not as nepotism but an investment in human resources. They believe that this makes the organization's culture more stable and brings inimitable value to the company.

But this is not all. Sławecki also demonstrates how double relations between the founder and an employed close family member result in the adoption of a double set of cultural norms. This feature is a source of tension in the organization's culture and can be a cause of conflict but it may also strengthen the normative control in organization. If the company needs more employees, family is also helpful in recommending candidates to work. Sometimes it brings in some diversity, if the family has access to social milieus different than those known to the entrepreneur. The family's role consists not only in recommending people but also in assessing the candidate's qualifications. The family plays a role similar to professional recruitment agencies. All this is regulated only by the ethics of the people involved, such as moral imperatives that forbid one to do harm to one's family members. The values and norms almost always stretch to the organization, seen as a close family member in its own right.

Edgar Schein (1991) narrates three interesting stories of organizations where the founder's influence on the company's cultural system in discernible over a longer period of time. The first is the story of a company active in the food business, founded by an immigrant who came from a family of small shopkeepers. He knew, then, how to run a shop but dreamed about building a large chain of shops, a largish organization. He succeeded in realizing his dream and became one of the most important entrepreneurs in his region. However, he looked after his organization as if it was his family shop, making sure that clients never felt cheated or unhappy with their purchase. He wanted to provide clients with high-quality products; he made sure that the shop interiors were clean and nice, and he always replaced the product with a better one when a client complained about their purchase. He believed that the manager should be available to clients, just like the owner in a small shop. These private, small shop rules became the basis of the company's policy, even when it became a large retail chain. Even after the founder's death, after a period of crisis resulting from the absence of the founder and of management, his principles survived in the organization's culture and continue to be its trademark today.

The second example comes from a company manufacturing advanced technology. Today the firm is big, and is still managed by its founder. The entrepreneur wanted to exert a strong influence on the company from the very beginning, he knew exactly what he wanted his company to be and parted ways with partners who did not share his business ideas. The most important among his convictions was his faith in teams and communication. All important decisions, all ideas, and even everyday procedures, were discussed in groups and implemented as a result of collective actions. Many of his other habits and rules were connected with his education. As an engineer, he treated all issues as problems that needed to be defined and solved, and the solutions he took into consideration were usually technical or, at least, very practical. In his opinion, one of these solutions was hierarchy – a practical arrangement that ensured effectiveness but nothing more, certainly not a revealed truth guaranteeing the high quality of the decisions made by people on the top of the hierarchy. Therefore, in practice, he combined hierarchy with teamwork and did not perceive the two solutions as contradictory. He also employed people whose thinking was similar to his own and so a pragmatic team culture permeated all the company's activities.

The last example provided by Schein is a chain of financial services providers founded by a salesman. The firm focused on selling its services and the results were measured and compared. The founder did not interfere with any of the spheres of the company's activities. Therefore the company, as it grew, developed in its subsidiaries and branches various norms and values that often had nothing to do with one another and with the person of the founder. Paradoxically, this can be seen as a perfect reflection of the founder's values and beliefs. Schein summarizes his examples with the conclusion that culture is created in the course of a long-term process of learning that initially inspires it or gives it direction.

These examples show that small and medium-sized companies are culturally influenced by the owner. There also exist large organizations where the figure of the founder constantly exerts a considerable influence on the company. A famous example of such a company is IKEA. Miriam Salzer-Mörling (1998) recalls how many times during her ethnographic study carried out in IKEA she had heard the story of the company's beginnings. Some of her interviewees were visibly much too young to remember such a distant past but kept telling her these stories anyway. Some employees spontaneously approached the researcher and wanted to share the story. Their narratives would always begin with an empty space, a barren landscape and a poor, cold part of the world. Then Ingvar Kamprad, a boy from a family of humble farmers, appears on the scene: he is ambitious and hard-working and is not afraid of dreaming of impossible things or treading where no one has trod before. He builds his company from scratch: at first, it is tiny, then it grows, and finally it turns into a global giant. The organization is a reflection of his dreams, continues to be innovative and, as opposed to other giants, never loses its soul. From the very beginning, the young entrepreneur had to face numerous obstacles and combat villains, and he managed to win thanks to his cunning and hard work. In the beginning IKEA was boycotted by large Swedish furniture manufacturers who felt threatened by its low prices. The story of IKEA is a narrative about how David defeated several Goliaths. For example, Ingvar Kamprad was not allowed to participate in furniture fairs and exhibitions. Once, he managed to smuggled himself into an important furniture fair hidden in a rolled-up carpet. No matter how hard the opposition of big competitors, however, IKEA furniture appealed to clients and it sold very well. IKEA grew recognized and slowly also began to slowly gain the competitors' acceptance and reluctant respect. People abroad also liked the modest, fresh and economic products that the company offered. The firm entered foreign markets and opened its first international subsidiaries. All the time the founder took great care that the IKEA spirit did not die, and he personally makes sure that IKEA stays IKEA all over the world, without being imperialistic or chauvinistic, but by staying true to the dream. For many of the employees who insisted on telling this story of the organization's foundation, it is an expression of their collective consciousness, and it helps to make sense of reality. In a mythical way it explains how the company works, and also gives hope. Salzer Mörling

believes that the story is the company's Genesis, a story about the creation
of the IKEA world.

14.3   CREATIVITY AND ORGANIZATION

In the 1950s Alex Faickney Osborn published a book ([1953] 1963) in
which he characterized a creative thinking technique called brainstorming, a technique that enables innovation on an everyday basis. Usually,
groups have a negative influence on the creative thinking of individual
members. Osborne's technique makes it possible to raise the creativity
level by eliminating the mechanisms that typically limit innovativeness,
such as conformism or the fear of making a mistake in front of others.
Moreover, brainstorming makes the group more coherent, better integrated and more cooperative. The author defines brainstorming as a
method by which the group tries to find a solution to a given problem by
making a list of all possible solutions proposed by all the members of the
group. Brainstorming differs from an ordinary meeting or council in the
set of rules that the participants have to follow. First of all, the participants should refrain from assessing the ideas as they are being formulated.
No ideas should be rejected at this stage, even the 'impossible' ones. The
participants should propose as many ideas as possible and not focus on
the quality of their ideas. At the next stage they should inspire one another
and propose improvements and modifications to the ideas that have been
proposed. Only in the final phase of the session are the best ideas chosen
and their usefulness assessed. It can also be advisable to combine some of
the proposed ideas to produce synergetic effects. Even if brainstorming
does not enhance the innovativeness of creative individuals, it remains
a good way of introducing creativity into everyday organizational life.
A regular use of brainstorming as a method of management is the basis
for a set of contemporary ideas for innovative organizations, including
aesthetic management.

According to Pierre Guillet de Monthoux ([1993] 2004) management
can be seen as a kind of art. All human actions have an aesthetic dimension and this is also true of organization, and its specific form that is
business organization. This does not mean that aesthetic criteria always
should replace financial criteria, but that they are at least as important.
In the writings of Adam Smith one can find the awareness of the importance of the aesthetic perspective for good management. Nowadays, as so
many have come to believe in the significance of creativity and innovation,
organizations are all the more in need of a language in which they would
be able to communicate such ideas that have to do with these aspects with

the environment. Also leadership depends to a large extent on aesthetics. A charismatic leader can be seen as a person who skilfully manages the aesthetics of leadership. Aesthetic management consists in distancing oneself from everyday life and looking for new possibilities. The creative dimension of management can be supported through contact with art – managers can develop their creative potential by visiting galleries and museums. Guillet de Monthoux presents the mechanism of creative management, calling it *Schwung*. It is 'the pendulum movement between form and substance' (ibid., p. 20), between the ideal and the real. *Schwung* is a sensual impulse that appears in the space defined by nature, culture, body and soul, what I would call a kind of sensual inspiration. In contemporary management it functions as a mechanism for permanent innovativeness that can be used to create value, unforgettable experiences and positive associations. The encounter between practising artists and managers produces creative energy that organizations need. It also brings about genuine productivity, which encompasses both the material and the spiritual dimensions. Management can particularly profit from the encounters and creation can stop being only subjective. In a similar vein Wendelin Küpers (2002) argues that creation and creative attitudes do not have to be treated as individual activities. They can be considered on the plane of intersubjectivity and relationships, as a kind of a collective experience that can have particularly important role, as it is potentially transformatory.

Business seen as having a creative side is not what the mainstream culture would lead us to believe it is. Robert Solomon (2004) argues for adding to the idea of business the dimensions of aesthetics and morality. He believes that in the process of re-evaluation of management one should look for inspiration in Aristotle's philosophy, in which philosophy issues that have to with economy are inextricably interwoven with ethical issues. The connection between them was lost in the twentieth century, and this rupture has had numerous negative effects. With the help of Aristotle's writings, the contemporary reader can learn how to think in terms of big communities, *Polis*. Today these may very well include work organizations, regions or countries. Organizational goals and plans could with advantage be considered in the context not just of 'markets' or even 'environments', but of such broader communities. The division into private and social interests is illegitimate and harmful. Private and public interests always overlap, when viewed from the perspective of ethics. The virtue and dignity of an individual are related to the community. Therefore, a good community supports and develops the virtues and dignity of its members. Good work brings not only material profit but also happiness: moral and aesthetic. A company that is perceived as a community does not need constructs external to the human psyche to ensure participation, trust and motivation, because communities are the human being's natural environment. Manipulation is a characteristic of organizations that cannot be communities because of their single-mindedness and artificial concentration on one kind of goals only, that is, usually financial ones. Such manipulative 'motivation' breeds inauthenticity and stifles subtle feelings.

An example of an organization founded as a creative combination of art and business and is the Why Do You Shop? project (Venkatesh, 2000). The aim of the project is to collect knowledge related to shopping but it is also a business enterprise in its own right, involving sales made directly and through the Internet. The founder, Judith Wilske, is a graduate of studies in both theatre and economics. For her, the project came into being as a result of the encounter of the two important spheres of her life, but when they did meet they did so in the form of a question more than an answer. That is why the project's name took the grammatical structure of a question. Judith Wilske explains that her project also immediately took the shape of a product she wanted to sell. WDYS started as a portable boutique set up in a stylish camping trailer. The co-workers, and the entrepreneur herself, sell the firm's products: mugs, stickers and other gadgets as well as books, including children's books. They draw the buyers into a conversation about shopping, they ask questions about brands and products. This is much more than marketing, it is a kind of ethnography as well as a theatrical performance. For the entrepreneur, the act of buying is quite theatrical, it is a performance that can be consciously dramatized. The portable boutique's localization and appearance also combine art with marketing – the trailer is both an installation of high artistic quality and an object that attracts and interests clients. WDYS travels all over Europe and it is the founder's ambitions to reach other continents, and as many people as possible. Creativity is one of the project's central characteristics; this does not only refer to the founder's creative ideas transmitted to other people to be realized, but also, as she says, to the collective creativity of all the people involved. Judith Wilske does not separate the business and the artistic dimensions; she says that she does not want to decide whether her project is more art or enterprise. It is an art firm and can only exist as a combination of the two dimensions. The project has won the appreciation of both the art world and the world of science, and the Why Do You Shop? logo is one of the most readily recognizable brands in Germany (Venkatesh, 2000).

15. Soteriology

15.1 THE ARCHETYPES OF DEATH AND TRANSFORMATION

Soteriology is a branch of religious studies that examines different religions and systems of beliefs about salvation and the liberation from the limitations of earthly life, often connected with death, often understood as a boundary or an ultimate test. Soteriological archetypes include the ideas connected with death and immortality, afterlife and the continuity of identity. Death regarded as a soteriological archetype is the moment of passing from one stage to another. It can be an ultimate test or the last gateway behind which the individual is rewarded or punished for their earthly life; it can also mark a change of course, the beginning of a new cycle, such as the moment of passing from one incarnation to another. A frequent motif is the journey into the underground domain of the dead that the soul undertakes after the death of the body. Apart from the souls of the dead, this kingdom is often inhabited by deities and other supernatural creatures. In some beliefs, the souls can be rewarded or punished after death, depending on whether the deceased person led a sinful or a virtuous life. The souls either go to the kingdom of eternal bliss (paradise, heaven) or are condemned (hell). In other mythologies, such as the Greek, there is only one common spiritual space for all the dead. Death is not always a threshold but it is always an archetype of transformation. It can mean the end for the individual. Or it can mean the loss of identity – Hades is inhabited by the shadows of past people, with no memory or identity. It can, alternatively, be the moment of the adoption of a new identity, as in religions that believe in reincarnation. There are also beliefs in which a person's identity stays intact after death, but reaches a higher level; the new identity is broader, more abundantly filled with consciousness. Immortality is usually the property of several types of beings, metaphysical and superhuman, divine or demonic. Often, human souls can also experience immortality, with a more or less limited possibility of contacting metaphysical beings after death.

Carl Gustav Jung ([1959] 1990) speaks about the archetype of rebirth as one of the eternal human archetypes. He focuses on the role of

Figure 15.1   Soteriology
(photo: Monika Kostera)

transformation and participation that interplay in different ways at the different stages of the processes of rebirth and renewal. Rebirth can but does not have to bring about a change in the experiencing subject itself, but it is always a radical passage between different states of experience. Rebirth can trigger a broadening of the Self but it can also impoverish it, depending on the way in which the human being accepts the transformation and whether they make an attempt at using it to gain wisdom.

A good example from contemporary culture that uses soteriological archetypes is Ingmar Bergman's *The Seventh Seal* (1957). The film is set in the Middle Ages. A knight, Antonius Block, returns from the Crusades in the Holy Land to find his native Sweden ravaged by the plague. On his way the protagonist encounters Death, in the shape of a hooded man, who had come to take him. Block challenges Death to a duel – a chess match. If he wins, Death promises to spare him. As long as the game continues, the protagonist gains time. Antonius Block feels that he does not stand a chance in this game, but he seizes the time he gains thanks to the chess match. He feels he does not want to go just yet and justifies his reluctance by his desire to do a noble deed before he dies. In his heart of hearts, he longs to hear the voice of God or, if that is impossible, then at least the voice of the devil whom he could then ask about God. But God remains silent, and so does the devil. Block has trouble keeping his faith in face of this silence; during confession he confides in the priest that he is not sure if he believes in God and whether life has any meaning at all. He tells the priest that he is playing chess with Death and discloses his strategy. Suddenly he realizes that the confessor is not a priest but Death himself. This, he knows only too well, is the end of any chances of winning he might have had. Block continues the game nonetheless, day after day, move after move. In the meantime, he befriends a troupe of travelling actors and in particular a young couple, Mia and Jof, and their newborn son. The actors intend to travel to places particularly stricken by the plague and Block tries to dissuade them from going there. He is worried and decides to invite them to his castle instead, where they can find shelter from the plague. But Death has already been active. It turns out that one of the actors has died. The epidemic is drawing nearer and nearer to the protagonists. It seems that the fate of the knight's young friends is sealed. But Block has his moment of opportunity to do a good deed. While thinking about the next move, he suddenly pushes the chessboard. This equals loss, but it attracts Death's attention and lets Mia and Jof escape. Death checkmates Block and the film ends. But the last scenes present something extraordinary – Jof's vision – a *danse macabre*, the dance of death, featuring the knight, his wife and all his guests present in the castle.

The title of the film refers to the *Book of Revelation*. After the seventh seal has been broken, heaven becomes silent. Block desires to hear God's voice but God remains silent. Only Death answers his calls. But the protagonist's death does not end the story. The ending shows a symbolic transformation. The knight's good deed makes it possible for the young actors to flee, just like the Holy Family fled to Egypt. The viewer has no certainty as to the outcome, no clear endings are given, but an openness remains, everything is possible. Death itself is about transformation. The *danse macabre* is one of the few very powerful medieval symbols of equality. Death conquers everyone, and it makes all people equal.

Soteriological archetypes can only be used metaphorically with regard to organizations, as they have no soul or awareness. Because of this, I focus on some of the key archetypical motifs of this type without referring to larger soteriological or eschatological questions with which they are often linked by religions and mythologies. They are instead presented as a metaphorical frame for reflection on some of the important characteristics of contemporary work organizations.

Burkard Sievers (1994) argues that the myth of the immortality of modern-day organizations is deeply ingrained in our cultures. This issue is not tackled either by theories or by practical discourse, but all mainstream organizational practices seem to be based on the assumption that immortality is available to organizations and, through them, to humans taking part in them. Usually, these assumptions stay in the sphere of fantasy as they are never the object of conscious reflection. So, such organizational immortality is not a full presence but rather an absence; the absence of death that from mainstream organizational discourses. The system's survival becomes the ambition of the people who construct it, and it symbolizes their personal survival and becomes a sort of collective symbolic incarnation. The participants symbolically merge to create one collective super-person to whom they entrust their immortality. This attempt at joint embodiment is based on the illusion that the organization will last forever, and the lack of reflection over this belief may lead to fanaticism. The example of the collective megalomania called the Third Reich is a case in point. This kind of immortality can only be a substitute for the immortality of the soul, and not always a harmless one. Instead of the uncertainty connected with human life and death, or in order to avoid thinking of it, many people choose the illusory certainty granted by organizations that we create on this side of the Great Unknown. This is reflected in the ideological power connected with the discourse about the organization's survival. It is usually placed above individual persons, turning the organization into a deity that everyone has to serve and be subordinated to. Instead of searching for spiritual and psychological truths and constructively working on the development of our organizations, people often sacrifice their individuality and creativity for this kind of illusory collective immortality. Sievers points out that a significant cultural effort is made to support this illusion. The companies' founders, the entrepreneurs, try to immortalize themselves through their firms, by their efforts, creativity and also by an enforcement of structures. Managers and employees do this as well, believing that such management tools as strategy or brand will grant them a kind of immortality. Sievers compares contemporary organizations to ancient Greek gods who were granted immortality by their worshippers who wished to be immortal themselves. They themselves could not reach for it as the Greek deities' immortality precluded the participation of ordinary people. Organizations, like Olympians, only take but do not give blessings in exchange.

Is a genuine organizational salvation possible at all? Wiktor Stoczkowski (2009) uses the term 'secular soteriology' to describe the diversity ideal cherished by the United Nations Educational, Scientific and Cultural Organization (UNESCO). One of the organization's aims is contributing to world peace. One method of attaining this purpose is by the promotion of the idea of peace in people's minds. Typical tools include showing people the importance of diversity as well as teaching them about different cultures and habits. The organization defines its purposes and leads the way to a utopian future of an ideal union, the end of time and the solving of all human problems, a happy ending of all conflicts and the flourishing of humanistic values. According to Stoczkowski, this metaphysical and soteriological vision lies behind the organization's programme and influences the way the organization formulates its more tangible purposes; among other things, it influences the way UNESCO constructs its educational curricula that are the means to the organization's aims. So even if organizations do not save us, some of them may be means through which we try to save others.

15.2 DEATH IN ORGANIZATION, DEATH OF ORGANIZATION

The book *Fear of the Unknown* by Arthur Berger and Joyce Berger (1995) is dedicated to death and dying. The authors consider death and how it influences human life. They are mainly interested in death understood as a threshold, a passage into the unknown. Our beliefs about afterlife are reflected in the way we perceive ourselves and the people who surround us. The reverse is also true: a reflection on the deeper layers of human nature, a look inwards, beyond our rationalistic everyday life that the majority of our contemporary discourses is limited to, enables to see death in a different dimension. It is not only the end of our path in the world of natural phenomena but also an unknown point in the path of the soul. Berger and Berger reflect upon whether a person keeps their identity, knowledge and memory after death, whether they are aware of having passed on, through death, to a different dimension of life. If the answer is in the affirmative, can the people close to the deceased person, as well as other people such as scientists, experience it too? The authors, a tanatologist and a lawyer who specializes in bioethics, quote numerous stories, beliefs and recorded experiences related to these questions. There are many stories, ideas and incidents documented by doctors which demonstrate that death is a moment of passing into another state, into something unknown. There are also good arguments that support the opposite statement; that is, that death is the ultimate ending of individual existence.

Still, contemporary rational and popular discourses rarely reflect on these two positions and the arguments in their favour, and their consequences for our way of life and our understanding of the meaning of life. Religious discourses are also reluctant to investigate these questions in more depth and prefer instead to offer dogmas, sets of assumptions that are considered indisputable and non-verifiable, and adopt a tone of certainty, much like the rationalists. In fact, however, we do not know the truth. It is impossible to know for certain whether the afterlife is a fact or an illusion, or what it is like if it exists, but there are not many who are willing to discuss or ponder upon it at any length. The book encourages us to think and talk about death. If not, we are doomed to live a lie: with death looming constantly somewhere in a psychic blind spot, outside the field of vision, but pretending that we are physically immortal. Among many different possibilities, this is certainly not true. It is also unconstructive, as it helps people neither to live nor to die.

In the world of organizations, death is also usually passed over or at least put out of focus. This is surprising, since questions like 'What happens to an organization when an important leader dies?' or 'What happens to the people when an organization dies?' are quite important for the theory as well as for the practice of organizing and management. Paula Hyde and Alan Thomas (2003) reflect on the first of the two questions. In their article based on empirical studies of organizations that had lost their leaders, the authors talk about employees' reactions and the influence of the loss on the functioning of the organizations. An emotional response to the leader's death is mourning. It is often accompanied by anxiety and a sense of uncertainty, because important leaders have a major influence on group integration and the definition of group borders. Sometimes, the reactions include aggression and collective depression, especially if the employees had been dependent on their leader and not autonomous enough. Depending on the relationship between employees and the manager before the latter's death, the dominant emotion may either be the fear of the future or the lack of a sense of threat. People's reactions to the successor also differ. It is often hard to avoid comparing two people, especially in cases of the death of an important figure. People tend to be more severe in their assessment of the successor of a dead leader than in the case of an ordinary succession (not linked with the leader's death). The comparisons may or may not be favourable to the new manager. It is important to be aware of this as a natural process and not expect people to be fair or to blame them for whatever the outcome of such comparisons may be.

Contemporary organizations do not have any good strategies of dealing with emotions. Often bureaucracy and simple administrative work replace mourning and grief. Sometimes further strategies may be adopted, such as employees withdrawing from contact with the environment, including the clients. The death of a dominating leader leaves the employees full of fear, projections and the readiness to look for someone to blame. Sometimes people who mourn the deceased manager are afraid of being harassed by his or her opponents. In such organizations there may develop a paranoid mood, where people relieve the tension created by their fears by looking for scapegoats. A less dominating leader may leave conflicting feelings: a sense of loss and an openness to new possibilities. All this usually overlaps with collective mourning and it may discourage the team to look for constructive solutions. Nonetheless, a leader's death often gives rise to important organizational changes, including promotions and demotions, for which the team might be better or worse prepared. If the leader had been supporting a feeling of his or her omnipotence among the employees, then an adjustment to reality after the leader's death may prove extremely difficult. Hyde and Thomas conclude that different leadership styles demand different strategies for coping with the leader's death. The new leader has to bear all this in mind, if they want to facilitate the group's functioning after the loss, and if they want to minimize negative reactions to the succession. The death of an important manager changes the organization and it is important to be aware of this fact.

What happens when an entire organization dies? Henry Mintzberg (1984) talks about the death of an organization as one of the natural stages of its life cycle. Death occurs when an organization cannot or is not allowed to change together with its environment. In some cases it is necessary to accelerate an organization's death so that resources that can be successfully reutilized are not wasted. The participants' and stakeholders' interests are more important than the survival of an organization. Its death is not a happy occurrence; rather, when it happens it is a sad necessity, albeit a natural one. There are courses of events that are much more unfavourable and destructive for a firm and the people, such as the valuing of an organization's survival higher than of the well-being of the people involved. For example, Henry Ford extended autocratic control over his company in a way precluding attempts at adapting to the changing conditions or allowing managers and employees a more substantial input. It is not uncommon for autocratic management to lead to an organization's deterioration and downfall. Death may be preferable to the parasitical existence of an organization incapable of being reformed, toxic and unwilling to cooperate.

Sometimes the death of an organization may be experienced by people just like the loss of somebody close. In particular, this is what it may feel like for a founder losing their company. Dean Shepherd (2003) discusses the entrepreneur's mourning after the loss of their firm. According to Shepherd, a discussion about how to deal with the grief resulting from the failure of a firm is lacking in the management discourse. The recovery from such a loss is important for the entrepreneur if he or she is to learn from the experience. It is important both for owner-managers and for the society as a whole. Effective recovery from grief makes it possible for firms to become better than the ones that failed. The knowledge of owners then stays in the system. Learning by mistakes in management and entrepreneurship is valuable – success conserves behaviour and attitudes, not always constructive ones, whereas failure, if it is used as a lesson, triggers creativity and looking for new ways of operating. For this to become possible, an understanding of the relationship between the entrepreneur and his or her company is indispensable. For the entrepreneur the firm is not just a thing or construct external to him or her, a tool intended to bring in profit, but also a creation endowed with an identity and aesthetic qualities, an object of feelings such as love and pride, and sometimes it is the result of the collective effort of a whole family. It is not surprising, then, that the collapse of a firm often results in feelings of loss and grief. One of the typical feelings accompanying a company's death is disbelief that the firm no longer exists and unwillingness to accept the fact. Such feelings may interfere with the process of learning as the entrepreneur continues to live in the past, does not try to gain insights from what happened, and feels grief, anger and fear. Entrepreneurs may want to give vent to these feelings or blame someone who can be treated as being actually or symbolically responsible for the company's collapse. The owner-manager may also feel guilt and anxiety, which makes it difficult to plunge anew into an active life. They may try to deal with all these feelings, which are typical for the process of mourning, in a way that is similar to coping with mourning a dead person. After the loss the entrepreneur may recover by focusing on everyday work.

Founding a new company may help in coping with grief. However, there is the danger of making the same mistakes that led to the former firm's collapse. Therefore it is very important for the owner-manager to attempt at a conscious process of learning by their mistakes relatively soon after the company's death. This enables the entrepreneur to cope with mourning while, at the same time, learning from mistakes. This can be quite a helpful and constructive way of dealing with feelings and even at some point the entrepreneur may even regard the failure as an excellent lesson. It is crucial for the owner-manager not to be ashamed of their grief and to be willing to talk about the feelings and experiences connected to the failure. This also shows how important it is for entrepreneurs to have somebody to talk to.

Failure of a firm can be a misfortune for the entrepreneur and something that needs much emotional and intellectual effort. But is it possible for an organization to die well? Mitchell Lee Marks and Ronny Vansteenkiste (2008) provide an example of a good organizational death made possible thanks to the human resources (HR) department which managed to lead the team through the organization's death in a compassionate and effective way. A company was taken over by a large corporation that decided to liquidate it, despite its good performance and good reputation. From the beginning of the takeover process the personnel division was active, always one step forward, trying to facilitate the employees' passage from active participation in the life of a well-functioning company to the necessity of watching its death. Their leaving of the company was inevitable and the HR division wanted to help people with the transition. The division worked differently than is usually the case during takeovers: it did not passively wait for instructions from management, nor did it take the side of the new owners. Instead, its staff saw their role as helping the employees. They did not expect miracles; they were aware that the corporation would not change its plans. They wanted to facilitate a kind of 'life after the organization's death' for the employees. First of all, they tried to offer support so that the employees' self-respect would not suffer. They were loyal and highly qualified people who had made the company's success possible in the past. The HR department tried to help the employees to cope with the awareness of the organization's death, and help them function well professionally after the company's liquidation. Simultaneously, care was taken not to let clients suffer; organizational life was to go on as normally as possible until the end. The HR department staff organized meetings to discuss all the problems openly, including the feelings accompanying the company's death. Together with the other employees, they worked out a strategy of passage for all who had to leave, and that included the HR department. Finally, they organized a symbolic mourning ceremony, where they could together express their sense of loss and grief. The HR department also managed to secure assurance from the new management of the corporation that all employees would receive good employment reference letters.

15.3 FORGETTING

The German psychologist Hermann Ebbinghaus (1885; quoted in Wozniak, 1999) was one of the pioneers who investigated memory and forgetting. He experimented on himself by memorizing lists of meaningless sets of three letters, combined according to the pattern consonant–vowel–consonant. For a year he systematically attempted to learn the lists and then he observed the process of forgetting. Later, he repeated the entire experiment. Each time he revised all the material until he remembered everything exactly. Ebbinghaus was the first scientist to observe the so-called learning curve. He observed that forgetting begins very quickly and consists in an increasingly high loss of information, but after some time

Organizations and archetypes

the rate of loss reaches an even level. He also observed that memorizing a given set takes more time, the more syllables the set contains. Dividing the learning process into several stages proved more effective than attempts at mastering the material in one go, and it prevented immediate forgetting. Forgetting can also be counteracted by revising the material after it has already been fully mastered. A preliminary, even cursory look at the list is helpful in this process. Ebbinghaus noted that the elements that are most easily forgotten are the ones added in the intermediary stages, not at the beginning or at the end. Material that makes no sense is more easily forgotten than meaningful material.

Forgetting is human; it is also a feature of our organizations. Chris Argyris and Donald Schön (1978), authors known perhaps the best for their fundamental work on learning in organizations, define forgetting as negative learning that provokes a loss of knowledge. They point out, however, that sometimes it is better to forget about something, as remembering may strengthen uncreative single-loop learning[77] and block the search for new approaches to problems. Such an understanding of learning and forgetting is characteristic of the majority of works on the subject in the field of organization theory, the difference between them being the focus either on the loss of knowledge or on the strategic role of forgetting (for a literature overview see e.g. Ciuk and Kostera 2010). The most serious problem identified by the discourse is that of accidental forgetting, happening beyond control of organizations. It is perceived as the waste of valuable resources – competence and knowledge. However knowledge is not always necessary or good: sometimes it is better not to know something, such as that something 'cannot be done'. Knowing would prevent someone from trying, and without this knowledge there is a chance that somebody may transgress the boundaries of the impossible. This is how novelties come into being, including the novelties in the world of organizations. Finally, forgetting is simply a natural part of the learning process; something is gained, and something is lost – what counts is the constant exchange of knowledge between an organization and its context.

But there is also a forgetting on a different level, one that affects the organization's identity. It causes discontinuity, the loss of something more than merely knowledge. Memory of the past makes up a crucial part of learning processes, according to Karl Weick (2001), as well as the organization's ability to interpret itself within a broader context and, in the long run, create a sustainable identity. Sometimes managers, by manipulating the organization's culture, deliberately try to cause memory loss, particularly when they are afraid of managing a coherent, well-integrated team that has a set of established traditions (Ciuk and Kostera, 2010). They may believe in a possibility to create a more 'flexible' culture, easier to control and more predictable. This is not only immoral but it also may have very harmful consequences for the organization.

It also happens that this kind of memory loss is accidental, not fully intended, a side effect of other manifestations of toxic leadership. Together with a co-author (Ciuk and Kostera, 2010) I call this phenomenon second-loop forgetting, in analogy to second-loop learning (Argyris and Schön, 1978). It consists in forgetting that one has forgotten. We speak of it as an archetypical kind of forgetting and to depict it we use the myth of the river Lethe. According to Greek mythology, the souls of the dead, before passing to Hades, the kingdom of shadows, drink water from the river of forgetfulness. They forget who they are and what happened to them in the course of their lives. Lethe's waters release them from pain, anxiety and worries, but it also makes them lose their identity. Odysseus, one of the few mortals who went to Hades and returned to Earth, looked with sadness at the wandering shadows. Lethe deprives people of their memory, identity and a sense of meaningfulness:

> Obscure figures drift aimlessly among eternal mists, as if oblivious of each other and their surroundings. Who are they and why are they here? No one seems to remember. Shades of heroes wander among those of commoners. The lesser souls cluster around the greater ones, once charismatic shining heroes, now shades among shades. Addressed by Odysseus, who is said to have ventured into the Underworld, the great Achilles exclaimed that he would rather be an underling in life than the lord of the dead. The winners are as lost as the losers. Nothing touches, no one is moved.
>
> The darkness is all-pervasive but not necessarily evil; this is not hell. The vast domains of Hades are not devoid of riches and exude a mysterious beauty. But how does one embrace beauty, how does one conquer pain, when one has drunk from the waters of Lethe, the river of forgetfulness, that separate the light from the darkness? Whoever drinks from them attains a perpetual drowsiness, a spiritual sleepiness. They are a miracle anesthetic, a cure for life. (Ciuk and Kostera, 2010, p. 188)

This kind of forgetting is the opposite of wisdom and awareness. When it occurs in organizations, its consequences are in the long run lethal for organizational identity and culture. We use the identity-building model conceived of by Mary Jo Hatch and Majken Schultz (2002),[78] according to which organizational identity is a continuous cultural process that demands an exchange of information with the environment and self-reflection. When some of the elements that shape these processes are lost – for instance, due to a destructive, toxic or simply careless management – a break or an imbalance may ensue. If such an disorder continues for a long period of time, the organization loses its memory, a crucial element necessary for identity creation, and double-loop forgetting occurs. The processes that cause identity erosion are consolidated. The organization receives the material for self-presentation from a broken, discontinuous culture that cannot make sense of the links between the past, the present and the future. The self-presentation consists in presenting a random selection of elements that do not make a meaningful whole. Such an identity reinforces the incoherency of culture, it makes the culture even more fragmented. The sense of alienation and randomness deepens. Management's presentation of the company's identity to the outside world usually takes the shape of self-promotion or dramatization that is supposed to create a positive image of the company in the environment. In the case of double-loop forgetting, attempts at such presentation become instead attempts at seducing – the board tries to provoke the most positive feelings towards the organization possible, not offering in exchange any lasting bonds or tangible proofs of the board's declarations. The image is a typical façade[79] that hides emptiness and is supposed to provoke liking and enthusiasm in the stakeholders. The only signal from the environment that the management chooses to accept is approval which perpetuates the company's identity in an unchanged state, fragmentary and devoid of meaning. No other voices from the environment are taken into consideration, although both praise and criticism are important for the construction of a sustainable organizational identity. As a whole, the fragmentated identity is devoid of its core and exerts an increasingly demotivating and demoralizing effect on participants. This is regrettable, because a healthy identity is one of the most powerful sources of morale and cohesion in an organization.

As an example we present in the cited article the story of a company, a Polish subsidiary of an international concern, where managers changed very often. The people appointed to be new managers came from abroad used to treat the company as a kind of a springboard upwards and back home to their own country and mother company. They never stayed in Poland for more than two years. At a certain point, the position was given to an extremely ambitious man who thought this was an excellent occasion to prove himself. His did not care for the organization or its employees; his main purpose was his personal promotion. That goal he achieved in the end. However, the means of getting there meant brutal exploitation of the company's resources and organizational culture. He engaged in micromanagement to exert maximum control over the function of all the organization's systems. By doing so he did not care that he also destroyed all the organization's traditions and that the cost of the short-term productivity rise was demoralization and burnout, as his style of managing people mainly consisted in intimidation. Internal procedures were strengthened in order to facilitate control; employees were punished for not achieving the short-term productivity rise that the manager wished them to achieve, and rarely if ever rewarded for their accomplishments. However, new employees were rewarded, something the old ones interpreted as a way of showing them how worthless they were – even complete newbies did better. He had no respect for customs based on trust and he severely limited the employees' professional autonomy. Soon, the most competent employees started leaving the company and the others were afraid to stick their necks out and tried to become invisible. Clients also reacted negatively, but it took some time before the effects of this materialized in the company. The bubble burst after the ambitious manager had succeeded with his plan and was already promoted back in his home country. He left behind him an organization in ruins. The financial situation was really bad, and the employees' morale had reached rock bottom. A new manager took the place of the ambitious careerist and was greeted with enthusiasm. However, the damage was already done. It was too late to repair the identity – the employees had lost the memory of the organization, what it was before the destruction of their culture, of their traditions and customs, as well as of their collective sense of meaning-making direction. Attempts at building a new culture and a new identity were limited to introducing new rules and regulations. The dominant conviction was that the company could not be trusted. Simultaneously, the level of technical and professional knowledge returned to the initial level, or even exceeded it. The competences that were lost in the collective exodus were restored. However, the new management did not manage to rebuild the organization's identity: the people forgot that they had forgotten it.

15.4 TRANSFORMATION AND REBIRTH

Susan Cheever (2005) published a biography of Bill Wilson, the founder of Alcoholics Anonymous (AA). She tells the story of his transformation from a broken man, enslaved by his addiction, to an enlightened leader of an international organization that has saved the lives of millions of people throughout the world. The first part of Wilson's life was a continuous struggle with his alcohol addiction, a struggle which he was losing. In 1935 Bill Wilson met Robert Smith, a doctor and an alcoholic, and they decided to support each other in their battle with the habit. They based their programme on the famous Twelve Steps, which were invented by Wilson. To cut a long story short, the steps consist in acknowledging one's powerlessness towards alcohol and that one's life has become unmanageable, referring to a higher power and turning to it for help towards liberation, then acknowledging one's mistakes and the harm done to other people and making amends with those harmed. These steps lead towards a spiritual awakening and a life with constant awareness. People who participate in the programme try to remain sober each day, 'just for today', with the support of a sponsor who has undergone a similar transformation before. In the book, Wilson is presented as a man who was at first obsessed with dreams and ambitions that could not be fulfilled and then, as a result of his transformation, as a happy person, willing to share his happiness with others. After the transformation, he did not stop being himself; perhaps he even became himself to a greater extent. His greatness does not result from the fact that he achieved success or built a great ego, but on the modesty and compassion that characterized the second half of his life when he became the founder of the AA movement. The path that Wilson, and his movement, took does not consist in piety but in a deep spirituality and an openness to transformation. The energy for the transformation comes from forces bigger than a single human being and work not contrary to our human nature, but in accord with it. The movement started by Wilson supports the personal transformation of its participants without enforcing beliefs, ideas or lifestyles; especially, it does not propose a form of spirituality that would imply the choice of this or other religious system. AA today has members of all persuasions as well as agnostics, who are united by their common path but not a faith or rules to follow. The path is gentleness, forgiveness and the transformation of the heart.

A transformation of a person or a spiritual transformation is a major change in the system of meaning that serves as the basis for self-definition and making sense of life and one's main purposes (Paloutzian, 2005). In this sense, transformation resembles a religious conversion. A person who has experienced conversion divides their life into the life 'before' and 'after' the conversion; they change their basic beliefs; sometimes, some personality traits of the person can undergo change as well. During a transformation the set of features that can be called the personality core remain unchanged. What changes is the way they manifest themselves in a person's actions. The purposes the participants strive to attain, as well as their values and attitudes, transform. A spiritual transformation is something more than a conversion and it does not have to be a religious change; rather, it refers to the essence of a person, to their orientation in the system of meanings. A transformation may be triggered by various factors: a disturbance of equilibrium in one's life caused by a sudden, dramatic event, a crisis or a conflict between one's experiences and beliefs. In a transformation both cognitive and emotional factors play important roles. Together they take on the shape of an imbalance or a dissonance that we experience. There are weaker and stronger factors, and it is difficult to predict what combination of circumstances will trigger a transformation just as it is difficult to predict the consequences of the transformation. After this turning point a person starts building a new system of meanings and using his or her main traits in a new way. From time to time, though not often, there are transformations that the author calls 'remarkable', transformations that result in a complete change of a person's life.

Organizations can undergo transformations as well – usually, however, attempts at transformation do not bring the expected results. The question of change and renewal in organizations is discussed by Ola Alexandersson and Per Trossmark (1997). The authors have analysed changes in the Danish public radio service where the changes were supposed to 'adjust' the organization to a new context. On one side the managerialists, or actors who treated the radio as an organization that functions in the market according to the principles of managing traditional commercial companies, advocated change that would bring more profits. For them renewal meant 'market facilitation', 'commercialization' and depriving the organization of old 'habits' and 'old-fashioned forms'. On the other side were the professionals, who were also in favour of changes, although they understood them very differently. They believed in the organization's public mission, which they believed to be essential for the company's identity; they also stressed the importance of professional autonomy for the history of the organization from its beginnings until the present. They wanted to treat it as a foundation for building new content, new programmes, new structures. The renewal in the Danish radio service has not been successful: some of the changes were more or less successfully implemented but the reform process gave rise to at least as many new problems as it has solved. The management was hesitant and tried to join the perspectives of the two groups. They hoped for a reconciliation and an 'objective' solution but did not understand that change does not exist as something external to the organization, and that it is always linked to its past and tradition. This connection is crucial for understanding organizational transformation – the changing culture has to preserve the identity and use it in formulating and fulfilling new goals. It is important to grasp the core of the relationship between the past and the present and translate it into knowledge to be used in defining the shape of the changes. The managers of the radio service were looking for such knowledge, yet could not find it, so they used the opinions of the employees and the stakeholders and tried to balance them. This did not work in the way they intended, as opinions inhabit a much more superficial level of an organization's culture than does its identity. Instead of transformation, the approach resulted in chaos.

The knowledge needed for introducing transformative change is encoded deeply in an organization's cultural system. Jonathan Gosling and Peter Case (2010) argue that organizational roles are reservoirs of knowledge needed for renewal – faced with new tasks and duties social actors can discover, often unexpectedly to themselves, needed resources of knowledge about how to interact with the role. Assuming new roles, people have an opportunity to experience something new that they would perhaps not have experienced otherwise; and to learn to see reality from another perspective. A person can develop and broaden their identity through adopting new social and organizational roles. People who prepare for a change of job or post are in a situation that is often described as suspension, as if in the shadow sphere of social reality. They fantasize about the new role or try adopting it in their imagination. But roles have a dynamic of their own, like living shadows, possibilities that come alive as soon as they are 'inhabited' by people. Gosling and Case claim that roles are in fact much more than an outer shell: when an actor adopts a new role, he or she is given more than just a new set of rules. He or she undergoes a kind of rebirth. Roles are forms that are in many respects autonomous and also may shape the personalities and experiences of people who play them. The knowledge contained in a new role plays an active part, as if it 'possesses' the person; playing a role is much more than merely learning new tasks.

Gosling and Case chose Plato's story of the warrior named Er as their leading metaphor. Er was taken to be dead and laid on a funeral pyre. However, he woke up before the fire was set, and managed to tell the story of what he saw in the afterlife. He could remember it because he did not drink the water from Lethe. Er said that after they die people are judged and the ones who have led a good life go to heaven, whereas the people who are not worthy of a reward go to the nether regions. After having travelled through these spiritual regions, the souls return later to the Earth, in different states of mind. Those who return from heaven are cheerful and full of joy, whereas those returning from the nether world are shaken and tainted. They are given a choice of various human fates and incarnations – the conditions are defined, but human temperament and character are not. The way a person lives their life depends on them only. But the soul of the person also changes under the influence of the life on Earth. The soul shapes its life and the life shapes the soul.

According to Gosling and Case, a similar process takes place in the case of the change of social and organizational roles. Organizational life teaches and changes a person through the roles the person assumes. Just like reincarnation and rebirth, each of the roles has consequences for the self. The consequences apply to the future but we make our choices on the basis of our past experiences. Wise people can make their choices beyond the imperative of necessity; they can make their choices without being guided by ambition, greed and impatience. Even if they do not remember past lives, they can choose paths with the use of moral agency, in and between incarnations. And so it is also with entering new social roles. The moment of making a decision is like choosing which way to go in physical space. The choice of role has both moral and purely technical implications. Gosling and Case conclude that it is not necessary to look at organizations in the traditional way that only allows for the importance of two dichotomic states of life and death. In organization theory there is space for considering the processes of passage, transformation and change, from the point of view of both organizational roles and the system as a whole. Learning can take place when the actor is open to the experience of rebirth in a new role, and when he or she makes the effort not to forget on a deep spiritual level, beyond conscious remembering. Learning on this level is not about the acquiring of new content but about opening oneself to the content that already exists and is encoded in the role. Knowledge management on this level would, then, consist in reflection and the creation of space for reflection. This is something more than pondering about the past and the present – it is also the capability to participate in a sense of wholeness undivided into temporal units. Adopting roles is a part of the identity work, an actualization of systematic knowledge as well as an activation of the organization's potential undertaken by an individual.

Transformatory organizations are not very easy to find but there are some good examples, such as Alcoholics Anonymous which I have already mentioned in this chapter. It is open to people from different cultures, traditions, from different religious traditions, including agnostics, who want to change their lives and remain sober every day (Alcoholics Anonymous World Services, [1939] 2010). The organization distances itself from taking any ideological, religious and political positions; it does not comment on any social controversies, including those regarding the nature of addictions. The AA programme is often considered more effective than other therapies, even though most of the participants leave the movement in the course of their first year. Participation is based completely on free will. The organization has no formalized structure and no strict membership rules and it functions according to the principles that Bill Wilson used to call 'kind anarchy'. There is no hierarchy, no superiors, and individual members comply with the Twelve Step programme of their own accord or, more precisely, accept it as their own and try to follow it in their lives. The Twelve Steps refer to the individual's relationship with a higher power; they show the way to transformation from addiction to freedom through forgiveness and humility. With help of the programme the participants can not only change their behaviour and stay sober but also awaken spiritually and start a mindful life. The programme aims to be a path for the whole life, though the participants focus on the present day and avoid looking far into the future. A person stays an alcoholic for the rest of their life.

Becoming sober does not make a person free from the addiction. In order to stay sober the participants practise conscious living and kindness on an everyday basis and regularly participate in AA meetings. They try to help new members, and by that they enhance their own capability of staying sober. The organization also has a set of 12 traditions that define its functioning and aim at protecting its independence. The aim is mutual help in the participants' attempts at staying sober; nobody in AA can subordinate other people and the only condition for participation in AA meetings is the desire to break with addiction. The organization should not accumulate capital or make any external stakeholders financially dependent on it, and so on. The Alcoholics Anonymous movement is not a sect and it does not influence the core of its participants' identity, it does not require conversion and it certainly does not cause a severing of the participants' relationships. On the contrary, most people who join the AA manage to deepen their relationships with others, especially with family. The values promoted by AA belong in the mainstream of social values (Greil and Rudy, 1983) and by no means belong to the area of total and greedy institutions (Coser, 1974).

PART III

Methodological notes

16. On the studying of organizational myths and archetypes: methods

16.1 ETHNOGRAPHIC INSPIRATIONS

The methods of choice for a study of archetypes are first and foremost various types of ethnography and ethnographically inspired methods. The ethnographer collects stories in the field and pays attention to archetypical and mythical motifs and plots, either while still in the field or back home, during the phase of interpretation. I will briefly explain how this can be done, but let me first explain the role of ethnography in the study of organizations.[80]

Ethnography is one of classical methodologies used in the exploration of culture. It is being defined by the use of ethnographic methods: observation, open-ended interviews and text analysis; a narrative form where data is thickly described; and expresses a textual sensibility (Yanow et al., 2009). Organizational ethnography originates in the research tradition of cultural anthropology from which it spread to organization theory. It is believed that this took place in the course of the research conducted by Elton Mayo in a factory of Western Electric in Hawthorne, when at one point, an anthropologist named Roethlisberger was asked to join in order to gain a better understanding of the culture of the employees (Wright, 1994).[81] Ethnography is particularly useful for research questions starting with 'why' and 'how'. It is a way of exploring social phenomena in their authentic context. Such research is often described as naturalistic, which means that the researcher attempts to observe and describe reality as it appears in its 'natural state', without interference of the researcher. For the ethnographer it is particularly important to understand how people live and cope in different contexts, and to explain their systems of meanings and values. He or she may also want to compare the findings with the results observed in other similar situations. The results of ethnographic research are not generalized for whole populations – ethnography is not a methodology suited for such generalizations, or indeed interested in such an abstracted view of cultures. It is about a level of understanding from a perspective of groups and individuals, one that encompasses processes and patterns, and is based on research conducted during long periods. It allows one to present processes, how they follow one another, what is their outcome is, how they connect, and so on. Studies of this kind can be compared to a film, where the essential elements are the plots and the actors. The knowledge gained thanks to such studies is close to the perspective of social actors but not necessarily identical with it. It is usually more critical and not based on the taken-for-granted assumptions that everyday knowledge has its roots in.

The researcher does not accept any of what they observe as obvious, and is constantly problematizing the reality he or she encounters in the field. He or she may empathize with people in his or her field but do not identify with them. Often, 'going native' is considered a serious methodological fault that can affect research results because of the loss of distance and the adopting of the categories used in the area in question. A researcher is expected to have a perspective that goes beyond the present and beyond the present beliefs and social institutions. This is an intensive and at the same time distanced engagement that is quite demanding.

However, the merits of ethnography are really important: first, because it brings a profound understanding; and second, because a good ethnography never grows old. The human world is revealed in its complexity and dynamics; both what is typical and unusual becomes brought to light. What is unusual today, may become typical tomorrow. And, the more is known about human custom and behaviour, the better we know ourselves. Where do we come from, what are we, where are we going? These are the questions that ethnographers, and their audiences, are interested in.

The main protagonists of ethnographies are social actors, the people in the field (Yanow et al., 2009). In organizational ethnography usually several viewpoints are represented and it is rare for an ethnographer to adopt the point of view of management alone. It is usually an advantage to show as many levels and layers in the organization's culture as possible, or else to present life from the point of view of the underprivileged, the underdogs whose voice is seldom heard. It can also be seen as a special aim of ethnography to present so-called tacit knowledge (Polanyi, [1958] 1974), that is, the knowledge contained within practice, experienced but not verbalized. It is unlikely for a reader to become, say, a good accountant after having read an ethnography, but he or she may perhaps find it easier to learn the profession, if the need arises; and, more likely, to understand accountants that he or she will encounter. Ethnography can be compared to the books about travel and adventure that most people so enjoyed to read as children. Not only did they tell stories of exciting adventures that we could imagine ourselves taking part in, but also they taught us something about the world and other people.

Ethnographic research is carried in a real setting, such as an existing live organization (Kostera, 2007; Yanow et al., 2009). The duration of research in organization ethnography is usually somewhat shorter than in the case of standard cultural anthropology, and the researcher's involvement may be less intense. Organization ethnographers rarely use the most engaged methods that dominate in cultural anthropology, such as participant observation. Still, the research demands the researcher's presence in the field for a period long enough to observe the main processes (in practice, it usually means at least a year). Sometimes, the researcher focuses on selected areas and questions instead of studying the whole of the culture. Sometimes one particular group of actors is studied, such as the underprivileged in an organization. If an ethnography concerns managers, it never identifies their view with that of the entire organization. The researcher:

> interprets that which he or she observes, experiences, or was told by others, recording this cultural data in field notes and consciously and unconsciously letting it settle against a tableau of meaning structures within his or her own imaginings. The resulting ethnographic interpretations are reworked as time and data accumulate and permit (Van Maanen, 1987, p. 75), mediated by experiences in and out of the field. (Rosen, 1991, p. 2)

Ethnographers aim at presenting 'cultural portraiture and what it is like to be someone else', to use the words of John Van Maanen (1998, p. xx). They do so by using a set of methods that include observation, interview and text analysis (Kostera, 2007; Yanow et al., 2009). Observation consists in experiencing the studied reality without interpreting or evaluating it, in striving to describe it in terms of behaviour and actions, without omitting or overlooking anything as uninteresting or obvious. There are two main types of observation types: non-participant and participant. In the first, the researcher does not adopt any roles from the studied field and tries to describes everything that they see from the outside of the culture, without adopting any categories, as if everything observed was completely new and unknown. Participant observation demands that the ethnographer enter a role within the field and gain knowledge from its perspective. The ethnographer, however, does not adopt the point of view of an ordinary organizational actor but keeps the distance necessary for research. Sometimes, ethnographers are employed in the organizations they wish to study and, after the research has been completed, leave. The most popular form of observation in organization ethnography is an intermediary form, called direct observation, and consisting in staying among the organizational actors, perhaps not just in one area or department but moving around, and not adopting any roles in the field. This allows the ethnographer to be more flexible, to plan research and organize it so that it suits their schedule, allowing for other activities, such as teaching, at the same time as the field study.

Interviews as an ethnographic method are usually open, long-lasting, not structured and not based on a standard set of questions. The questions are more like interactions in a conversation where the interview talks more and the researcher listens more. Often the ethnographer explicitly asks for stories about everyday life in the organization: what the person does, with whom he or she works, what his or her work is about. Some ethnographers like returning several times to the same main interviewees as this helps in telling their stories over in time and aids us in understanding processes and their consequences. An ethnographer does not search for a representative sample of interlocutors; instead, they look for people who are interesting, willing to trust the researcher and will help him or her understand what is like to work in the field, as seen from their perspective.

There is also a set of methods for analysing texts in which contemporary organizations abound. Some of the methods are borrowed from literary studies and allow one to analyse rhetorical style and plots, characterize the protagonists and describe textual strategies that define the relation with the model reader of the texts.

It is an advantage if the research is conducted in a reflexive way, that is, challenging the researcher:

> to address fundamental questions about the nature of reality, knowledge and our own ways of being – to take a leap into a constantly shifting ocean rather than studying organizational life from the security of the shore. Specifically, reflexivity raises a need to be critical of any self-sealing processes in our research, and the possibility of transforming our contexts as social actors and researchers (Jun, 1994; Lewandowski, 2000; Weick, 1999). (Cunliffe, 2003, p. 999)

By adopting a reflexive stance, it is possible to inquire into the deeper layers of culture, and this provides insights into questions about the nature of knowledge and reality, as well as our own part in it as researchers.

After the researcher has concluded his or her engagement with the field and left the premises of the organization, he or she begins to interpret the material. This is the stage where it is preferable to look for archetypical plots and motifs, such as, in particular, archetypical tales.[82] A significant part of the examples quoted in this book are such archetypical plots drawn from the research carried out by myself and others. It can be a good idea to look for broader categories that overlap with archetypes and connect with other categories, forming relatively coherent plots, characteristic of some archetype. For instance, if a leader tends to appear in much of the materials, it may be good to look for plots that occur in the material, if any coherent categories can be found, and whether these categories constitute elements in a narrative characteristic for the archetype of the King.

This is how I, together with my co-author (Kostera and Postuła, 2011), looked for archetypical plots in the material gathered during an ethnographic study. The research focused on professional roles of information technology (IT) specialists and brought abundant material that came from interviews and observation. We found only one archetype around which we could build an archetypical tale. The archetype was identified on the basis of numerous categories that formed many different narrative relationships. The archetype was linked with how the IT specialists defended their professional autonomy against other groups, and in particular, against the management. We called this phenomenon the Aegis archetype and we used it to describe how the IT specialists use their unique competences and education as a protective shield against external interference and control. They distance themselves from the definitions and labels that other people direct at them and create for themselves a space of professional freedom. Aegis was the powerful shield of Zeus and Athena. After having killed the monstrous Medusa, who killed everyone who looked at her, Perseus presented Athena with her severed head. The goddess attached the head to her shield, making it even more lethal. Now just looking at the shield would kill an opponent. The archetype of the Aegis involves using powerful symbols to dispose of enemies, or unwanted interfering presences. In the case of the IT people such symbols included mathematical and technical language. People outside of IT often have a serious fear of such terms and concepts, and a persistent usage of them may be a successful tool in deflecting society's gaze.

16.2   THE NARRATIVE COLLAGE

Ethnographic research results in realistic stories that refer to things actually happened or to the opinions of actors encountered in the course of field studies. If the area of study is mainly located in the domain of the imagination, as opposed to reality, the method of preference can be one that I call 'narrative collage' (Kostera, 2006). It consists in the collection of fictitious stories created by the interlocutors. The researcher asks the interviewees, whom I call authors, to compose stories on a given subject or to finish a story that begins with a sentence provided by the researcher. The authors decide how the story is going to develop; they create the plots, invent new characters and may also choose the genre. After having collected the material, the researcher becomes editor and joins the materials to create a coherent whole. The researcher can also review or interpret the material, or respond to the stories collected by writing their own story. The whole collage should shed new light on the cultural context of organization contained in the sphere of imagination. Imagination is also a sort of reality – even though it is not actualized, but potential. It is this reality that gives birth to creativity and innovation.

There is also a consulting version of this method, proposed by Henrietta Nilson (2009). Its purpose is to draw a map of an organization's creative potential. The process of collecting material is quite similar to that of the narrative collage in research, but the author expanded the method to include music and art. The collected narrative material is passed on to artists to draw illustrations and to musicians to compose and perform music resonating with the plots and characters in the stories. Nilson recommends jazz because it is so strongly based on improvization and uses many accords and nuances. The stories, art and music are then used during a presentation for the client organization. It is an excellent way of describing the imaginative reality of the employees and at the same time stimulating it and inspiring them to develop even further. The clients were very satisfied with what this kind of consulting project offered them. After each session the level of creative thinking in the company rises for some time.

The principles for conducting research with the aid of the narrative collage may differ depending on the needs of the research situation. The process of collage creation begins with the initiative of the researcher who conceives of the topic of study. This can be different aspects of the cultural context of organizing, or the imaginative potential of an organization's participants. The researcher comes up with the topic or the first sentence of a narrative, and sometimes also selects its genre. Then complete stories are requested and later collected during personal meetings with the authors or by email. When a sufficient number of stories have been collected, they are analysed and interpreted. The analysis can be semiotic, semantic, rhetorical or archetypical. Synergetic effects can be looked for, as well as common directions of plots and metaplots. The researcher can also seek out thematic groups, ways in which the plot is presented, relationships between protagonists, and so on. If the researcher creates his or her own story, it can constitute a sort of ending. If he or she interprets or reviews the stories, then it may be a good idea to try to compare and contrast the material and describe the boundaries of the imaginative space created by the collected stories.

Ethnography and collage differ also as to the role of the researcher. An ethnographer seeks to investigate phenomena in their natural context, and tries to influence them as little as possible. A story collector plays an active role, initiates actions, and selects the topic and the scope of study.

However, similarly to the ethnographer, the story collector is open to the voices of others, and refrains from enforcing his or her ideas or suggesting outcomes of plots.

The ultimate shape of the collage is up to the authors and the researcher. They all play creative roles – the authors invent the stories; the researcher creates, using the materials they have provided, like an artist working on a collage. In the process, everyone uses imagination and the researcher strives to combine individual imagination in a common, intersubjective imaginative space.

An example of how the main differences between ethnography and the narrative collage works is the following story from my own research experience. In the beginning of the 1990s, I conducted ethnographic research among Polish managers who had been active as managers since before 1989. This was the first field study undertaken on my own and, due to my lack of experience, I formulated the research problem somewhat unfortunately: 'Polish managers' visions for the future'. Unsurprisingly, my interlocutors did not reply to a question posed this way. Still, I was lucky because I managed to collect quite a lot of interesting material, thanks to the willingness of my interviewees to talk about their experiences and forget all about the question. And, fortunately, I soon realized that I had to reformulate my question to fit what my interlocutors wanted to talk about: that is, mainly the past, and to a certain degree the present. Now I know that my initial topic referred to an imagined and not an experienced reality, and so was not suited for an ethnographic study. When I changed my research problem to the historical roots of Polish management from before 1989 and their potential for the shaping of the present in the new political and economic system, the field was more than willing to contribute. The effect of my research was an ethnographic study of management in the People's Republic of Poland (Kostera, 1996).

If I had stuck to my initial topic, I may have, if the method had existed at that time, used the narrative collage to explore the domain of imagination. I would then have asked the managers to write fictitious stories, perhaps in the genre of science fiction, opening with the sentence: 'On the first day at work in the new year 2020, the CEO of the company X [the name of the company managed by my interlocutor] was sitting behind his desk and thinking.' I might have then looked for plots indicating the authors' visions of the future, regarding the management of their companies. Then, I would perhaps have written my own story about management in the future, based on my interlocutors' ideas.

If the researcher is interested in archetypes, he or she can design the narrative collage study in such a way as to direct it towards archetypical themes and plots. Whereas an ethnographer looks for archetypical tales in the material and it may very well turn out that there are none to be found, the narrative collage collector may use the method explicitly in a way that focuses it on archetypes from the very beginning. The interlocutors can be asked to write a story about a specific archetype, perhaps linking the archetype with organizing or management. The first sentence of a story can invite thinking along these lines, or asking the authors to compose a poem or a piece of music or produce a drawing. Other forms of expression are also possible, though I have never encountered researchers of consultants collecting sculptures or films as part of a narrative collage. This does not mean that such forms are impossible – the method of the narrative collage is young and invites us to interpret and use it in new ways.

The following example comes from my recent study. Together with a co-author (Kociatkiewicz and Kostera, 2012b) I am investigating the potential of the archetype of the King in the cultural context of organizing. We have asked authors from academia and practice to invent stories beginning with the line: 'Upon a certain Anniversary Day the good manager had come from London, and held a very magnificent reception at the HQ as was fitting on such a day'.[83] The stories we have gathered show a rather dark vision of the protagonist. The stories are sarcastic or ironic and end in disaster and death. In one story the protagonist intends to blow up the party; in another, he is diagnosed with cancer and is going to die but first he sells his company to a corporation and betrays the employees; in another, the manager sets his own company on fire . . . Only a few stories expressed hope and faith.

We analysed the stories on several planes, using Roman Ingarden's (1960) model of phenomenological reading texts, according to which a text should be read on several levels in order to uncover the different layers of meanings and symbols. On the first, most superficial level we found two archetypes: that of the King and of Goodness. Goodness is mostly used as an instance of managerial newspeak, the language of the depraved and cynical King. It is but a label covering a sinister reality. In most of the stories, there is a clear tragic shade of the plot. However, the reader does not sympathize with the manager, who just got what he or she deserved. The outcome of the plot, leadership encountering goodness, falls into any of three categories: disenchantment, nostalgia and death. Disenchantment means that the reader realizes that goodness was only a deceptive façade. Nostalgia expresses an insight that goodness perhaps was meaningful sometime in the past, but is not any more. Death is usually literal: the hero, the company or other protagonists die.

On the second, underlying level the same archetypes form a different pattern. The King is still a fallen leader. But the narratives express support for the fight against an unjust system and they seem to convey some kind of hope beyond the exterior external layer of the stories. It is due to Goodness, which here is a hidden archetype – both the reader and the narrator know that it exists somewhere beyond the plot and its setting, but it is not articulated openly. Here Goodness is an empty place, a shadow of an ideal, perhaps a utopia.

On the third level, the main role is played by the archetype of Death. Here, Death and transformation create a new narrative space, a potential for change or revelation. On this level, Goodness is the background against the plot unravels. It casts a shadow, visible on the more superficial levels, but it is only on this, more profound level that it gives a deeper meaning to the stories and their protagonists' actions.

Finally, the fourth and most profound layer holds Goodness as a root metaphor of all the narratives. Used on this level, it is a powerful hidden archetype, compelling the protagonists to undertake transformative quests for revelation, healing and change. On this level, goodness in management is its Holy Grail (Kociatkiewicz and Kostera, 2012b).

16.3   WHY STUDY ORGANIZATIONAL ARCHETYPES?

Instead of a more traditional ending, I will now, still using the image of the Grail, say why I believe it is worthwhile to talk about archetypes in organizations. I will do so with the help of the story of Perceval.[84] As it happens, this youngest among King Arthur's knights was the one who first found the Grail. He found it only to lose it again. And this is what took place on that fateful day and night.

Perceval meets the Wounded King who invites him to stay the night at his castle. During a sumptuous dinner organized in his honour, he observes astounding and truly astonishing things. A procession of youths carry strange and powerful artefacts. Then a beautiful young girl enters carrying the Grail itself. It is so brilliant that all the surrounding lights appear dim and faint. It is made of gold and precious stones of incomparable beauty. The procession goes by him and leaves the room. All he sees surpasses his imagination and leaves him speechless. By the way, he has been taught not to talk too much, as it does not befit a knight. So he says nothing, dazzled and petrified, and after the dinner, he goes to sleep. Only later does he learn that he should have asked questions, engaged in a conversation about all the amazing symbols he saw. Then the King and his barren land would have been healed and the Grail would have become his. But he did not speak, he could not, lacking a language and a mindset for such unusual things. So instead, he wakes up the next day, alone. The

Grail is gone and so is the King and, indeed, the castle. He lies wide awake with his head resting on a stone.

It is important to be able to talk about the important things in our lives, also in organizational life, because organizations are so crucial in our times. All the significant things, sometimes strange, sometimes terrifying, beautiful, astounding, the procession of symbols before our eyes – let us not remain speechless before them, so as not to wake up in the midst of a wasteland with a stone for a pillow under our heads. They need to be and should be addressed, questions need to be asked; we, organization researchers and participants, need to recognize and talk about the most fundamental issues of what it means to be human and part of a living planet. Only then can we hope for a healing of ourselves and our environment and address some of the most serious and damaging problems of our times. We are not helpless in the face of an impersonal omnipotent Invisible Hand, nor fated to live bleak lives where only standards, quotas, rates, indexes and other figures count, but such things as goodness, happiness, compassion and responsibility are irrelevant because of a lack of language and mindset. This language exists and is there for us to use. It is accessible and free for us to obtain – from the humanities.

Notes

1. Figures are from 2009.
2. Poland, figures from 2006/07, students of economic sciences (which, in Poland, include management).
3. The systematic approach is only one of many structures-oriented approaches to organizations. See, for example, Ackoff (2010).
4. 'As a scientific discipline strategic management is a theory of the company's effectiveness. It is a difficult discipline – technical and interdisciplinary, combining modern micro-economy, finance theory, the theory of organizations, marketing with quantitative methods and social psychology. Put in practice, strategic management means looking for the best path of development for the company. Therefore, the simplest definition of strategy is a consistent and effective response to the challenges of the environment. Strategy is not the working out of a plan and budget, nor a hundred PowerPoint slides, or a list of the company's key competencies. It is a consistent plan of action based on only few key and mutually complementary choices that – by enabling the company to use its chance or gain advantage over competing companies – are to guarantee the company an outstanding performance' (Obłój, 2010, p. 13).
5. For example, *Studies in Cultures, Organizations and Societies*, the predecessor of *Cultures and Organizations*, a journal still published.
6. For example, *Organization Studies, Administrative Science Quarterly, Journal of Management, Journal of Management Studies*.
7. For example, the Standing Conference on Organizational Symbolism, a global academic network, organizing a conference each year.
8. For example, Pharmacia created a new department: Personnel and Business Culture.
9. More about archetypes in Chapter 3.
10. In other academic disciplines, dealing with society, language and culture, myths are often conceived of as fictions built by a certain social group for a certain goal. In literary theory and the constructivist philosophical reflection based on it, for instance, Roland Barthes (1957/1973) sees myth as a type of speech, a semiological system – the dominant ideology of its time serving to naturalize the social order in the interests of the bourgeoisie.
11. Here, Campbell's interpretation agrees with Barthes' diagnosis. For Campbell, however, such validation of a sociological system is not an end in itself; myth is not equivalent with the governing group's ideology.
12. For more information see Miller and Friesen (1980) and Greenwood and Hinings (1988).
13. In Chapter 2, section 2.4.
14. Adam Smith was an outstanding moral philosopher; unfortunately, contemporary economic education programmes often tend to disregard this. I

believe that the organizational world would be a better place if the ethical dimension of Smith's thought was taken into serious consideration.

15. For more see Chapter 2, section 2.1.

16. Often, companies introduce changes at the stage of interpretation, through communicating and, if necessary, explicating new rules. This strategy is not effective and can be risky. New ideas introduced at the stage of interpretation are naturally absorbed and interpreted by culture according to old assumptions. When a change is introduced in a radical and aggressive manner, it can be overturned and destroyed.

17. For more see Chapter 13, section 13.2.

18. An example taken from the research of Hatch and Schultz (2008).

19. The example comes from my own research.

20. Wisdom will be discussed in Chapter 8.

21. The example comes from Aleksander Chrostowski's (2006) research.

22. The described company also did really well in terms of customer satisfaction and economic results. Alas, in the current climate of disregard of anything other than constant shareholder value growth, it has been taken over by a large multinational corporation, the former management has been fired and all of the described reforms have been halted and abandoned. Many of the most competent employees left the organization and people are still leaving (postscript by Aleksander Chrostowski, private communication, 2011).

23. The term was introduced by Abraham Maslow (1965/1998) and refers to a manager who supports the self-actualization of their cooperators; a eupsychic organization consists of self-actualizing people whose self-actualization process is in no way interfered with.

24. More about the method in Chapter 16, section 16.2.

25. More on the subject in Chapter 10.

26. Chapter 4, section 4.5.

27. Not Invented Here.

28. I discuss this in more detail in Chapter 7, section 7.2.

29. Private communication, 2005; the professor wanted to remain anonymous.

30. The example comes from my research material.

31. The example comes from my research material.

32. The example comes from my research material.

33. The example comes from my research material.

34. The example comes from my research material.

35. Death in organizations is the topic of Chapter 15.

36. The example is a combination of two cases: one by Yiannis Gabriel (2008) and one by Ciuk and Kostera (2010).

37. See Chapter 3, section 3.3.

38. Both examples come from my research material.

39. An example from my research material.

40. Finally, she discloses to her aunt and uncle that she is Tosia and not Tomek because she does not want to have her hair shaved off. However, she does that after passing all 'masculinity tests' and becoming accepted by her cousins as a brave, yet well-behaved little boy.

41. An example from the research of a doctoral student who wants to remain anonymous.

42. Together with Chaos, Tartarus and Gaia. All my stories inspired by Greek,

Norse and other mythologies are mainly based on Kempiński (2001, 2009) and the images of popular culture.

43. It does not mean that technology is always praised. The author is also critical of many negative effects of technical progress.

44. Example from my research material.

45. Gandalf returns as Gandalf the White, a more powerful but qualitatively different representation of the Sage: much more distant from the world, more unambiguously good, but less intensely involved.

46. This kind of knowledge resembles Michael Polanyi's tacit knowledge (1958/1974).

47. The example comes from my research material.

48. Throughout the chapter I will use the term 'King' as referring to both the masculine and the feminine gender. From the perspective of archetypes, the Queen Regnant is identical with the King. This is supported by philosophical tradition: Plato's Philosopher King was neither a man nor a woman, or perhaps both. Jadwiga was crowned King of Poland in 1384. This is not a universal approach, but one suitable for this particular approach to leadership: that is, its being a collective pattern. The archetype of the King is 'a place where to stand' rather than 'a body to be'. One 'stands in the place of the King' which is not that one 'becomes King' (Kociatkiewicz and Kostera, 2012b).

49. There are numerous Arthurian legends and stories, sometimes mutually exclusive, often very different. I chose the stories to suit the purpose of this chapter. My main source of inspiration was Chrétien de Troyes' (1170/1988) epic poem. I also used Internet resources, *Arthurian Legend* (Taylor 2004/2007).

50. Namely, in Chapter 10.

51. The example comes from my teaching experience (an assignment at a training session consisting of a description of one's own leadership style).

52. For an overview see for example Hersey et al. (1996/2007).

53. The example comes from my research material.

54. The example comes from my research material.

55. The example comes from various materials published in the Swedish press: *Dagens Nyheter* and *Dagens Industri*.

56. A federation was a structure above a group of state-owned companies. Its aim was to make management more effective and to strengthen control over the companies; in practice, however, federative actions were perceived as limiting the autonomy of management and having a negative effect on companies (this included their economic performance). The managers of pre-1989 enterprises I interviewed were all very negative towards federations, claiming that they were extremely politicized and anti-management (Kostera, 1996).

57. An example from my teaching practice.

58. I do not want to suggest the sportspeople are troublemakers or psychopaths. Skilling is a model example of an Adventurer who searches for adventure at all cost – at work and outside his workplace.

59. It is not certain whether this is a conscious inspiration. Similar ideas were also formulated by other thinkers. Bakunin, however, was the first to express them in the field of the history of ideas, and his 'creative passion', which is at the same time a 'passion for destruction', seems very close to the archetype of the Adventurer.

60. In Chapter 9, section 9.1.
61. More about mythical and historical tricksters as alternative organizers can be found in Martin Parker's fascinating book on outlaws and business (2012).
62. A contestant in Senate elections organized a group of helpers who voted for him several times in different places. The inhabitants of the quarter investigated by Foote Whyte, Italians by descent, realized that their candidate had no chance of winning if they did not do the same. The young researcher was asked if he was willing to take part in the fraud and, after some hesitation, he agreed. He voted four times for one candidate and even tried to vote under a different name, but his vote was questioned by the officials. Also, his fraud could have been easily detected. Worried about consequences, he backed out of the endeavour.
63. Meeting quotas of the central plan was the main aim of all enterprises in the pre-1989 Poland and Eastern Bloc. The consequences of not doing so could be quite serious for the organization and usually meant loss of autonomy but could go as far as liquidation.
64. Heterarchy is a structure based on decentralization and diversity, where power is dispersed and every actor's uniqueness is recognized (Grabher, 2001).
65. From the Latin *ludere* – to play.
66. Knowledge management is discussed in Chapter 8, section 8.3.
67. For more, see for example Chaffey (2002/2007) and Razi et al. (2004).
68. The classic archetypes, however, include the Mother archetype, see Chapter 6, section 6.3.
69. According to Hesiod, other primordial deities, apart from Gaia, include Chaos (who was creating spontaneously out of nothingness in the very beginning), Tartarus and Eros. For more see Chapter 5, section 5.11.
70. Music by Philip Glass.
71. The director invited viewers to make their own interpretations.
72. Colonialism is understood in a broad sense, including both what used to be known as the 'Third World' and the softly, that is, mainly economically, subordinated countries (this includes, for example, the former Eastern Bloc). See definition further in this chapter.
73. Currently the Body Shop is part of the L'Oréal corporation. Anita Roddick died in 2007.
74. In the USA Ruby was banned from the shop windows after Mattel sent a cease-and-desist order to the Body Shop, where it claimed that Ruby was a anti-Barbie propaganda tool.
75. The primeval Kronos is not equivalent to Chronos, a much later god of time.
76. 'Actants' is a term coined by Bruno Latour (1987) to include all kinds of social and organizational actiors: human and non-human.
77. Various ways of learning are discussed in Chapter 4, section 4.4.
78. See Chapter 4, section 4.2. for more on the model and organizational identity.
79. Various organizational images are discussed in Chapter 7, section 7.2.
80. I write more extensively on ethnography in Kostera (2003/2007); see also, for example, Yanow (2007), Czarniawska-Joerges (1992) and Van Maanen (1988).
81. I write more about culture in Chapter 2. The study of Mayo's team is described in Wright (1994).

82. See Chapter 3, section 3.2.
83. The sentence is a paraphrase of Chrétien de Troyes' (1170/1988) sentence from his long poem on King Arthur: 'Upon a certain Ascension Day King Arthur had come from Caerleon, and had held a very magnificent court at Camelot as was fitting on such a day.'
84. My reading of the Perceval legends, mainly based on de Troyes (1170/1988). I also used Internet resources (Taylor, 2004/2007).

References

Note: I give the bibliographic details of English versions of publications if they exist; unless I have not read any significant part of the English version. In that case the entry here is the one I have been using the most extensively, with an English translation of the title in parenthesis.

Aaltio, Iiris (2008), 'Louhi, the Mistress of Northland: The power of the loner', in Monika Kostera (ed.), *Organizational Olympians: Heroes and heroines of organizational myths*, London: Palgrave, pp. 17–29.

Abrahamson, Eric (1992), 'Management fashion', *Academy of Management Review*, **21** (1), 253–85.

Accenture (2010), 'Accenture's Spirit of Flexibility Brings Working Mother's "100 best" Recognition', accessed 6 April 2010 at http://careers3.accenture.com/Careers/Global/Careers-News/0911-Working-Mother-Recognition.htm.

Ackoff, Russell, L. (2010), *Systems Thinking for Curious Managers*, Axminster: Triarchy Press.

Adler, Nancy (2011), 'Leading beautifully: the creative economy and beyond', *Journal of Management Inquiry*, **20** (3), 208–21.

Albert, S. and D.A. Whetten (1985), 'Organizational identity', in L.L. Cummings and M.M. Staw (eds), *Research in Organizational Behavior*, Greenwich, CT: JAI Press, pp. 263–95.

Alcoholics Anonymous World Services ([1939] 2010), *The Big Book Online*, accessed 19 May 2010 at www.aa.org/bigbookonline/en_table ofcnt.cfm.

Alexandersson, Ola and Per Trossmark (1997), *Konstruktion av förnyelse and organisationer*, Lund, Sweden: Lund Universitet.

Alvesson, Mats (1994), 'Talking in organizations: managing identity and impressions in an advertising agency', *Organization Studies*, **15** (4), 535–63.

Alvesson, Mats and P.O. Berg (1988), *Företagskultur och organisations-symbolism: Utveckling, teoretiska perspektiv och aktuell debatt*, Lund, Sweden: Studentlitteratur.

Alvesson, Mats and Yvonne Due Billing ([1997] 1999), *Kön och organisation*, Lund, Sweden: Studentlitteratur.

Anderson, Carl and Elizabeth McMillan (2005), 'Of ants and men: self-organized teams in human and insect organizations', *Emergence*, **5** (2), 29–41.

Arendt, Hannah ([1958] 1999), *The Human Condition*, Chicago, IL: University of Chicago Press.

Argyris, Chris (1999), *On Organizational Learning*, Oxford: Wiley-Blackwell.

Argyris, Chris and Donald Schön (1978), *Organizational Learning: A Theory of Action Perspective*, Reading, MA: Addison Wesley.

Aristotle (1998), *The Metaphysics* (with an introduction by H. Lawson-Tancred), London: Penguin.

Armstrong, Karen ([2005] 2006), *A Short History of Myth*, Edinburgh: Canongate.

Bakunin, Michael (1842), *The Reaction in Germany: From the Notebooks of a Frenchman*, accessed 10 October 2008 at www.marxists.org/reference/archive/bakunin/works/1842/reaction-germany.htm.

Banerjee, Subhabrata Bobby and Anshuman Prasad (2008), 'Introduction to the Special Issue on Critical Reflections on Management and Organizations: a postcolonial perspective', *Critical Perspectives on International Business*, **4** (2–3), 90–98.

Barley, Stephen R. and Gideon Kunda (1992), 'Design and devotion: surges of rational and normative ideologies of control in managerial discourse', *Administrative Science Quarterly*, 37, 363–99.

Barthes, Roland ([1957] 1973), *Mythologies*, London: Paladin.

Bateson Gregory (1972), *Steps to an Ecology of Mind*, New York: Ballantine Books.

Bateson Gregory (1979), *Mind and Nature: A Necessary Unity*, Toronto, ON: Bantam Books.

Bauman, Zygmunt ([1991] 1993), *Modernity and Ambivalence*, Cambridge and Oxford: Polity Press.

Bauman, Zygmunt (1998), *Globalization: The Human Consequences*, Cambridge: Polity.

Bauman, Zygmunt (2000), *Liquid Modernity*, Cambridge: Polity.

Bauman, Zygmunt (2003), *Liquid Love*, Cambridge: Polity.

Bauman, Zygmunt (2004), *Identity: Conversations with Benedetto Vecchi*, Cambridge and Malden: Polity Press.

Bauman, Zygmunt (2011), *Collateral Damage: Social Inequalities in a Global Age*, Cambridge and Malden: Polity Press.

Berger, Arthur S. and Joyce Berger (1995), *Fear of the Unknown*, Westport, CT and London: Praeger.

Blikle, Andrzej (2009), *Przemówienie na 140-lecie firmy,* accessed 11 March 2010 at www.blikle.pl/index.php?option=com_content&view=category&layout=blog&id=39&Itemid=217&lang=pl.

Boddy, Clive Roland (2006), 'The dark side of management decisions: organizational psychopaths', *Management Decision*, **44** (10), 1461–75.

Böhm, Steffen and Vinícius Brei (2008), 'Marketing the hegemony of development: on pulp fictions and green deserts', *Marketing Theory*, **8** (4), 339–66.

Boje, David (1995), 'Stories of the storytelling organization: a postmodern analysis of Disney as "Tamara-land"', *Academy of Management Journal*, **38** (4), 997–1035.

Boje, David M. (2001), *Narrative Methods for Organizational and Communication Research*, London, Thousand Oaks, CA, and New Delhi: Sage.

Boje, David M. and Rita Durant (2006), 'Free stories!', *Tamara Journal*, **5** (3), 19–37.

Bornstein, David (1998), 'Changing the world on a shoestring', *Atlantic Monthly*, **281** (1), 34–9.

Bornstein, David (2007), *How to Change the World: Social Entrepreneurs and the Power of New Ideas*, New York: Oxford University Press.

Boucouvalas, Marcie (1999), 'Following the movement: from transpersonal psychology to a multidisciplinary transpersonal orientation', *Journal of Transpersonal Psychology*, **31** (1), 27–39.

Bowles, Martin (1991), 'The organization shadow', *Organization Studies*, **12** (3), 387–404.

Bowles, Martin L. (1993), 'The gods and goddesses: personifying social life in the age of organization', *Organization Studies*, **14** (3), 395–418.

Branson, Richard (2009), *Business Stripped Bare: Adventures of a Global Entrepreneur*, London: Virgin Books.

Brei, Vinícius and Steffen Böhm (2009), '1L=10L for Africa: the postcolonial marketing of bottled water', Essex Business School working paper 09/08, University of Essex, Colchester.

Brook, Peter ([1968] 1995), *The Empty Space*, New York: Touchstone.

Burke, Kenneth (1945), *A Grammar of Motives*, Berkeley, CA: University of California Press.

Burnham, James ([1941] 1960), *The Managerial Revolution,* Bloomington, IN: Indiana University Press.

Burns, Bernard and Rachael Pope (2007), 'Negative behaviours in the workplace: a study of two primary care trusts in the NHS', *International Journal of Public Sector Management*, **20** (4), 295–303.

Burrell, Gibson (1997), *Pandemonium: Towards a Retro-organization Theory*, London: Sage.

Burrell, Gibson (1988), 'Modernism, postmodernism and organizational analysis: the contribution of Michel Foucault', *Organization Studies*, **9** (2), 221–35.

Burton, Dawn (2001), 'Critical marketing theory: the blueprint?', *European Journal of Marketing*, **35** (5–6), 722–43.

Burton, John C. and Robert J. Sack (1991), 'Time for some lateral thinking', *Accounting Horizons*, **5** (2), 118–23.

Butler, Stephen A. (2010), 'Solving business problems using a lateral thinking approach', *Management Decision*, **48** (1), 58–64.

Campbell, Christina (2006), 'Inside the Googleplex', *Canadian Business*, **79** (22), 59–61.

Campbell, Joseph ([1949] 1993), *The Hero with a Thousand Faces*, Princeton, NJ: Princeton University Press.

Campbell, Joseph ([1972] 1988), *Myths to Live by: How we Recreate Ancient Legends in our Daily Lives to Release Human Potential*, New York, Toronto, ON, Sydney, NSW and Auckland, New Zealand: Bantam Books.

Campbell, Joseph (1988), *The Inner Reaches of Outer Space: Metaphor as Myth and as Religion*, New York: Harper & Row.

Campbell, Joseph (2004), *Pathways to Bliss: Mythology and Personal Transformation*, Novato, CA: New World Library.

Carr, Adrian (2002), 'Jung, archetypes and mirroring in organizational change management: lessons from a longitudinal case study', *Journal of Organizational Change Management*, (5), 477–89.

Case, Peter (2006), 'Management education and the philosophical life: a reply to John Hendry', *Management Learning*, **37** (3), 283–9.

Case, Peter and Jonathan Gosling (2007), 'Wisdom of the moment: premodern perspectives on organizational action', *Social Epistemology*, **21** (2), 87–111.

Cassirer, Ernst (1946), *Language and Myth*, translated by S. Langer, New York: Dover.

Chaffey, Dave ([2002] 2007), *E-business and E-commerce Management*, Harlow: Prentice Hall.

Cheever, Susan (2005), *My Name Is Bill: Bill Wilson – His Life and the Creation of Alcoholics Anonymous*, New York: Washington Square Press.

Chomsky, Noam (2005), *Chomsky on Anarchism*, Edinburgh and Oakland, CA: AK Press.

Chrostowski, Aleksander (2006), 'Metoda Action Research w procesie doradztwa strategicznego', PhD thesis, Akademia Leona Koźmińskiego, Warsaw.

Ciuk, Sylwia and Monika Kostera (2010), 'Drinking from the Waters of Lethe: a tale of organizational oblivion', *Management Learning*, **41** (2), 187–204.

Collinson, David and Jeff Hearn (eds) (1996), *Men as Managers, Managers as Men: Critical Perspectives on Men, Masculinities and Managements*, London: Sage.

Collinson, David and Jeff Hearn (2001), 'Naming men as men: implications for work, organization and management', in Stephen M. Whitehead and Frank J. Barnett (eds), *The Masculinities Reader*, Cambridge: Polity Press, pp. 144–69.

Connell, R.W. (1995), *Masculinities*, Berkeley, CA and Los Angeles, CA: University of California Press.

Cooke, Graham (2005), 'The disabling shadow of leadership', *British Journal of Administrative Management*, **46**, 16–17.

Cooper, Robert (2006), 'Making present: autopoiesis as human production', *Organization*, **13** (1), 59–81.

Coser, Lewis (1974), *Greedy Institutions: Patterns of Undivided Commitment*, New York: Free Press.

Costea, Bogdan, Norman Crump and John Holm (2007), 'The spectre of Dionysus: play, work and managerialism', *Society and Business Review*, **2** (2),153–65.

Csikszentmihályi, Mihály (1990), *Flow: The Psychology of Optimal Experience*, New York: Harper & Row.

Csikszentmihályi, Mihály (2003), *Good Business: Leadership, Flow, and the Making of Meaning*, New York: Penguin.

Cunliffe, Ann (2003), 'Reflexive inquiry in organizational research: questions and possibilities', *Human Relations*, **56** (8), 983–1003.

Cunliffe, Ann and Matthew Eriksen (2011), 'Relational leadership', *Human Relations*, **64** (11), 1425–49.

Cyert, Richard M. and James G. March (1963), *A Behavioral Theory of the Firm*, Englewood Cliffs, NJ: Prentice-Hall.

Czarniawska, Barbara (1997), *Narrating the Organization: Dramas of Institutional Identity*, Chicago, IL: Chicago University Press.

Czarniawska, Barbara (2000), *A City Reframed: Managing Warsaw in the 1990s*, London: Harwood.

Czarniawska, Barbara (2004), *Narratives in Social Science Research*, London, Thousand Oaks, CA, and New Delhi: Sage.

Czarniawska, Barbara (2005), 'Fashion in organizing', in Barbara Czarniawska (ed.) *Global Ideas: How Ideas, Objects and Practices Travel in the Global Economy*, Copenhagen and Malmö, Sweden: CBS Press, pp. 129–46.

Czarniawska, Barbara (2008), 'Humiliation: a standard organizational product?', *Critical Perspectives on Accounting*, 19, 1034–53.

Czarniawska, Barbara (2009), *A Theory of Organizing*, Cheltenham, UK and Northampton, MA, USA: Edward Elgar.

Czarniawska, Barbara and Carl Rhodes (2006), 'Strong plots: the relationship between popular culture and management theory and practice', in Pasquale Gagliardi and Barbara Czarniawska (eds), *Management and Humanities*, Cheltenham, UK and Northampton, MA, USA: Edward Elgar, pp. 195–218.

Czarniawska-Joerges, Barbara (1992), *Exploring Complex Organizations: A Cultural Perspective*, Newbury Park, CA, London and New Dehli: Sage.

Czarniawska-Joerges, Barbara (1993), *The Three-Dimensional Organization: A Constructionist view*, Lund, Sweden: Studentlitteratur.

Czarniawska-Joerges, Barbara (1994), 'Nauka o zarządzaniu – dyscyplina praktyczna czy akademicka', *Przegląd Organizacji*, **1**, 16–17.

Czarniawska-Joerges, Barbara and Rolf Wolff (1991), 'Leaders, managers, entrepreneurs on and off the organizational stage', *Organization Studies*, **12** (4), 529–46.

de Beauvoir, Simone ([1949] 1997), *The Second Sex*, London: Vintage.

De Bono, Edward ([1967] 2007), *Myślenie lateralne: Idee na przekór schematom*, Gliwice, Poland: Helion/OnePress.

de Troyes, Chrétien ([1170] 1988), *Arthurian Romances*, New York: Everyman's Library.

Derber, Charles ([1979] 2000), *The Pursuit of Attention: Power and Ego in Everyday Life*, Oxford: Oxford University Press.

Dew, Nicholas (2009), 'Serendipity in entrepreneurship', *Organization Studies*, **30** (7), 735–53.

Diderot, Denis ([1773] 2009), *Le paradoxe sur le comédien*, Paris: Gallimard.

Dixon, Sarah E.A. and Anne Clifford (2007), 'Ecopreneurship – a new approach to managing the triple bottom line', *Journal of Organizational Change Management*, **20** (3), 326–45.

Douglas, Mary (1966), *Purity and Danger: An Analysis of Concepts of Pollution and Taboo*, New York: Praeger.

Douglas, Mary ([1985] 2004), *Risk Acceptability According to the Social Sciences*, Oxford and New York: Routledge.

Drucker, Peter ([1985] 1993), *Innovation and Entrepreneurship: Practice and Principles*, Harper Collins.

Dutton, J. and Dukerich, J. (1991), 'Keeping an eye on the mirror: image and identity in organizational adaptation', *Administrative Science Quarterly*, **39** (3), 239–63.

Durant, Rita (2002), 'Synchronicity: a post-structuralist guide to creativity and change', *Journal of Organizational Change Management*, **15** (5), 490–501.

Eco, Umberto ([1973] 1989), *The Open Work*, Cambridge, MA: Harvard University Press.

266

Ehrenreich, Barbara (2005), *Bait and Switch: The (Futile) Pursuit of the American Dream*, New York: Metropolitan Books.

Eliade, Mircea ([1932] 1961), *Images and Symbols: Studies in Religious Symbolism*, London: Harvill Press.

Eriksson, Michael and Mats Sundgren (2005), 'Managing change: strategy of serendipity – reflections from the merger of Astra and Zeneca', *Journal of Change Management*, **5** (1), 15–28.

Finnigan, Annie, Susan Goldberg, Patty Orsini, Joanna Ramey, Sarah Scalet and Vicki M. Young (2010), '*Working Mother* 100 best companies 2009', *Working Mother*, accessed 6 April 2010 at www.workingmother.com/BestCompanies/work-life-balance/2009/08working-mother-100-best-companies-2009.

Foote Whyte, William ([1943] 1993), *Street Corner Society: The Social Structure of an Italian Slum*, Chicago, IL, and London: Chicago University Press.

Fotaki, Marianna and Nancy Harding (2012), 'Lacan and sexual difference in organization and management theory: towards a hysterical academy?', *Organization*, forthcoming, DOI:10.1177/1350508411435 280.

Foucault, Michel ([1975] 1991), *Discipline and Punish: The Birth of the Prison*, London: Tavistock.

Fromm, Erich ([1941] 1994), *Escape from Freedom*, New York: Henry Holt.

Fromm, Erich ([1968] 2001), *The Revolution of Hope: Toward a Humanized Technology*, New York: American Mental Health Foundation.

Fuller, Robert W. (2001), 'A new look at hierarchy', *Leader to Leader*, **21** (Summer), 6–12.

Fuller, Robert W. (2003), *Somebodies and Nobodies: Overcoming the Abuse of Rank*, Gabriola Island, BC: New Society Publishers.

Furusten, Staffan (2009), 'Management consultants as improvising agents of stability', *Scandinavian Journal of Management*, **25**, 264–74.

Gabriel, Yiannis (2000), *Storytelling in Organizations: Facts, Fictions, and Fantasies*, Oxford: Oxford University Press.

Gabriel, Yiannis (2004), 'Introduction', in Yiannis Gabriel (ed.,) *Myths, Stories and Organizations: Premodern Narratives for Our Times*, Oxford: Oxford University Press, pp. 1–10.

Gabriel, Yiannis (2008), 'Oedipus in the land of organizational darkness', in W.M. Kostera (ed.), *Organizational Epics and Sagas: Tales of Organizations*, London: Palgrave Macmillan, pp. 39–52.

Gabriel, Yiannis, Stephen Fineman and David Sims ([1992] 2000), *Organizing and Organizations: An Introduction*, London, Thousand Oaks, CA, and New Delhi: Sage.

Gaffen, David (2007), 'Hemlines are dropping, sell!' *Wall Street Journal*, **250** (58), B4-0.

Gaiman, Neil ([2005] 2006), *Anansi Boys*, New York: Harper Collins.

Galbraith, John Kenneth (2004), *The Economics of Innocent Fraud: Truth for our Time*, Boston, MA and New York: Houghton Mifflin.

Galea, Christine (2006), 'All you really need is love', *Sales and Marketing Management*, **158** (2), 24–8.

Geertz, Clifford (1973), Thick description: toward an interpretive theory of culture', in *The Interpretation of Cultures*, New York: Basic Books, pp. 3–30.

Geus, Marius de (2002), 'Ecotopia, sustainability and vision', *Organization and Environment*, **15** (2), 187–201.

Ginsberg, Benjamin (2011), *The Fall of the Faculty: The Rise of the All-administrative University and Why it Matters*, Oxford: Oxford University Press.

Glinka, Beata (2008), *Kulturowe uwarunkowania przedsiębiorczości w Polsce*, Warsaw: PWE.

Goffman, Erving (1959), *The Presentation of Self in Everyday Life*, Harmondsworth: Penguin.

Goffman, Erving ([1961] 1991), *Asylums: Essays on the Social Situation of Mental Patients and other Inmates*, London: Penguin.

Goll, Monika (2009), 'Barbie Girls – pierwszy polski lesbijski kabaret', *Wysokie Obcasy.pl*, accessed 20 February 2012 at www.wysokieobcasy.pl/wysokie-obcasy/1,53662,7175455,Barbie_Girls___pierwszy_polski_le sbijski_kabaret.html.

Gosling, Jonathan and Peter Case (2010), 'Taking up a role as an affordance of knowledge: a psychodynamic interpretation of the rebirth motif in Plato's Myth of Er', Exeter Business School working paper.

Grabher, Gernot (2001), 'Ecologies of creativity: the village, the group, and the heterarchic organization of the British advertising industry', *Environment and Planning*, **33**, 351–74.

Greenwood, Robert and C. Royston Hinings (1988), 'Organizational design types, tracks and the dynamics of strategic change', *Organization Studies*, **9** (3), 293–316.

Greil, Arthur L. and David R. Rudy (1983), 'Conversion to the world view of Alcoholics Anonymous: a refinement of conversion theory', *Qualitative Sociology*, **6** (1), 5–29.

Guillet de Monthoux, Pierre ([1993] 2004), *The Art Firm: Aesthetic Management and Metaphysical Marketing from Wagner to Wilson*, Stanford, CA: Stanford Business Books.

GUS (2010) *Portal informacyjny*, accessed 2 June 2010 at www.stat.gov.pl/gus/index_PLK_HTML.htm.

Hamel, Gary (2006), 'The why, what and how of innovation', *Harvard Business Review*, **84** (6), 1–13.

Hannan, Michael and John Freeman (1977), 'The population ecology of organizations', *American Journal of Sociology*, **82**, 929–64.

Haraway, Donna J. ([1985] 1991), 'A cyborg manifesto: science, technology, and socialist-feminism in the late twentieth century', in Donna Haraway, *Simians, Cyborgs and Women: The Reinvention of Nature*, New York: Routledge, pp. 149–81.

Hart, David W. and F. Neil Brady (2005), 'Spirituality and archetype in organizational life', *Business Ethics Quarterly*, **15** (3), 409–28.

Hartley, David (1995), 'The "McDonaldization" of higher education: food for thought?', *Oxford Review of Education*, **21** (4), 409–23.

Hatch, M.J. (1993), 'The dynamics of organizational culture', *Academy of Management Review*, **18** (4), 657–63.

Hatch, Mary Jo (1997), *Organization Theory: Modern, Symbolic and Postmodern Perspectives*, Oxford: Oxford University Press.

Hatch, Mary Jo, Monika Kostera and Andrzej K. Koźmiński (2005), *Three Faces of Leadership: Manager, Artist, Priest*, London: Blackwell.

Hatch, Mary Jo and Majken Schultz (2002), 'The dynamics of organizational identity', *Human Relations*, **55** (8), 989–1018.

Hatch, Mary Jo and Majken Schultz (2008), *Taking Brand Initiative: How to Align Strategy, Culture and Identity through Corporate Branding*, San Fransisco, CA: Jossey-Bass/Wiley.

Hayles, Katherine N. (1999), *How We Became Posthuman: Virtual Bodies in Cybernetics, Literature and Informatics*, Chicago, IL and London: University of Chicago Press.

Hedblom Jacobson, Kaaren (1993), 'Organization and the mother archetype: a Jungian analysis of adult development and self-identity within the organization', *Administration and Society*, **25** (1), 60–84.

Hepso, Vidar (2008), '"Boundary-spanning" practices and paradoxes related to trust among people and machines in high-tech oil and gas environment', in Dariusz Jemielniak and Jerzy Kociatkiewicz (eds), *Management Practices in High-Tech Environments*, New York: Information Science Reference, pp. 1–17.

Hersey, Paul, Kenneth H. Blanchard and Dewey E. Johnson ([1996] 2007), *Management of Organizational Behavior: Leading Human Resources*, London: Pearson Education.

Hesiod (2008), *Theogony and Works and Days*, translated by M.L. West, Oxford: Oxford Paperbacks.

Hjorth, Daniel (2003), *Rewriting Entrepreneurship: For a New Perspective on Organizational Creativity*, Copenhagen, Malmö, Sweden and Oslo: CBS Press-Liber-Abstrakt.

Hochschild, A. (1983), *The Managed Heart: Commercialization of Human Feeling*, Berkeley, CA: University of California Press.

Hollis, James (2000), *The Archetypical Imagination*, College Station, TX: Texas A&M University Press.

Höpfl, Heather (2002), 'Strategic quest and the search for the primal mother', *Human Resource Development International*, **5** (1), 11–22.

Höpfl, Heather and Linstead S. (1993), 'Passion and performance: suffering and the carrying of organizational roles', in S. Fineman (ed.), *Emotion and Organization*, London, Thousand Oaks, CA, and New Delhi: Sage, 76–93.

Hrebniak, Lawrence G. and William F. Joyce (1985), 'Organizational adaptation: strategic choice and organizational determinism', *Administrative Science Quarterly*, **30**, 336–49.

Huczynski, Andrzej A. ([1993] 1996), *Management Gurus: What Makes Them and How to Become One*, International Thompson Business Press.

Huizinga, Johan ([1938] 2003), *Homo Ludens*, London: Routledge & Kegan Paul.

Hunter, Carolyn, Dariusz Jemielniak and Agnieszka Postuła (2010), 'Temporal and spatial shift within playful work', *Journal of Organizational Change Management*, **23** (1), 87–102.

Hyde, Paula and Alan B. Thomas (2003), 'When a leader dies', *Human Relations*, **56** (8), 1005–24.

Illies, Jody J. and Roni Reiter-Palmon (2008), 'Responding destructively in leadership situations: the role of personal values and problem construction', *Journal of Business Ethics*, **82**, 251–72.

Ingarden, Roman (1960), *O dziele literackim: Badania z pogranicza antologii, teorii języka i filozofii*, Warsaw: PWN.

Isaak, Robert (2007), 'The making of the ecopreneur', in Michael Shaper (ed.), *Making Ecopreneurs: Developing Sustainable Entrepreneurship*, Aldershot: Ashgate, pp. 13–25.

Isaack, Thomas (1978), 'Intuition: an ignored dimension of management', *Academy of Management Review*, **3** (4), 917–21.

Jackall, Robert (1988), *Moral Mazes: The World of Corporate Managers*, Oxford: Oxford University Press.

Jacobs, Claus D. and Loizos Heracleous (2007), 'Strategizing through playful design', *Journal of Business Strategy*, **28** (4), 75–80.

Jemielniak, Dariusz (2007), 'Managers as lazy, stupid careerists? Contestation and stereotypes among software engineers', *Journal of Organizational Change Management*, **20** (4), 491–508.

Jemielniak, Dariusz and Jerzy Kociatkiewicz (2009), 'Knowledge management: fad or enduring organizational concept?', in Dariusz Jemelniak and Jerzy Kociatkiewicz (eds), *Knowledge-Intensive Organizations*, New York: Information Science Reference, pp. 552–61.

Johannisson, Bengt (1987), 'Anarchists and organizers: entrepreneurs in network perspective', *International Studies of Management and Organization*, **17** (1), 49–63.

Johannisson, Bengt (2005), *Entreprenörskapets väsen (Istota przedsiębiorczości)*, Lund, Sweden: Studentlitteratur.

Jonnergård, Karin (2008), 'The witchcraft of professionalism: the attractiveness of ideal types of professions', in Monika Kostera (ed.), *Organizational Olympians: Heroes and Heroines of Organizational Myths*, London: Palgrave, pp. 184–94.

Jung, Carl Gustav (1993), *Synchronicity: An Acausal Connecting Principle*, Bollingen, Switzerland: Bollingen Foundation.

Jung, Carl Gustav ([1921] 1971), *Psychological Types, The Collected Works of C.G. Jung*, vol. 6, Princeton, NJ: Princeton University Press.

Jung, Carl Gustav ([1928] 1972), 'Two essays in analytical psychology', *The Collected Works of C. G. Jung*, vol. 7, Princeton, NJ: Princeton University Press.

Jung, Carl Gustav ([1934–1954] 1968b), *Aion*, collected works vol. 9, London: Routledge and Kegan Paul.

Jung, Carl Gustav ([1935] 1969), 'Psychological commentary on 'The Tibetan Book of the Dead', *The Collected Works of C.G. Jung*, vol. 11, Princeton, NJ: Princeton University Press, pp. 509–26.

Jung, Carl Gustav ([1938] 1966), *Psychology and Religion*, New York: Yale University Press.

Jung, Carl Gustav ([1959] 1990), 'The archetypes and the collective unconscious', *The Collected Works of C.G. Jung*, vol. 9, Princeton, NJ: Princeton University Press.

Jung, Carl Gustav ([1960] 1981), *The Structure and Dynamics of the Psyche*, New York, Bollingen, Switzerland and Princeton, NJ: Princeton University Press.

Jung, Carl Gustav (ed.) ([1964] 1968), *Man and His Symbols*, New York: Dell.

Kant, Immanuel ([1781] 2008), *The Critique of Pure Reason*, Forgotten Books, accessed 20 April 2010 at www.forgottenbooks.org/info/9781440078828.

Kanter, Rosabeth Moss ([1977] 1993), *Men and Women of the Corporation*, New York: Basic Books.

Kempiński, Andrzej M. (2001), *Encyklopedia mitologii ludów indoeuropejskich*, Warsaw: Iskry.

Kempiński, Andrzej M. (2009), *Ilustrowany leksykon mitologii Wikingów*, Swarzędz, Poland: Kurpisz.

Kerfoot, Deborah and David Knights (1996), '"The best is yet to come?" The quest for embodiment in managerial work', in David Collinson and Jeff Hearn (eds), *Men as Managers, Managers as Men: Critical Perspectives on Men, Masculinities and Managements*, London: Sage, pp. 78–98.

Kets de Vries, Manfred (1998), 'Charisma in action: the transformational abilities of Virgin's Richard Branson and ABB's Percy Barnevik', *Organizational Dynamics*, **4**, 7–21.

Kets de Vries, Manfred (2003), '"Doing an Alexander": lessons on leadership by a master conqueror', *European Management Journal*, **21** (3), 370–76.

Kets de Vries, Manfred (2006a), 'The spirit of despotism: understanding the tyrant within', *Human Relations*, **59** (2), 195–220.

Kets de Vries, Manfred (2006b), *The Leader on the Couch: A Clinical Approach to Changing People and Organizations*, New York: John Wiley.

Kets de Vries, Manfred (2009), *Reflections on Character and Leadership: On the Couch with Manfred Kets de Vries*, San Fransisco, CA: Jossey Bass.

Kidd, Bruce (1987), 'Sports and masculinity', in Michael Kaufman (ed.) *Beyond Patriarchy: Essays by Men on Pleasure, Power and Change*, Toronto, ON and New York: Oxford University Press, pp. 250–65.

Kiddle, Thomas (2009), 'Recent trends in business casual attire and their effects on student job seekers', *Business Communication Quarterly*, September, 350–54.

King, Sandra and Dave M. Nicol (1999), 'Organizational enhancement through recognition of individual spirituality: reflections of Jaques and Jung', *Journal of Organizational Change Management*, **12** (3), 234–42.

Klein, Naomi (2000), *No Logo: Taking Aim at the Brand Bullies*, New York: Picador.

Kociatkiewicz, Jerzy (2000), 'Dreams of time, times of dreams', *Studies in Cultures, Organizations, and Societies*, **6** (1), 71–86.

Kociatkiewicz, Jerzy (2004), '*The social construction of space in a computerized environment*', PhD thesis, IFiS PAN, Warsaw, accessed 14 April 2010 at www.kociak.org/files/drweb.pdf.

Kociatkiewicz, Jerzy (2007), 'Of angels, demons, and magic items: the experience economy of everyday objects', in Daniel Hjorth and Monika Kostera (eds), *Entrepreneurship and the Experience Economy*, Copenhagen: Copenhagen Business School Press, pp. 93–113.

Kociatkiewicz, Jerzy (2008), 'The cosmogonic duel', in Monika Kostera (ed.), *Organizational Epics and Sagas: Tales of Organizations*, London: Palgrave, pp. 142–55.

Kociatkiewicz, Jerzy and Monika Kostera (2005), *Gender and Technology: Images of Humans and Computers in Polish Press*, Cambridge: 4th International Critical Management Studies Conference.

Kociatkiewicz, Jerzy and Monika Kostera (2010), 'Experiencing the shadow: organizational exclusion and denial within experience economy', *Organization*, **17** (2), pp. 257–82.

Kociatkiewicz, Jerzy and Monika Kostera (2012a), 'The speed of experience: the co-narrative method in experience economy education', *British Journal of Management*, 28, pp. 162–72.

Kociatkiewicz, Jerzy and Monika Kostera (2012b), 'The good manager: an archetypical quest for morally sustainable management', *Organization Studies*, forthcoming, DOI: 10.1177/0170840612445124.

Konecki, Krzysztof ([2003] 2007), 'How the identity of the observed person becomes the identity of the researcher', in Monika Kostera (ed.), *Organisational Ethnography: Methods and inspirations*, Lund, Sweden: Studentlitteratur, pp. 64–6.

Kostera, Monika (1995), 'The modern crusade: missionaries of management come to Eastern Europe', *Management Learning*, **26** (3), pp. 331–52.

Kostera, Monika (1996), *Postmodernizm w zarządzaniu*, Warsaw: PWE.

Kostera, Monika (1997), 'The kitsch-organization', *Studies in Cultures, Organizations and Societies*, **3**, 163–77.

Kostera, Monika (2003), 'Reflections of the other: images of women in the Polish business press', *Human Resource Development International*, **6** (3), 325–42.

Kostera, Monika (2005), *The Quest for the Self-actualizing Organization*, Malmö, Sweden and Copenhagen: Liber.

Kostera, Monika (2006), 'The narrative collage as research method', *Storytelling, Self, Society*, **2** (2), 5–27.

Kostera, Monika (2007), *Organisational Ethnography: Methods and Inspirations*, Lund, Sweden: Studentlitteratur.

Kostera, Monika (2008a), 'The mythologization of organization', in Monika Kostera (ed.), *Organizational Epics and Sagas: Tales of Organizations*, London: Palgrave-Macmillan, pp. 9–13.

Kostera, Monika (2008b), 'Introduction,' in Monika Kostera (ed.), *Organizational Olympians: Heroes, Heroines and Villains of Organizational Myths*, London: Palgrave-Macmillan, pp. 9–16.

Kostera, Monika (2011), *Fast Poetry*, accessed 14 February 2012 at www.kostera.pl/haiku.htm.

Kostera, Monika and Agnieszka Postuła (2011), 'Holding up the aegis: on the construction of social roles by Polish IT-professionals', *Tamara Journal for Critical Organization Inquiry*, **9** (1–2), 75–84.

Kostera, Monika and Martyna Śliwa (2010), *Zarządzanie w XXI wieku*, Warsaw: WAiPP.

Koźmiński, Andrzej K. (1986), 'Zarządzanie w przyszłości', *Przegląd Organizacji*, **2**, 3.

Küpers, Wendelin (2002), 'Phenomenology of aesthetic organising: ways towards aesthetically responsive organizations', *Journal Consumption, Markets and Cultures*, **5** (1), 31–68.

Kwiatkowski, Stefan (2001), 'Join us for the knowledge café on intellectual entrepreneurship for sustainable development . . .', in Stefan Kwiatkowski and Charles Stowe (eds), *Knowledge Café for Intellectual Product and Intellectual Capital*, Warsaw: Wydawnictwo WSPiZ, pp. 7–25.

Lakoff, George and Mark Johnson ([1980] 1983), *Metaphors We Live By*, Chicago, IL: Chicago University Press.

Latour, Bruno (1987), *Science in Action: How to Follow Scientists and Engineers Through Society*, Cambridge, MA: Harvard University Press.

Leck, Joanne and Bella Galperin ([2005] 2006), 'Workplace violence and young workers', *International Journal of the Diversity*, **5** (4), 49–57.

Lee, Monica (2008), 'Goddess: a story of myth and power', in Monika Kostera (ed.), *Organizational Epics and Sagas: Tales of Organizations*, London: Palgrave, pp. 40–50.

Lemon, Mark and P.S. Sahota (2004), 'Organizational culture as a knowledge repository for increased innovative capacity', *Technovation*, **24**, 483–98.

Letiche, Hugo (2000), 'Phenomenal complexity theory as informed by Bergson', *Journal of Organizational Change Management*, **13** (6), 545–57.

Lewin, Kurt, Ronald Lippit and Ralph K. White (1939), 'Patterns of aggressive behavior in experimentally created social climates', *Journal of Social Psychology*, **10**, 271–301.

Lindgren, Astrid ([1945] 2003), *The Best of Pippi Longstocking: Three Books in One*, Oxford: Oxford University Press.

Lindstedt, Gunnar (2001), *Boo-com och IT-bubblan som sprack*, Stockholm: MånPocket.

Linsley, Philip M. and Philip J. Shrives (2009), 'Mary Douglas, risk and accounting failures', *Critical Perspectives on Accounting*, **20**, 492–508.

Lipton-Blumen, Jean (2005), 'Toxic leadership: when grand illusions masquerade as noble visions', *Leader to Leader*, **1**, 29–36.

Lovelock, James ([1979] 2000), *Gaia: A New Look at Life on Earth*, Oxford and New York: Oxford University Press.

Lovelock, James ([2006] 2007), *The Revenge of Gaia*, London: Penguin.

Ludwicki, Tomasz (2008), 'Krytyczne badania nad doradztwem

organizacyjnym', in Monika Kostera (ed.), *Nowe kierunki w zarządzaniu*, Warsaw: WAiP, pp. 259–75.

Luhmann, Niklas ([1995] 1996), *Social Systems*, Stanford, CA: Stanford University Press.

Lutgen-Sandvik, Pamela, Sarah J. Tracy and Jess K. Alberts (2007), 'Burned by bullying in the American workplace: prevalence, perception, degree and impact', *Journal of Management Studies*, **44** (6), 837–62.

Lyons, Denise (1997), 'The feminine in the foundations of organizational psychology', *Journal of Applied Behavioral Science*, **33** (1), 7–26.

Machiavelli, Niccolò ([1532] 2007), *Książę* [*The Prince*], Kęty, Poland: Marek Derewiecki.

MacIntyre, Alisdair (1981), *After Virtue: A Study in Moral Theory*, London: Duckworth Press.

Magala, Sławomir (2009), *The Management of Meaning in Organizations*, London: Palgrave Macmillan.

Mangham, Iain L. and Michael A. Overington (1987), *Organizations as Theatre: A Social Psychology of Dramatic Appearances*, Chichester, New York, Brisbane, QLD, Toronto, ON, and Singapore: John Wiley.

Marks, Mitchell Lee and Ronny Vansteenkiste (2008), 'Preparing for organizational death: proactive HR engagement in an organizational transition', *Human Resource Management*, **47** (4), 809–27.

Maslow, Abraham ([1962] 1968), *Toward a Psychology of Being*, New York, Cincinnati, OH, Toronto, ON, London, and Melbourne, VIC: Van Nostrand.

Maslow, Abraham ([1965] 1998), *Maslow on Management*, New York: Wiley.

Matthews, Robin (2002), 'Competition archetypes and creative imagination', *Journal of Organizational Change Management*, **15** (5), 461–76.

McKinlay, Alan and Ken Starkey (eds) (1998), *Foucault, Management and Organization Theory: From Panopticon to Technologies of Self*, Thousand Oaks, CA: Sage.

Merton, Robert K. ([1965] 1993), *On the Shoulder of Giants: A Shandean Postscript*, Chicago, IL: Chicago University Press.

Merton, Robert K. and Elinor Barber ([1958] 2004), *The Travels and Adventures of Serendipity: A Study in Sociological Semantics and the Sociology of Science*, Princeton, NJ: Princeton University Press.

Milczarczyk, Aneta (2008), 'Fenomen przedsiębiorczości społecznej', in Monika Kostera (ed.), *Nowe kierunki w zarządzaniu*, Warsaw: WAiP, pp. 277–91.

Miller, Danny and Friesen, Peter H. (1980), 'Archetypes of organizational transition', *Administrative Science Quarterly*, **25**, 268–99.

Mills, C. Wright ([1959] 2007), *Wyobraźnia socjologiczna* [*Sociological Imagination*], Warsaw: PWN.

Mintzberg, Henry (1984), 'Power and organization life cycles', *Academy of Management Review*, **9** (2), 207–24.

Mintzberg, Henry (1999), 'Managing quietly', *Leader to Leader*, **1**, 24–30.

Mitchell, Austin, Tony Puxty, Prem Sikka and Hugh Willmott (1994), 'Ethical statements as smokescreens for sectional interests: the case of the UK accountancy profession', *Journal of Business Ethics*, **13** (1), 39–51.

Monks, Claire P., Peter K. Smith, Paul Naylor, Christine Barter, Jane L. Ireland and Iain Coyne (2009), 'Bullying in different contexts: commonalities, differences and the role of theory', *Aggression and Violent Behavior*, **14**, 146–56.

Moore, Henrietta L. ([1988] 1995), *Feminism and Anthropology*, South Minneapolis, MN: University of Minnesota Press.

Morgan, Gareth ([1986] 2006), *Images of Organization*, Thousand Oaks, CA, London and New Delhi: Sage.

Morgan, Gareth (1993), *Imaginization: New Mindsets for Seeing, Organizing and Managing*, Thousand Oaks, CA, London and New Delhi: Sage.

Moss Kanter, Rosabeth ([1977] 1993), *Men and Women of the Corporation*, New York: Basic Books.

Mukherjee, Sanjoy (2007), 'Non-conventional entrepreneurial learning: spiritual insights from India', *Journal of Human Values*, **13** (1), 23–34.

Nielsen, Jeffrey (2004), *The Myth of Leadership: Creating Leaderless Organizations*, Palo-Alto, CA: Davies-Black.

Nilson, Henrietta (2009), *Henriettas collage: Kreativa kvinnor i familjeföretag*, Vaxjö, Sweden: Drivkraft.

Nonaka, Ikujiro (1991), 'The knowledge-creating company', *Harvard Business Review*, **69** (6), 96–105.

Nonaka, Ikujiro and Hirotaka Takeuchi (1995), *The Knowledge Creating Company: How Japanese Companies Create the Dynamics of Innovation*, New York: Oxford University Press.

Norcia, Vincent di (1996), 'Environmental and social performance', *Journal of Business Ethics*, **15**, 773–84,

Novicevic, Milorad M., Thomas J. Hench and Daniel A. Wren (2002), '"Playing by ear"... "in an incessant din of reasons": Chester Barnard and the history of intuition of management thought', *Management Decision*, **40** (10), 992–1002.

Obłój, Krzysztof (2001), *Strategia organizacji: W poszukiwaniu trwałej przewagi konkurencyjnej*, Warsaw: PWE.

Obłój, Krzysztof (2010), *Pasja and dyscyplina strategii*, Warsaw: Poltext.

Obłój, Krzysztof and Monika Kostera (1994), 'Polish privatization program: action, symbolism and cultural barriers', *Industrial and Environmental Crisis Quarterly*, **8** (1), 7–21.

Organisation for Economic Co-operation and Development (OECD) (2011), 'Graduates by field of education', *Higher Education and Adult Learning*, accessed 20 October 2011 at www.oecd.org.

Olson, Bradley John, Debra L. Nelson and Satyanarayana Parayitam (2006), 'Managing aggression in organizations: what leaders must know', *Leadership and Organization Development Journal*, **27** (5), 384–98.

Osborn, Alex Faickney ([1953] 1963), *Applied Imagination: Principles and Procedures of Creative Problem Solving*, New York: Charles Scribner's Son.

Ozbilgin, Mustafa and Ahu Tatli (2008), *Global Diversity Management: An Evidence Based Approach*, London: Palgrave Macmillan.

Ożogowska, Hanna ([1961] 2007), *Dziewczyna and chłopak czyli heca na 14 fajerek*, Łódź, Poland: Akapit-Press.

Palmer, Catherine (2002), '"Shit happens": the selling of risk in extreme sport', *Australian Journal of Anthropology*, **13** (3), 323–37.

Paloutzian, Raymond F. (2005), 'Religious conversion and spiritual transformation: a meaning-system analysis', in Raymond F. Paloutzian and Crystal L. Park (eds), *Handbook for the Psychology of Religion and Spirituality*, New York: Guilford, pp. 331–47.

Parker, Martin (2008), 'Heroic villains: the badlands of economy and organization', in Monika Kostera (ed.), *Organizational Epics and Sagas: Tales of Organizations*, London: Palgrave, pp. 105–17.

Parker, Martin (2009), 'Pirates, merchants, anarchists: representations of international business', *Management and Organizational History*, **4** (2), 167–85.

Parker, Martin (2012), *Alternative Business: Outlaws, Crime and Culture*. *London*, New York: Routledge.

Patwardhan, Abhijit, Stephanie M. Noble and Ceri M. Nishihara (2009), 'The use of strategic deception in relationships', *Journal of Services Marketing*, **23** (5), 318–25.

Payne, Roy L. (2000), 'Eupsychian management and the millennium', *Journal of Managerial Psychology*, **15** (3),219–26.

Pearson, Christine M., Lynne M. Andersson and Christine L. Porath (2000), 'Assessing and attacking workplace incivility', *Organizational Dynamics*, **29** (2), 123–37.

Pedersen, Sanna (2007), Världens bästa Astrid', *Dagens Nyheter*, accessed 18 March 2010 at www.dn.se/kultur-noje/film-tv/varldens-bas ta-astrid-1.731568.

Perrow, Charles (1991), 'A society of organizations', *Theory and Society*, **20**, 725–62.

Piątkowski, Przemysław (2007), 'Filadelfia – organizowanie jako walka na murach oblężonej twierdzy', in Monika Kostera (ed.), *Kultura organizacji: Badania etnograficzne polskich firm*, Gdańsk, Poland: GWP, pp. 211–33.

Piłat, Bartosz (2009), 'Leszek Czarnecki: Zdecydowałem się na książkową inwestycję i . . .', *Gazeta Wyborcza*, accessed 3 November 2010 at http://gospodarka.gazeta.pl/firma/1,31560,6658633,Leszek_Czarnecki__Zdec ydowalem_sie_na_ksiazkowa_inwestycje.html.

Pink, Daniel H. (2009), *Drive: The Surprising Truth about What Motivates Us*, New York: Riverhead Hardcover.

Pinnington, Ashly and Timothy Morris (2003), 'Archetype change in professional organizations: survey evidence from large law firms', *British Journal of Management*, **14**, 18–99.

Plato (1999), *The Apology*, accessed 15 March 2010 at the Project Gutenberg website, www.gutenberg.org/etext/1656.

Plato (2007), *The Republic*, London: Penguin.

Pleck, Joseph H. (1983), *The Myth of Masculinity*, Cambridge, MA: MIT Press.

Polanyi, Michael ([1958] 1974), *Personal Knowledge: Towards a Post-critical Philosophy*, Chicago, IL: University of Chicago Press.

Powell, Sarah (2007), 'Spotlight on Edward de Bono', *Management Decision*, **45** (6), 1058–63.

Pratt, Michael (2000), 'Building an ideological fortress: the role of spirituality, encapsulation and sensemaking', *Studies in Cultures, Organizations and Societies*, **6**, 35–69.

Pratt, Michael G. and Anat Rafaeli (1997), 'Organizational dress as symbol for multilayered social identities', *Academy of Management Journal*, **40** (4), 862–98.

Propp, Vladimir ([1928] 1968), *Morphology of the Folk Tale*, Austin, TX: University of Texas Press.

Qi, Yan and Joseph Meloche (2009), 'The power of play in knowledge management', paper presented at the International Conference on New Trends in Information and Service Science, Institute of Electrical and Electronics Engineers, Beijing.

Rafaeli, Anat and Michael G. Pratt (1993), 'Tailored meanings: on the meaning and impact of organizational dress', *Academy of Management Review*, **18** (1), 32–55.

Raz, Aviad E. and Judith Faldon (2005), 'Managerial culture, workplace culture and situated curricula in organizational learning', *Organization Studies*, **27** (2), 165–82.

Razi, Muhammad A., J. Michael Tarn and Faisal A. Siddiqui (2004), 'Exploring the failure and success of dotcoms', *Information Management and Computer Security*, **12** (3), 228–44.

Reason, Peter (2007), 'Education for ecology: science, aesthetics, spirit and ceremony', *Management Learning*, **38** (1), 27–44.

Rehn, Alf and Saara Taalas (2004), 'Crime and assumptions in entrepreneurship', in Daniel Hjorth and Chris Steyaert (eds), *Narrative and Discursive Approaches in Entrepreneurship: A Second Movements in Entrepreneurship Book*, Cheltenham, UK, and Northampton, MA, USA: Edward Elgar, pp. 144–59.

Ritzer, George (1996), *The McDonaldization of Society*, London: Pine Forge Press.

Roper, Michael (2001), 'Masculinity and the biographical meanings of management theory: Lyndall Urwick and the making of scientific management in inter-war Britain', *Gender, Work and Organization*, **8** (2), 182–204.

Rosen, Michael (1991), 'Coming to terms with the field: understanding and doing organizational ethnography', *Journal of Management Studies*, **28** (1), 1–24.

Rutenberg, David P. (1970), 'Organizational archetypes of a multinational company', *Management Science*, **16** (6), 337–49.

Ryland, Elizabeth (2000), 'Gaia rising: a Jungian view at environmental consciousness and sustainable organization', *Organization and Environment*, **13** (4), 381–402.

Said, Edward (1978), *Orientalism*, New York: Vintage.

Salzer-Mörling, Miriam (1998), 'As God created the earth . . . a saga that makes sense?', in David Grant, Tom Keenoy and Cliff Oswick (eds), *Discourse and Organization*, London, Thousand Oaks, CA, and New Delhi: Sage, pp. 104–18.

Sandilands, Lloyd (2010), 'The play of change', *Journal of Organizational Change Management*, **23** (1), 71–86.

Sapir, Edward (1931), 'Fashion', in *Encyclopaedia of the Social Sciences*, New York: Macmillan, pp. 139–44.

Sarasvathy, Saras D. (2008), *Effectuation: Elements of Entrepreneurial Expertise*, Cheltenham, UK and Northampton, MA, USA: Edward Elgar.

Saren, Michael (2007), 'Marketing is everything: the view from the street', *Marketing Intelligence and Planning*, **25** (1), 11–16.

Sargent, Alice G. (1981), 'Training men and women for androgynous behaviors in organizations', *Group and Organization Studies*, **6** (3), 302–11.

Schaper, Michael (2005), 'Understanding the green entrepreneur', in Michael Shaper (ed.), *Making Ecopreneurs: Developing Sustainable Entrepreneurship*, Aldershot: Ashgate, pp. 3–12.

Schein, Edgar H. (1991), 'The role of the founder in the creation of organizational culture', in Peter J. Frost, Larry F. Moore, Meryl Reis Louis, Craig C. Lundberg and Joanne Martin (eds), *Reframing Organizational Culture*, Newbury Park, CA, London and New Delhi: Sage, pp. 14–25.

Schott, Richard L. (1992), 'Abraham Maslow, humanistic psychology and organization leadership: a Jungian perspective,' *Journal of Humanistic Psychology*, **32** (1), 106–20.

Schreyögg, Georg and Heather Höpfl (2004), 'Theatre and organization: editorial introduction', *Organization Studies*, **25** (5), 601–704.

Schumpeter, Joseph (1949), 'Economic theory and entrepreneurial history', in *Change and the Entrepreneur*, prepared by the Research Center in Entrepreneurial History, Harvard University, Cambridge, MA: Harvard University Press, pp. 63–84.

Schwartz, Howard (1990), *Narcissistic Processes and Corporate Decay: The Theory of the Organizational Ideal*, New York: New York University Press.

Segal, Lynne (1990), *Slow Motion: Changing Masculinities, Changing Men*, New Brunswick, NJ: Rutgers University Press.

Seidl, David and Kai Helge Becker (2006), 'Organizations as distinction generating and processing systems: Niklas Luhmann's contribution to organization studies', *Organization*, **13** (1), 9–35.

Senge, Peter ([1990] 2006), *The Fifth Discipline: The Art and Practice of the Learning Organization*, London: Random House.

Sennett, Richard (1998), *The Corrosion of Character: The Personal Consequences of Work in the New Capitalism*, New York: Norton.

Sennett, Richard (2006), *The Culture of the New Capitalism*, New Haven, CT: Yale University.

Sexton, Carol (1994), 'Self-managed work teams: TQM technology at the employee level', *Journal of Organizational Change Management*, **7** (2), 45–52.

Shakespeare, William ([1600–1602] 2007), *Hamlet*, Kraków, Poland: Zielona Sowa.

Shepherd, Dean A. (2003), 'Learning from business failure: propositions of grief recovery for the self-employed', *Academy of Management Review*, **28** (2), 318–28.

Shepherd, Dean A. and Evan Douglas (1998), 'Is management education developing or killing the entrepreneurial spirit?', *Entrepreneurship Theory and Practice*, **23** (3), 11–27.

Sievers, Burkard (1994), *Work, Death and Life Itself: Essays on Management and Organization*, Berlin: De Gruyter.

Sievers, Burkard (2000), 'Competition as war: towards a socio-analysis of war in and among corporations', *Socio-Analysis*, **2** (1), 1–27.

Singer, June (1976), *Androgyny: Toward a New Theory of Sexuality*, New York: Anchor Books.

Sjöstrand, Sven-Erik (1998), 'Företagsledning', in Barbara Czarniawska (ed.), *Organisationsteori på svenska*, Malmö, Sweden: Liber, pp. 22–42.

Sławecki, Bartosz (2010), *Zatrudnianie po znajomości*, Warsaw: Beck.

Śliwa, Martyna and Geirge Cairns (2009), 'Towards a critical pedagogy of international business: the application of phronesis', *Management Learning*, **40** (3), 227–40.

Smircich, Linda (1983), 'Concepts of culture and organizational analysis', *Administrative Science Quarterly*, **28** (3), 339–58.

Smircich, Linda and Gareth Morgan (1982), 'Leadership: the management of meaning', *Journal of Applied Behavioural Studies*, **18**, 257–73.

Smith, Adam (1799), *Essays on Philosophical Subjects*, Basildon: James Decker.

Smith, Charles and Michael Elmes (2002), 'Leading change: insights from Jungian interpretations of The Book of Job', *Journal of Organizational Change Management*, **15** (5), 448–60.

Solomon, Robert C. (2004), 'Aristotle, ethics and business organizations', *Organization Studies*, **25** (6), 1021–43.

Stevenson, Robert Louis ([1886] 2007), *The Strange Case of Dr Jekyll and Mr Hyde*, London: Penguin Classics.

Steyaert, Chris (2004), 'The prosaic of entrepreneurship', in Daniel Hjorth and Chris Steyaert (eds), *Narrative and Discursive Approaches in Entrepreneurship: A Second Movements in Entrepreneurship Book*, Cheltenham, UK, and Northampton, MA, USA: Edward Elgar, pp. 8–21.

Stoczkowski, Wiktor (2009), 'UNESCO's doctrine of human diversity: a secular soteriology?', *Anthropology Today*, **25** (3), 7–11.

Stogdill, Ralph M. (1974), *Handbook of Leadership: A Survey of the Literature*, New York: Free Press.

Styhre, Alexander (2004), 'Rethinking knowledge: a Bergsonian critique of the notion of tacit knowledge', *British Journal of Management*, **15** (2), 177–99.

Styhre, Alexander (2008), 'The element of play in innovation work: the case of new drug development', *Creativity and Innovation Management*, **17** (2), 136–49.

Sun Tzu (2008), *The Art of War*, London: Penguin.

Svensson, Göran and Greg Wood (2005), 'The serendipity of leadership effectiveness in management and business practices', *Management Decision*, **43** (7–8), 1001–9.

Tadajewski, Mark and Douglas Brownlie (2008), 'Critical marketing: a limit attitude', in Mark Tadajewski and Douglas Brownlie (ed.), *Critical*

Marketing: Issues in Contemporary Marketing, Chichester: John Wiley, pp. 1–8.

Takala, Tuomo and Jaana Uripainen (1999), 'Managerial work and lying: a conceptual framework and an explorative case study', *Journal of Business Ethics*, **20** (3), 181–95.

Tarde, Gabriel (1902), *La psychologie economique, Vol.1*, Paris: Alcan.

Tarde, Gabriel ([1903] 1962), *The Laws of Imitation*, Gloucester, MA: Peter Smith.

Taylor, Patrick ([2004] 2007), *Arthurian Legend*, accessed 15 April 2010 at www.arthurian-legend.com/search/search.pl.

Tepper, Bennett J. (2000), 'Consequences of abusive supervision', *Academy of Management Journal*, **43** (2), 178–90.

Thomas, Janice Lynne and Pamela Buckle-Henning (2007), 'Dancing in the white spaces: exploring gendered assumptions in successful project managers' discourse about their work', *International Journal of Project Management*, **25**, 552–59.

Thompson, Hunter ([1966] 2003), *Hell's Angels: The Strange and Terrible Saga of the Outlaw Motorcycle Gangs*, London: Penguin.

Tolkien, J.R.R. ([1945–55] 2008), *Władca pierścieni [Lord of the Rings]*, Warsaw: Muza.

Van Maanen, John (1975), 'Police socialization: a longitudinal examination of job attitudes in an urban police department', *Administrative Science Quarterly*, **20** (2), 207–28.

Van Maanen, John (1978), 'People processing: strategies of organizational socialization', *Organizational Dynamics*, **7** (1), 18–36.

Van Maanen, John (1988), *Tales of the Field: On Writing Ethnography*, Chicago, IL and London: University of Chicago Press.

Van Maanen, John (1990), 'The smile factory: work at Disneyland', in Peter J. Frost (ed.), *Reframing Organizational Culture*, London, Thousand Oaks, CA and New Delhi: Sage, pp. 58–76.

Van Maanen, John (1998), 'Different strokes: qualitative research in the *Administrative Science Quarterly* from 1956 to 1996', in John Van Maanen (ed.), *Qualitative Studies of Organizations*, Thousand Oaks, CA, London and New Delhi: Sage, pp. ix–xxxii.

Vanderstraeten, Raf (2000), 'Autopoiesis and socialization: on Luhmann's reconceptualization of communication and socialization', *British Journal of Sociology*, **51** (3), 581–98.

Veblen, Thorstein (1899), 'Dress as an expression of the pecuniary culture', in *The Theory of the Leisure Class: An Economic Study of Institutions*, New York: Macmillan.

Venkatesh, Alladi (2000), 'Why do you shop?', *Consumption, Markets and Culture*, **3** (4), 297–330.

Venkatesh, Sudhir (2008), *Gang Leader for a Day: A Rogue Sociologist Crosses the Line*, London: Allen Lane.

Wajcman, Judy (1998), *Managing Like a Man: Women and Men in Corporate Management*, Cambridge: Polity Press.

Wang, Ying and Brian H. Kleiner (2005), 'Defining employee dishonesty', *Management Research News*, **28** (2–3), 11–22.

Weber, Max ([1947] 1964), *Theory of Social and Economic Organization*, London: Macmillan.

Webster, Jane and Joseph J. Martocchio (1993), 'Turning work into play: implications for microcomputer software training', *Journal of Management*, **19** (1), 127–46.

Weick, Karl E. ([1969] 1979), *The Social Psychology of Organizing*, Reading, MA: Addison-Wesley.

Weick, Karl, E. (1995), *Sensemaking in Organizations*, Thousand Oaks, CA: Sage.

Weick, Karl E. (2001), *Making Sense of Organization*, Oxford: Blackwell.

Weick, Karl E. (2004), '*Vita Contemplativa*. Mundane poetics: searching for wisdom in organization studies', *Organization Studies*, **25** (4), 653–68.

Weick, Karl E. (2005), 'Organizing and failures of imagination', *International Public Management Journal*, **8** (3), 425–38.

Whitehead, Stephen M. and Frank J. Barrett (2001), 'The sociology of masculinity', in Stephen M. Whitehead, and Frank J. Barrett (eds), *The Masculinities Reader*, Cambridge: Polity Press, pp. 1–26.

Whyte, William H. ([1956] 2002), *The Organization Man*, Philadelphia, PA: University of Pennsylvania Press.

Wilde, Oscar ([[1895] 2007), *The Importance of Being Earnest*, London: Penguin.

Wood, Jennifer L., James M. Schmidtke and Diane L. Decker (2007), 'Lying on job applications: the effects of job relevance, commission, and human resource management experience', *Journal of Business and Psychology*, **22** (1), 1–9.

Wozniak, Robert H. (1999), *Classics in Psychology, 1855–1914: Historical Essays*, Bristol: Thoemmes Press.

Wright, Susan (1994), 'Culture in anthropology and organizational studies', in Susan Wright (ed.), *Anthropology of Organizations*, London and New York: Routledge, pp. 1–31.

Yanow, Dvora, Sierk Ybema, Harry Wels and Frans Kamsteeg (2009), *Organizational Ethnography: Studying the complexities of Organizational Life*, Los Angeles, CA, London and New Delhi: Sage.

Zammuto, Raymond F. (1988), 'Organizational adaptation: some implications of organizational ecology for strategic choice', *Journal of Management Studies*, **25** (2), 105–20.

Zanetti, Lisa A. (2002), 'Leaving our father's house: micrologies, archetypes, and barriers to conscious femininity in organizational settings', *Journal of Organizational Change Management*, **15** (5), 523–37.

Index